# JOURNEY OF FAITH

Published by Vantage Point Press, Saratoga, California

© 2002 Vantage Point Press, Inc.

Photos © the photographers, with the exception of photos
by Ken George, © Threemark Entertainment, LLC

Musical score © Threemark Entertainment, LLC

Library of Congress Control Number 2002108442

ISBN 0-9721661-0-6

Editors: Anita Schiller and Randy Davis

Design: Toki Design, San Francisco

Printed in Singapore

www.vantagepointpress.com

# JOURNEY OF FAITH

## THE MAKING OF

the Other side of Heaven

IN THE WORDS OF THE FILMMAKERS

MITCH DAVIS  JOHN GARBETT  GERALD R. MOLEN

VANTAGE POINT PRESS

# INTRODUCTION

BASED ON THE MEMOIRS OF JOHN H. GROBERG, *The Other Side of Heaven*, was completed in January 2001. It opened in theaters in Utah the following Christmas. After playing in select cities, it opened nationally on April 12th, 2002, culminating a nearly four-year filmmaking odyssey.

The earliest steps of this journey were taken by a boy from Idaho in 1954, when he left the security of his home and family to accept a call to serve a mission in a foreign land for the Church of Jesus Christ of Latter-day Saints. John Groberg had barely even seen the ocean before, let alone crossed it, when he accepted his call to serve three years in the remotest corner of the South Pacific.

Groberg arrived at the Tongan island of Niuatoputapu to find that none of its inhabitants spoke a word of English; indeed, most of them had never seen a white person before. For his part, Groberg didn't speak a word of Tongan but knew that the Lord had called him to be this people's teacher.

"In the end, they taught me much more than I ever taught them," he says fondly.

This book is written in response to numerous letters, e-mails and questions received by the filmmakers since the movie's opening. It takes the reader on three interwoven journeys: the journey of the real John Groberg; the journey found within the movie's storyline; and the journey of the filmmakers, themselves. Included are photos and other items from Groberg's actual experiences, stills from the movie, and a behind-the-scenes look at the filmmaking process.

Our special thanks to the incredibly talented photographers whose images grace this book: Anita Schiller, Ken George, and Hugh Hogle, your work is beyond reproach, as is that of the book's designer, Michi Toki of Toki Design in San Francisco. Additional thanks to John Groberg and his lovely wife, Jean, for their enormous faith and inspiring works.

WE HAD A DREAM: TO MAKE A MOVIE THAT SAID SOMETHING ABOUT MORMONISM, and to make that movie "boldly, nobly and independent." But the dream was large and we were small, until others joined us to help make that dream real.

There were investors in California, Utah, Texas, Washington and New York. There were actors from New Zealand, the Cook Islands, New York and California. There were filmmakers from Australia, New Zealand and the United States. There were special-effects teams in Canada, musicians in London, Los Angeles and Prague.

There were ministers of many faiths who prayed the rain away during our eight weeks of shooting in the Cook Islands. There were car accidents and motorcycle accidents, broken bones and broken hearts. There was an actor who gave his life for our movie, and a composer who gave many sleepless nights.

So now the dream is real, as is our gratitude for all those who made it possible. To the hundreds who took the journey of faith with us, we thank you with all our hearts for your capacity and your companionship. To the thousands who will read this book, we hope it inspires you to pursue your dreams and take your own journey of faith.

'Ofa Atu –

*Producers John Garbett and Jerry Molen, writer/director Mitch Davis*

JERRY MOLEN HAS WORKED IN HOLLYWOOD MOST OF HIS ADULT LIFE and has a considerable treasure chest of amazing stories. If you're lucky enough to coax one out of him, you might learn that his very first job as a studio driver was on a little movie called *Psycho,* directed by Alfred Hitchcock.

Remember the movie's opening shot from inside the car as it drives toward the Bates Hotel? That car was driven by Jerry Molen.

"There he was, Alfred Hitchcock, breathing right over my shoulder," Jerry recalls with a grin. "He didn't shout like some directors, just whispered very calmly: 'Alright, let's move ahead slowly. Now to the left. Alright, now, stop the car slowly. Now, cut. Print.'"

Jerry's encounter with that film giant was only the beginning of a storybook career that has spanned more than forty years. Jerry's legendary work ethic and extraordinary people skills allowed him to grow from the lowly station of studio driver to one of Hollywood's all-time greatest producers.

Jerry's credits include dozens of hit films, among them *Absence of Malice, Tootsie, The Color Purple, Rain Man, Hook, Jurassic Park, The Flintstones, Casper* and *Minority Report.* He is perhaps best known as the Academy Award–winning producer of *Schindler's List.*

"I was in Austria one evening at a promotional event for *Schindler's List,*" Jerry recounts. "As I stood in a reception line with Steven Spielberg and fellow producer Branko Lustig, a woman stepped up to me and, in broken English, asked me what I had done on the film. I told her I was one of the producers. As she shook my hand she said matter-of-factly, 'But you are not Jewish.'

"'No ma'am,' I replied. 'I am not.'

'Then what are you?' she asked.

"'I am Mormon,' I began. But before I could finish, Steven took the woman by the hand and guided her in his direction. As the evening came to an end, Steven and I had a moment alone, and he asked me if I had been put off by the woman's questioning. I assured him that I had not. Then Steven asked me a very surprising question: 'Jerry, what is a Mormon?'

"At that moment, I promised myself that someday I would help tell the story of Mormonism in the same way *Schindler's List* tells a story of modern Judaism. I think we have done that with *The Other Side of Heaven.* The next time anyone asks me about my faith, I can tell them there's a little movie I'd like them to see."

AFTER STINTS IN TELEVISION AT ABC AND FOX, JOHN GARBETT was hired by the Walt Disney Company where he oversaw the production of some 25 Disney Sunday Movies. Later, John shepherded films such as *Three Men and a Little Lady, Father of the Bride* and *Alive* in the feature film division. After Disney, he acted as a production consultant for Amblin Entertainment, Warner Bros. and Universal Studios, working on a number of feature films, including *The Matrix* and *Shrek*.

"I had been at Disney a few years when I heard there was an intern in the Creative Group who was a member of the church," John explains. "That intern was Mitch Davis. We became friends and stayed in touch over the years, even after our paths diverged. One day, when Mitch mentioned that he wanted to make a movie about the Mormon missionary experience, I suggested he read John Groberg's book about his mission in Tonga. Fourteen years after we first met, we were making *The Other Side of Heaven* together."

A few years before Mitch and John's pivotal collaboration, John was asked by filmmaker Robert Zemeckis to supervise the production of Peter Jackson's thriller *The Frighteners*, starring Michael J. Fox. He accepted the position and moved his family to New Zealand. After living there for a time, John and his family fell in love with the country and its people.

"From that day forward, I was on the lookout for stories that would take us back to the people and place we had come to love. When I read Mitch's adaptation of Elder Groberg's book, I realized that in addition to being a great story, it was also a great film to be made in and around New Zealand."

With John and Jerry teamed up to lead production, the project was ready to begin in earnest.

MITCH DAVIS' QUEST TO BRING *THE OTHER SIDE OF HEAVEN* to the big screen began more than twenty years ago, while he was serving as a missionary in Argentina.

"I remember the exact moment in the city of Cordoba in 1979. I was walking down a narrow street with my companion, Elder Anderson, when I received an impression that someday I was to make a movie about what it means to be a Mormon missionary," Mitch relates.

The first step to fulfilling that dream was graduating with a degree in English from Brigham Young University.

"I focused on creative writing, hoping to use those skills to write for film. I soon learned, however, that screen-writers have no control over what they write once they hand their screenplay over to a director, so I decided I had to become a director to protect the integrity of my material."

As a result, Mitch decided to attend USC film school, where he earned a Master's Degree in film production.

"I got an internship at Disney that turned into a job as a junior executive. It was there I met John Garbett. I had enormous respect for him, and we talked a few times about wanting to make a movie together."

Mitch eventually moved to Columbia Studios, where he met Jerry Molen.

"Jerry was making *Hook* on the sound stage next door to my office. One day I visited the set and introduced myself. I told him I was a fellow Mormon filmmaker, and asked if we could go to lunch. He made the mistake of saying yes, and it was then that our friendship began. As with John, we vowed we'd someday make a movie together. Looking back, I think I may have been a bit more committed to that notion than Jerry was, but he still let me believe it could happen."

Many years and twists and turns later, Mitch finally came across Elder Groberg's book, which at that time was called *In the Eye of the Storm*.

"I realized this was the version of the Mormon missionary story I had to make into a movie. It was easy to know with whom I wanted to make it. I sent the first draft of the script to John and Jerry, and couldn't believe my good fortune when they both threw their weight behind it and said 'Let's make this thing!' There is no question in my mind that without the support of John and Jerry there would not be a movie called *The Other Side of Heaven*.

"Someone once asked me if I believed the spirit of the Lord assisted me in the making of this film, if it somehow guided or directed me," Mitch continues. "My honest answer was that not only had the Spirit guided me, but that it had driven me. I had no choice but to make this movie. I am so very grateful for all those who put their arms around me and helped make the dream real."

*Garbett, Davis, Joe Folau ("Feki"), effects supervisor John Gajdecki, art director Mark Grenfell*

*Christopher Gorham ("Elder Groberg"), Davis*

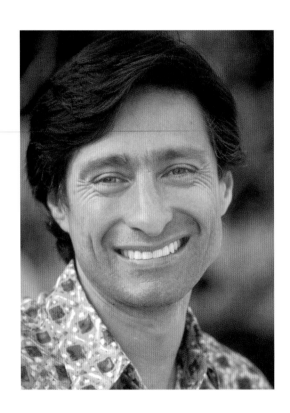

STEVE RAMIREZ ALWAYS KNEW HE WANTED TO BE IN THE MOVIE BUSINESS.

"I initially wanted to become a cinematographer," Steve reveals. "Somehow I had this romantic notion of being in the middle of an African desert, sitting atop a crane filming some great epic. My father explained what it would be like, leaving my family to go on location for long periods of time, and suggested I work towards being an editor."

Steve took his father's advice and developed an impressive resume as an editor, including films such as *Being There, Driving Miss Daisy, The Devil's Advocate,* and *Double Jeopardy.* Given this track record, it's no surprise that Steve was the first guy John Garbett thought of when looking for an editor for *The Other Side of Heaven*.

"When John mentioned that the film was going to be shot in Rarotonga, I didn't even know where that was. He told me that it was a Polynesian island with white sand beaches, warm waters, and fruit falling off the trees. Right away I asked, "When do I go?"

Steve already was thinking about missionaries at the time since his oldest son, Skyler, was preparing to leave for a mission in New York. It also didn't hurt that Steve's friendship with John Garbett dated back almost twenty years.

"In all that time, John never once spoke to me about working together, so I knew this project must have been really important to him," Steve says, "and I wasn't disappointed. *The Other Side of Heaven* provided such unique experiences that I fear it will never be equaled by regular Hollywood fare."

Steve worked closely with John, Jerry and Mitch to test the movie for general audiences during post-production.

"We decided we would only preview the film to non-LDS audiences, and it surprised us how many members of other Christian denominations were visibly moved by its spirit," Steve relates. "I am a witness to how films like this can bring so much good into our lives."

*John and Jean Groberg in Rarotonga, 2000*

WHEN ASKED HOW HE FEELS ABOUT BEING THE SUBJECT OF A MAJOR MOVIE, John Groberg replies with characteristic humility:

"I can tell you it sure never crossed my mind while I was serving my mission on that tiny island in the South Pacific that anyone would ever want to make a movie about it. And sitting together on our swing set under the stars, Jean and I never imagined we'd see ourselves on the silver screen."

Groberg's humility is outstripped only by his obedience, which is the main reason he wrote the book that eventually spawned the film. "A good friend of mine, a Church leader, requested that I record my mission experiences in book form," recalls Elder Groberg, adding with a smile, "He was the kind of friend you just shouldn't say no to."

Thus was born *In the Eye of the Storm*, a quietly successful book published by Bookcraft in 1993. You can imagine the Grobergs' surprise when Mitch approached them in 1999 about turning their story into a major motion picture.

Elder Groberg wasn't sure what to say, so he consulted with Jean, who knew exactly what to say: "Absolutely not!" he explains, "We were concerned that the movie accurately reflect the true spirit of the book, which doesn't often happen in Hollywood."

Thankfully, the Grobergs gave the proposal some thought and prayer before making their final decision.

"I looked into these people. I found out about their credentials and their track record, and began to feel very good about them," Elder Groberg relates. "These were serious filmmakers who wanted to make a movie for the world. I came to appreciate their motives and their vision for the film."

Having put their hands to the plow, the Grobergs did not look back. They consulted with the filmmakers to help get many details right, and even spent their personal vacation time visiting the sets in the Cook Islands and New Zealand. Although they did not supervise the screenplay or the movie's production, their tireless support and encouragement proved invaluable to the team.

"It is important to know that this movie was entirely an independent, commercial venture. In no way was it initiated, supervised or funded by the Church, and the Church doesn't stand to benefit from it financially or otherwise," Elder Groberg clarifies.

In the end, the Grobergs are glad they overcame their initial fears and allowed the movie to go forward. "You know, I think they really got it right," praises Elder Groberg. "They took a 300-page book and turned it into a 100-page screenplay, which inevitably required some compromises. But the spirit of the movie is exactly right."

*Groberg family (John, back row, second from left), circa 1944*

*Groberg siblings (John third from left), circa 1952*

*John Groberg, circa 1944*

CHURCH OF JESUS CHRIST OF LATTER DAY SAINTS

OFFICE OF THE FIRST PRESIDENCY

SALT LAKE CITY 1, UTAH

June 22, 1954

Elder John Holbrook Groberg
255 - 12th Street
Idaho Falls, Idaho

Dear Elder Groberg:

You are hereby called to be a missionary of the Church of Jesus Christ of Latter-day Saints to labor in the Tongan Mission. Your presiding officers have recommended you as one worthy to represent the Church of our Lord as a Minister of the Gospel.

It will be your duty to live righteously, to keep the commandments of the Lord, to honor the holy Priesthood which you bear, to increase your testimony of the divinity of the Restored Gospel of Jesus Christ, to be an exemplar in your life of all the Christian virtues, and so to conduct yourself as a devoted servant of the Lord that you may be an effective advocate and messenger of the Truth. We repose in you our confidence and extend to you our prayers that the Lord will help you thus to meet your responsibilities.

The Lord will reward the goodness of your life, and greater blessings and more happiness than you have yet experienced await you as you serve Him humbly and prayerfully in this labor of love among His children.

We ask that you please send your written acceptance promptly, endorsed by your presiding officer in the ward or branch where you live.

Sincerely your brother,

David O. McKay

President

I DON'T FEEL MY MISSION WAS ANY MORE IMPORTANT than anyone else's mission. The mission wasn't really my mission, the book I wrote about it was not my book, and the movie was not my movie. It all belongs to the Lord. —*John Groberg*

*First assistant director Carey Carter, Garbett, Davis, director of photography Brian Breheny*

**To:** Investors
**Date:** Sun, 30 Apr 2000 02:27:19
**Subject:** INVESTOR UPDATE

Hello everyone!

We now have 21 people working full-time to "mount" the production. Most of these people are working out of our New Zealand production offices, primarily on costuming, props and set design.

Since we will be making the film on a rather remote island, it is necessary for us to ship everything we need for the production--cars from the 1950's period, construction supplies for the three villages we are building, wind machines for the hurricane scene, etc. We will be filling a few containers to put on a freighter that leaves New Zealand for Rarotonga next week.

Because a significant element of our film will be the music of Tongan choirs, we recently attended services at the Tongan Free Methodist Church. At the conclusion of the meeting, we visited with the choir director outside. We mentioned that the name of the Mormon missionary whose story we are telling is John Groberg, or "Kolipoki." The choir director's eyes lit up.

"Kolipoki?" he asked. We nodded. The choir director smiled broadly.

"I know him!"

Turns out this man, Semi Telefoni, was born and raised in the city of Pangai, where Elder Groberg finished his mission. He had heard Elder Groberg teach, probably when he returned as a mission president. Then another woman standing outside the church joined in the conversation.

Seems her aunt was Mormon and had once shown her a videotape of Elder Groberg teaching at a conference in Nuku'alofa. This woman said she couldn't believe how well Elder Groberg spoke the language--"Better than us Tongans!"--and that he was surely a powerful preacher.

We are proceeding with the movie, full steam ahead.

'Ofa Atu--

Jerry, John and Mitch

**To:** Investors
**Date:** Fri, 19 May 2000 01:12:37
**Subject:** INVESTOR UPDATE

Hello everyone!

A lot has happened since we last updated you, and it's all good news. We have set our lead actor in the movie! Christopher Gorham, an accomplished actor with significant film and television credits, has signed on to do the role.

As part of our talent search, our casting director met with the head of casting for the WB network. She asked, "Who is the best potential breakout star from among the WB's shows?"

The head of casting strongly recommended Chris, who is a lead in the WB series "Popular." After testing some 200 other actors, we auditioned him and he gave by far the best performance we saw.

We are especially excited about Chris' ability to make the Elder Groberg character fun and humorous. Chris combines a lot of the boyish charisma of Jimmy Stewart ("You want the moon? Just say the word, and I'll go on up there and lasso it for you!") and the tenderhearted humor of Tom Hanks.

I also wanted to take a moment to highlight another of our major hires, that of our cinematographer, Brian Breheny, an Australian director of photography with an exceptional string of films under his belt. Brian's last two pictures have both been featured at major festivals: *My Mother Frank*, Official Selection, Berlin Film Festival, 2000; and *Siam Sunset*, Official Selection, Critics Week, Cannes Film Festival, 1999. Prior to those two films, Brian helmed such critically acclaimed features as *Forever Fever* for Miramax, *Heaven Is Burning* starring Russell Crowe, and *Priscilla, Queen of the Desert*, starring Terrance Stamp.

Brian's experience with our movie is representative of those of many of our crew members. Most of the films Brian has worked on in the last several years have been fairly dark and amoral. He had grown quite weary of such assignments but rarely, if ever, came across a script that allowed him to take his career in another direction.

When he read Elder Groberg's story, however, he felt a powerful, affirmative spirit. He arrived for his interview fairly bubbling with enthusiasm for the opportunity to create images consistent with what he felt while reading the script. He has asked us a number of times if Elder Groberg is ever going to visit the set because, in his own words, "It's not every day you get to meet a chap with the kind of spirit that man must have."

We hope all is well with you and yours. We'll keep you posted on our progress.

All the best.

Mitch, John and Jerry

WE DECIDED EARLY ON THAT WE WOULD HIRE THE BEST ACTORS and filmmakers possible. Of the hundreds of people who formed the cast and crew, only a handful were of the LDS faith. Nonetheless, everyone was captivated by the spirit of John Groberg's story and approached it respectfully. I think the diversity of people working on the project helped us to tell the story more effectively to a broader audience.—*John Garbett*

IT WAS REALLY QUITE A THRILL SEEING ALL THOSE NON-LDS ACTORS and crew members working so hard to make the movie as good as it could be. To tell you the truth, they seemed like a pretty worldly crowd, but I could really tell they were taking great care to get the movie right, and they did. —*John Groberg*

**To:** Investors

**Date:** Sat, 27 May 2000 15:39:06

**Subject:** INVESTOR UPDATE

✉

Hello everyone! Or, as they say in Tonga, "malo lei lei!"

Our project continues moving forward at a brisk clip. Most of the actors have arrived in Rarotonga and we have begun rehearsals. We also have most of our eighty-member crew on the island
now. They are working at the wardrobe, props and construction warehouses around the island,
preparing the show.

There is only one road around the island of Rarotonga, and it seems like most of the trucks
headed one way or the other are hauling either our equipment or our building materials. We are
hiring lots of the locals for labor, so we are quite well-liked here. So far no casualties,
other than a construction laborer who had to be hospitalized after--yes, it's true--a coconut
fell on him. Looks like he is going to be okay.

Earlier this week, we made an offer to a great actress to play the role of Jean Sabin Groberg.
We hope to have good news on that front next week. We don't shoot any scenes with Jean until the
last two weeks of production, so we actually have quite a lot of time to lock that part down.

I have spent most of my rehearsal time so far working with Chris Gorham (Elder Groberg) and Joe
Folau (Feki, Elder Groberg's Tongan companion). Today we walked out onto the beach and rehearsed
a scene in which Feki encourages a rather downbeat Elder Groberg by telling him the "Hurrah for
Israel!" story from the pioneer apostles. I found it hard to contain my gratitude as I watched
these two non-LDS actors bring all their skills to bear on a scene already enriched by the
spirit of the Lord.

Many of you have commented that you are keeping our production in your thoughts and prayers. We
so appreciate that consideration and can only encourage more of it. We need the right weather,
the right light, the right sunsets, the right waves, the right performances. We need magical
things to happen that we could never consciously plan or orchestrate. We need physical health
and strength, and (as time goes on) harmony amongst a sleep-deprived cast and crew.

Thanks again to all of you for making this movie possible.

'Ofa Atu --

Mitch, John and Jerry

Dear Faithful Believers,

Greetings, one and all. I am now in Rarotonga.

I wanted to personally take this opportunity to convey my thoughts and observations since arriving at this oasis in the South Pacific. Simply put--all is well.

The day we have all been waiting for is just around the corner. The countdown is very real-- four days until we first hear the call, "Roll camera!"

There is a definite buzz, a mixture of excitement, anticipation and eagerness to begin the process.

Mitch is focused, doggedly determined, dedicated to the task at hand and a bit nervous (as are all great directors). But he is also beaming with the pride and excitement of a parent about to give birth. In a way, that's what he is.

The cast, the crew and the support groups on the island are a comfort and a blessing for their willingness and dedication to purpose. John has been brilliant in putting together a team that equals any I've ever seen.

So, go ahead; please feel the excitement and the joy of fulfillment in knowing that your spirit is with us, that because of you and your belief in Mitch and the project, the dream is becoming reality. We are about to begin the journey, and you are with us.

It is my prayer that our Father in Heaven bless each of you always in all ways.

On behalf of Mitch and John, I am

Yours and His,

Jerry Molen

THE DAY BEFORE WE BEGAN PRINCIPAL PHOTOGRAPHY, a prayer service was held to bless our production. The Polynesian elders of Rarotonga and ministers from many different churches were in attendance, along with our entire cast and crew. When asked if there was anything they could do to help us, I told them they could pray it wouldn't rain.

I guess I shouldn't have been surprised when they took my suggestion quite seriously. From that day forward, countless islanders from many different denominations began praying that the weather would be kind to us.

We had some pretty close calls, but never once did we get rained out during nearly two months of filming in Rarotonga. The day we finished shooting and got on our plane for New Zealand, it started to rain and didn't stop for five days. —*John Garbett*

WE WERE SHOOTING IN THE MOUNTAINS OUR FIRST DAY, and it was still dark when I was dropped off at the trailhead to our location. It was raining, and I was feeling apprehensive as I hiked by flashlight with a fellow named Rat, our key grip who never used his real name. He was sort of a grizzled guy, kind of a cross between Willie Nelson and Harry Dean Stanton, and he must have sensed my first-day jitters. As we were hiking up the trail, Rat called out to me, "Hey Mitch!" I turned and he just smiled and said, "May the spirit be with you." At that moment I knew every-thing was going to be alright. If Rat's arms were around me, everyone else's would be too. —*Mitch Davis*

*Rat*

ELDER GROBERG WAS VISITING THE SET THE DAY WE SHOT THIS STUNT. It was a pretty impressive feat, and a large crowd of islanders "oohed" and "aahed" every time the stunt man leapt to the tree. Surprisingly, Elder Groberg sort of took it in stride. "Feki could do that," he shrugged. "Feki could do just about anything." —*Jerry Molen*

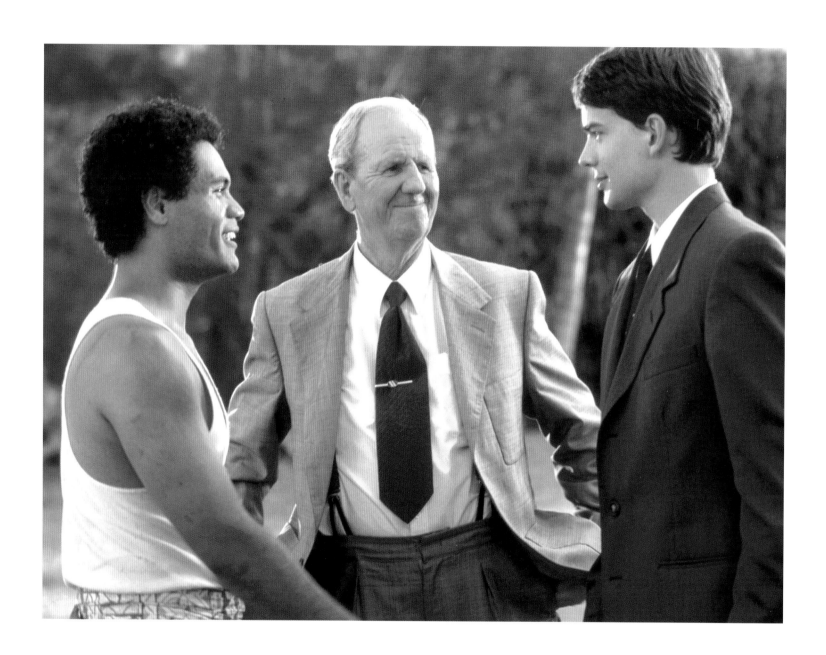

IT'S A WELL-KEPT SECRET THAT, IN ADDITION TO BEING A HIGHLY SUCCESSFUL PRODUCER, Jerry Molen is also an accomplished actor, having appeared in films like *Rain Man, Days of Thunder, Jurassic Park* and *Amistad*. He was a natural for the part of Elder Groberg's first mission president, although it wasn't easy talking him into doing it. Unlike any of his previous roles, the President Coombs part required that he shave his beloved mustache. But he did it, and he delivered a great performance. His paternal warmth and strength came through perfectly. I'm really grateful to have him in the movie. —*Mitch Davis*

*Joe Folau as "Feki"*

*Feki Po'uha, circa 1955*

IN THE CASE OF ELDER GROBERG'S MISSIONARY COMPANION, FEKI, we adhered very faithfully to the true character's story, with one exception: We combined Feki's story with that of another man whose father had been an abusive alcoholic before converting to the gospel.

We cleared that addition to Feki's character with some of the members of his family. When the movie came out, a few family members who were unaware of the addition were surprised by it, since Feki's actual father was a devout man of God who never let liquor touch his lips.

I got a phone call at home as I was rushing out to church one Sunday morning. An elderly, serene voice spoke to me with a Tongan accent from the other end of the line.

"Brother Davis?"

"Yes?" I replied.

After a brief exchange of pleasantries, she said, "I am very sad today, Brother Davis. You make a movie about Elder Groberg and my brother, Feki Po'uha."

"Yes!" I lit up, finally realizing who this was—one of Feki's sisters. "How I came to love your brother during the making of the movie!"

"Then why you tell lies about him?" came the sweet but firm reply. I was completely stunned.

"Lies?"

"You say Feki's father a drinking man. Feki's father, my father, he never drink. He never beat my mother. You make our family very sad."

We were going to be late for church. My kids were out in the car, honking the horn. Nonetheless, I launched into my best possible explanation of the concept of composite characters. I explained how important it was for us to show the impact the gospel has on real lives, and how this scene with Feki was the best place in the movie to achieve that. After a thoughtful pause, she asked, "But why you have to hurt people to preach the gospel?"

I realized there was no way I could effectively communicate with this dear woman unless I could speak her native tongue. I told her I was late for church and asked her if we could talk more at the end of the day. She graciously agreed.

All I could think about at church that day was this beautiful sister and how the movie had hurt her feelings. I prayed for the means to explain to her what we had done and why we had done it.

That afternoon the phone rang again. I heard the familiar, sweet voice on the other end.

"Brother Davis, I hope my phone call this morning did not keep you from enjoying the Sabbath day," she said. Before I could answer, she continued: "It was fast Sunday today, and I fast about the things you and I talk about. During Sacrament meeting, I pray in my heart to God to help me understand and help me forgive you.

"And Feki, he come to me. He comfort me. He say much good will come from this movie, and it's alright. 'The truth will come out in the end,' he tell me. And I know what he say is true. Somehow a miracle will happen and the truth about my father will come out.

"So, I want you to know, Brother Davis, it's alright. I'm alright now. I'm sorry if I bother you earlier. Feki told me everything is alright."

With that she hung up and I just stood there, realizing I had just been speaking with an angel. —*Mitch Davis*

IT'S NOT EVERY DAY THAT ONE GETS TO MAKE A MOVIE ABOUT A MAN like John Groberg, and meeting him only made my admiration for him grow. I was surprised to learn how much we had in common. For instance, about the time Elder Groberg decided to go on a mission, I decided to join the Marines. About the time he got on the S.S. Ventura to leave for New Zealand, I got on a troop carrier ship, headed for the Atlantic. And on the same nights he walked to the end of the pier and talked to Jean 'across the sky,' I was talking to Pat, my sweetheart, from the bow of my ship. —*Jerry Molen*

FORM NUMBER TS-1

37459/rj

## MATSON NAVIGATION COMPANY    THE OCEANIC STEAMSHIP COMPANY
### IDENTIFICATION CHECK
## ONE WAY FIRST CLASS CONTRACT TICKET

SERIAL NUMBER  37658

FROM _Los Angeles Harbor_    TO _Pago, Pago - Samoa_

☞ THIS IDENTIFICATION CHECK IS TO BE RETAINED BY PASSENGER UNTIL COMPLETION OF VOYAGE

| NAMES OF PASSENGERS IN FULL | AGE | NUMBER OF | | | | |
|---|---|---|---|---|---|---|
| | | WHOLE | HALF | QUARTER | INFANT | SERVANT |
| Groberg, Mr. John Holbrook | ad | One | | | | |
| | "Basis three in room" | | | | | |

TAX PAID  Exempt

REMARKS

"Ports & dates of departure or arrival subject to change."
Pls phone R. Jones, VA. 2421, between 4:30 & 5 p.m. on Oct. 11 for boarding hour.

NOTICE—NOT GOOD FOR PASSAGE UNTIL RESERVATION FOR A SPECIFIED SAILING HAS BEEN SECURED.

GROSS VALUE OF TICKET . . . . . . . . $ 262.00

### RESERVATIONS
CARRIER  The Oceanic Steamship Co.
FROM  L.A. Harbor    TO  Pago Pago, Samoa
S.S.  Ventura    DATE  on or abt. Oct. 12, 1954    HOUR Indef.
ROOM  3    BERTH  D
ROOM      BERTH

### ORDER HONORED
FORM  TS43    NO. 28725    VALUE 262.00
AGENT  Franklin J. Murdock, T.A.
STREET  47 E. South Temple St.
CITY  Salt Lake City, Utah (jr)

### SPECIAL NOTICE TO PASSENGERS FROM HONOLULU

RESERVATION FOR THE JOURNEY FROM HONOLULU, AS SHOWN ABOVE, IS AVAILABLE TO FIRST CALIFORNIA PORT ONLY. UPON ARRIVAL THERE THE PURSER WILL, IF NECESSARY TO CHANGE ROOM, ASSIGN COMPARABLE ACCOMMODATION BEYOND.

## IDENTIFICATION CHECK
### TO BE RETAINED DURING THE VOYAGE
#### (NOT GOOD FOR PASSAGE)

PRINTED IN U.S.A.

# Bon Voyage

## by
## WESTERN UNION

1297

PR.IFA034  PD=IDAHO FALLS IDA 13 940AMM=

1954 OCT 13  AM 9 26

ELDER JOHN H GROBERG=

VENTURA MATSON LINES LOSA=

=MAY THE LORD BLESS YOU ON YOUR OCEAN TRIP AND DURING YOUR

ENTIRE MISSION BON VOYAGE OFA ATU ALL OUR LOVE=

MOM AND DAD=

OFA ATU

This helped alot - as no one
was there - nobody anyway - to say Goodby.

Ships Course —

1954

Oct. 13 | Wednesday - Boarded at 7:00 P.M. Left 8:15 P.M.
From Wilmington. Port of Los Angeles
Both 160 - To Pago 4204 M.

14 | Thursday - Noon Report   Travelled 220 M.
From L.A. 220 To Pago 3984

15 | Friday - Noon Report: Travelled 366 Miles.
From L.A. 586 To Pago 3618
Lat. 27°49' N. Long. 127°08' W.
Ave. Speed 15.25 Knotts.

16 | Saturday - Noon Report - Travelled 384 M.
From L.A. 970 To Pago 3234
Lat. 23°32' N Long. 132°22' W.
Ave. Speed 15.67 Knotts.

17 | Sunday - Noon Report - Travelled 374 M.
From L.A. 1344 To Pago 2860
Latt. 19°19' N. Long. 137°14' W.
Ave. Speed 15.54+

18 | Monday - Noon Report - Travelled 380 M.
From L.A. 1724 To Pago 2480
Latt. 14°51' No. Long. 141°52' W.
Ave. Speed 15.51 Knotts.

19 | Tuesday - Noon Report - Travelled 379 M.
From L.A. 2103 To Pago 2101
Latt. 10°25' N. Long. 146°25'
Ave. Speed 15.79 Knotts

1954

Oct. 20 | Wednesday - Noon Report Travelled 362 M.
Latt. 5°51' No. Long. 150°21' W.
Course 220°38' - From L.A. 2465 M.
To Pago 1739 Ave. Speed 14.78 Knotts

Oct. 21 | Thursday - Noon Report: Travelled
Latt. 1°48' No. Long. 154°16' W
From L.A. 2805 To Pago 1399
Course 224°10' Ave. Speed 14.16 Knotts

Oct. 22 | Friday - Noon Report - Travelled 382 Miles
Latt. 2°59' S. Long. 158°25' W
From L.A. 3187 To Pago 1017
Course 221°07' Ave. Speed 15.6 Knotts

Oct. 23 | Saturday - Noon Report - Travelled 370 M.
Latt. 7°25' S. Long. 162°40' W
From L.A. 3557 To Pago 647
Course 223°52' Ave. Speed 15.11 Knotts

Oct. 24 | Sunday - Noon Report - Travelled 386 M
Latt. 11°39' So. Long. 167°15' W
From L.A. 3943 To Pago 261
Course 227°04' Ave. Speed 15.7+ Knotts

Oct. 25 | Monday —

*Elder Groberg's log of the ship's progress on his trip from Los Angeles to Tonga*

Ship *Ventura* from Southampton to Boston.

Richards Hall 109
Provo, Utah
U.S.A.

PROVO, UTAH
JAN 1?
5-PM
1955

Elder John H. Groberg
Box 58 Nukualofa
Tongatapu, Tonga F.I.

Air Mail

Perhaps by this time you are already
in Niuatoputapu. Did your boat arrangements
finally get worked out?
I hope they don't keep you waiting for
boats too much and that things keep
right on being wonderful down there in Tonga.
"Ofa atu."
Jean

WE HIRED MUCH OF OUR CREW from the mountain-climbing adventure *Vertical Limit*, which had been shooting in the wintry New Zealand Alps. Camera operator Peter McCaffrey was among those who were happy to move to the sunnier climes of Rarotonga. —*John Garbett*

WE DIDN'T REALLY HAVE A PART FOR GLYNNIS when we auditioned her, but she was so full of mischief that we knew we had to cast her. We ended up combining several small roles into one—"The Postmistress"—just for Glynnis. She stole every scene she was in. —*John Garbett*

ONE OF MY BIGGEST CHALLENGES WAS DIRECTING the large crowd scenes. We were working with a mixture of experienced actors and inexperienced extras. Sometimes it was pretty frustrating trying to get everyone doing the right thing at the right time. —*Mitch Davis*

WE HIRED A TONGAN SCHOOLTEACHER WHO LIVED ON RAROTONGA to coach Chris on his Tongan language scenes. During the first read-through Chris did with all the Polynesian actors, we got to a long Tongan speech. Everyone assumed he would just skip over it, but he dove right in and pronounced the whole thing perfectly from start to finish. The Polynesian actors couldn't believe it! Chris gained their instant affection and admiration. —*Jerry Molen*

Date **Tuesday March 1, 1955**

I spoke a little while. I really haven't done all I could to get this language. I have got to do more i the future. I shook hands with all of the people - especially the kids. - There are some wonderful people here - I hope I can do my part to help them - John.

I was able to pray in the Falehitu here for a while - Lord - Give me a tongue to speak to these people - seemed to be my prayer. Oh have I ever learned a lot. The reason a mission is so wonderful is because it is so hard - The strengtheny we receive from the Lord is worth it all.

*Elder Groberg's missionary journal*

Saturday I was going to fast – In treating Caoi's leg, I just couldn't refuse their Keke – Then *noʻe loko* at *atu ʻae aukai* – Kai teu loko ongói ʻae [pale] ʻi he po ko ia = just sweet peaceful assurance. But Sunday – We preached to the Kau Popula – toki hau teu teuteu ha malanga – FK tomala – FK molemole – FK ngalói. Naʻe ikai teu loko lava be teuteu ia ke lelei, ka siʻi ʻao taimi toki ʻalu ʻaki ʻae Lotu ʻi hoku loto – Oh the joy – the sweet joy. I just talked – They understood – The various fakamaoni – all fit together so perfectly. –

*aukai*

*Within a few short months, Elder Groberg began to master the language*

Thank you for my first lesson in Tongan.
I'll try to study it really hard so I
can be ready for lesson number two. The
language is certainly a challenging one.
I do hope your success with this language
will continue and increase rapidly,
as needed, for you to take your great
message to the Tongan people.

*Letter from Jean to John, 1955*

*Elder Groberg's photos of Feki building their house, 1955*

*Joe Folau ("Feki") and Chris Gorham ("Elder Groberg") build their house*

## Ordinances.

NAMES, ADDRESSES, AND
IMPORTANT DATES TO REMEMBER

| NAME | Place | ADDRESS Ordinance | DATE 1955. |
|------|-------|---------|------|
| Saula Vakata | Hihifo N.T.T. | Sealed Annointing | Nov. 28 (Hanga |
|  | " " | Anointed | Nov. 29, 1955 (Tamak |
| " " | | | |
| Nuku Fonua | Vaipoa N.T.T. | ANNOINNTED | Jan. 2, 456 (F |
| Lulu Faingaanuku Liva | Vaipoa N.T.T | Confirmed member of | Jan 1, 956 |
|  | " " | ANNOINTED | Jan 5, 1956 (f |
| Lavenia Foliaki Paau | | | |

Monday we played our band in Vaipoa - then down
in the afternoon the big fall came. Nuku (one) the Saint
fell from a Mangoe Tree a was really dead. I think

...ally dead - or very, very close. We carried him to our house,
...e applied artificial respiration and then we administered
him. I know that the Lord hears the prayers and acknowledges
...faith of these saints. You can't doubt it after what I've seen.
...o one except the parents really expected him to live. The
...mily was angry for keeping him here, but I felt it not.
...eally did some praying and I know these saints' faith was
...ecognized. It's wonderful yet terrifying to come close to the
...d. Death or the expectation of it brings one close to the great
...ealities in life. There isn't a lot that's important. Just to love,
...elp, serve others. We are here to serve, not to be served. There
...re countless opportunities to serve if we but will. Jria & his family
...ame Sunday. There's beauty in those kids, because of their un-
...elfishness. I suppose unselfishness makes most anyone most
...eautiful. I wish I had more of it. To really think of the
...ood of others. We stayed up all Monday night, all Tuesday, all
...uesday night (mostly awake) and most of Wednesday. Slept a little
...ednesday, as Niuku seemed better. Thursday he was able to get
...p and walk a little. It's been a great humbling experience
...or me. I hope I can be more unselfish - more willing
...o help others - live closer to the Lord. Use the
...riesthood more effectively, etc. There's a lot to life. I will
...ust be unselfish. — Ofa' atu — John.

Wednesday, January 11, 1956 - Sometimes a week
seems to sort of drag, but at the end of it, there has been an
awful lot done during it. It's all necessary, and some of
the most essential things in life - I feel certain - are
accomplished in a rather quiet, unassuming period.

IT WAS KIND OF IRONIC THAT WE PICKED probably the most hyperactive kid on the entire island to play a dead boy named Nuku. Ben had to lie perfectly still for several minutes at a time, and he showed remarkable self-control, but the instant the cameras stopped rolling, he would jump up and start terrorizing the set. —*Mitch Davis*

*Nuku Fonua, 2001*

*Nuku (far right) with his family, 1960s*

PEOPLE ALWAYS ASK IF THE STORY about the rats eating my feet really happened. They also wonder how it was possible for such a thing to happen without me waking up. The answer to the first question is yes, it definitely happened. I don't know why I didn't wake up, but I am told the rats probably only ate the dead flesh—the calluses— leaving only a thin layer of live skin. I felt fine when I woke up that morning, but when I stood up, the weight of my body caused the bottoms of my feet to split open.

The scene in which the soles of my feet are healed in the sun is also true. In fact, years later I ended up with skin cancer on my feet. The doctor who treated me told me that, in all his years of practice, he had never seen skin cancer in such an unlikely place. —*John Groberg*

*Miriama Smith ("Lavania") and Apii McKinley (Lavania's mother, "Noli")*

SIMAIMA'S MOTHER WAS VERY ANGRY AND HURT that I had rejected her daughter's advances. No matter what I said, it seemed to make things worse. I had just about decided the situation was hopeless when I remembered something that had come in the mail for me the day before: a picture of my sweetheart, Jean, from back home.
—*John Groberg*

I DON'T THINK IT WAS A COINCIDENCE that I sent the letter when I did, nor did I have any idea John had sent me a photo of himself at precisely the same time. We like to joke that our photos passed each other in the air somewhere over Hawaii. But as much as I treasured John's photo, by all accounts the one I sent him came in handier.
—*Jean Groberg*

WHEN I HANDED SIMAIMA'S MOTHER JEAN'S PHOTO, it seemed like her maternal loyalties divided, as if suddenly she had two daughters with competing interests. As she caressed Jean's photo lovingly with her thick, brown hands, I sensed she realized that giving her daughter what she wanted meant taking it away from someone else.
—*John Groberg*

*Jean Sabin (Groberg), 1955*

*Simaima Tulua with her husband-to-be Sione, 1959*

*Simaima Tulua, 2001*

IN THE MOVIE, LAVANIA IS A COMPOSITE character based mostly on the girl called Simaima in my book. The movie's time limitations made it impossible to share some of the highlights of Simaima's story. Simaima was a very good girl whose conversion to the gospel was one of the sweetest experiences of my mission. She was subsequently married in the temple to a man who later served as bishop. Her children served missions and have been married in the temple. We remain good friends to this day. —*John Groberg*

PUA MAGASIVA WAS ONE OF OUR LEAST EXPERIENCED ACTORS, and we gave him one of the movie's most difficult scenes: He dies violently of lockjaw in Elder Groberg's arms. The night before we filmed that scene, Pua confided to his fellow Polynesians that he was worried about his upcoming performance. The next day, all of the male Polynesian actors stayed on the set all day to show their support for Pua. When the time came for him to actually "die" on camera, they took him off to a nearby building and held a Polynesian prayer with him. I've worked with a lot of generous actors in my life, but it's hard for me to imagine any of them showing the kind of consideration Pua's contemporaries showed him. Their efforts made for one of the most convincing deaths I've ever seen on film. —*Jerry Molen*

FOR THE SCENE IN WHICH THE RICH MAN COMES TO TRADE LIQUOR FOR FAVORS with the locals, our plans to rent a yacht and sail it into the bay were foiled when we discovered that it was too shallow. Thanks to a little movie magic and a terrific art department, we were able to create a shell of a yacht that looked like the real thing. —*John Garbett*

NAT LEES IS ONE OF THE PREEMINENT POLYNESIAN ACTORS in the world. After completing our film, Nat was hired to work in the *Lord of the Ring* trilogy, then was hired for both sequels to *The Matrix*.

We found Nancy Kareroa, who played Kelepi's daugthter, from an open casting call in Rarotonga. Nancy was from a nearby, undeveloped island called Mangaia, and happened to be going to school in Rarotonga when we held auditions. Her performances were always pure and natural, which is just the way Nancy is. —*John Garbett*

GROBERGS FLOATING POV ON KOLI

GROBERGS POV DOWN ON KULI, FLOATING

C.U. GROBE
FOR TOMAS

# HURRICANE
## EYE OF THE STORM

Camera Turn
Shot

WATCHING FROM SEA
CGI

Ring Fence for Animary

## EYE OF THE STORM

2A

TRACKING BACK WITH THE PAIR. MAYHEM
ANIMALS SCURRY. THE PAIR IS FULL OF
DEBRIS.  "DON'T STOP!"

3A

THEY GLIMPSE A SHEET OF IRON
AS IT IS RIPPED OFF A ROOF AND
HURTLES TOWARDS THEM.

1A

PAN WITH... AS HE RUNS AWAY.
GROBERG FOLLOWS. AS THEY RECEDE "WHERE
ARE WE GOING?"  "THE OLD WELL."

1B

See. MOUNTAIN B.G
CGI

WE FOLLOW AS THEY RUN. LIGHTING

2B

TRACKING
DIVE. TH
CAMERA
B

2C

THEY
"KEEP

THE CLIMAX OF THE HURRICANE SCENE OCCURS when our actors are running through a small village and the winds reach such intense levels that two of the huts are literally blown away. For obvious reasons, we saved that shot until the very end of the day. Once those huts were gone, we would have no set to shoot on anymore!

The time came for our final shot. Four cameras were positioned to record the stunt from various angles. First the rain towers and fire hoses began spewing water over the set, then the fans started blowing hurricane force winds. Our actors stood bravely in the midst of it all, awaiting their cue from me.

I was about to call "action" when I noticed something unusual—a huge torrent of water cascading perilously close to our actors. I followed its source to find one of our special-effects technicians up in a scaffold tower, holding a fire hose under one arm. Rather than pay attention to where that hose was pointed, he held his personal camcorder to his eye, intent on recording this moment for all posterity.

I asked my assistant director to call him on the radio. He tried, to no avail. The noise from the fans and rain towers was too loud for his radio to be heard. He tried the radio again, shouting this time. Still no use.

I grew frustrated and waved my arms to get this fellow's attention when suddenly, out of the corner of my eye, I saw our actors starting to run toward me, charging heroically through the wind and mud. I watched in horror as the first hut was blown away, followed by the second. The actors ran up to me, panting but proud of their performance.

"Well," they asked, "how'd it look?"

I turned to our director of photography, who could only shrug haplessly. None of the cameras had been rolling! I was furious, and ordered our assistant director to find out who had set off this horrible chain reaction, then retreated to my corner to pout.

A few moments later Carey Carter, our New Zealand assistant director, ventured over to me. "I don't know how to tell you this," he said, "but it was you, mate." He went on to explain that, when I waved my arms to get the attention of the guy with the fire hose, the actors thought I was cuing them. The special-effects crew saw the actors starting to run, and pulled the trigger on blowing the huts away, not knowing that the cameras weren't recording any of it.

Our construction crew spent that night rebuilding the set, and we all returned the next day to get the shot that almost was. —*Mitch Davis*

Shooting the hurricane sequence was a blast. Literally. —*Christopher Gorham*

IN THE MOVIE, THEY USE A JAR OF JAM to represent the can of jam given to me when I was starving after the hurricane. I recently ran into a missionary who served on the island of Niuatopatapu ten or twenty years after I served there. He told me that one day he was helping local members clean out the chapel and started to throw away a rusty old can he found sitting on a shelf. The branch members grabbed the can and scolded him. "Don't touch that can! That is the can of jam that saved Kolipoki's life after the hurricane!" —*John Groberg*

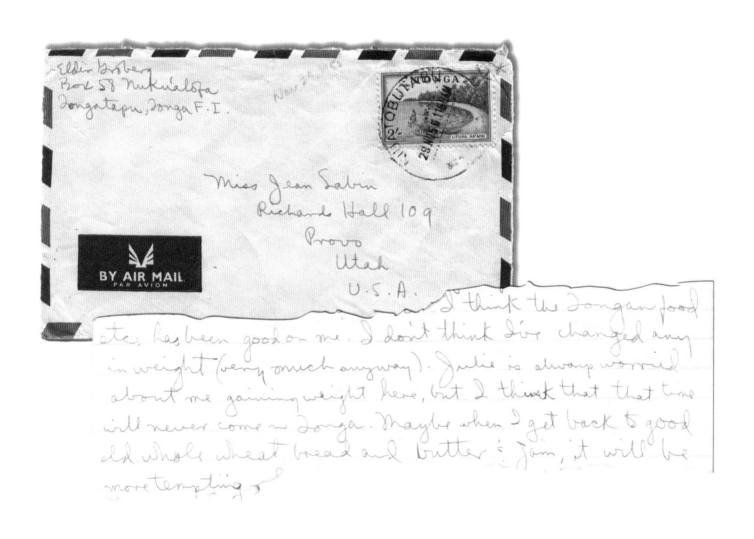

Elder Groberg
Box 58 Nukualofa
Tongatapu, Tonga F.I.

Nov 28 1955

Miss Jean Sabin
Richards Hall 109
Provo
Utah
U.S.A.

BY AIR MAIL
PAR AVION

and I think the Tongan food
etc. has been good on me. I don't think I've changed any
in weight (very much anyway). Julie is always worried
about me gaining weight here, but I think that that time
will never come in Tonga. Maybe when I get back to good
old whole wheat bread and butter & jam, it will be
more tempting.

ALVIN FITISEMANU WAS THE CLOSEST we had to an LDS actor in our movie. His parents are devout members of the Church, as are all of his brothers and sisters. Alvin, however, was raised outside of the church by his grandparents, who were Catholic. Ironically, Alvin's own children were raised by their grandparents—Alvin's parents—and all turned out to be faithful Mormons. One of Alvin's sons was serving his mission in Australia while we were shooting the movie in Rarotonga. —*John Garbett*

Samoa

Fiji                        - 3 -          NiuaToputapu                    Niue

                                    Vava'u

                                    Ha'apai

                                    Tonga

him until on my way home.
    The dotted line
shows the big
steamship line and the
solid line shows the small interTongan route. I stay within
this interTongan route. While Ch... ... Niuall Ht at ...
I think there are about 7 ne...
left there last February — ...
Tonga in December — I ...

... hind on letters, gifts etc. Have
... n't know
... gan food
... ged any
in weight (...                                    ... orried
about me                                         ... that time
will never ...                                   ... good
old whole ...                                    ... will be
more tempti...                                   ... hape as
far as c...

ALTHOUGH I WAS SERVING MY MISSION IN TONGA, I became aware of some of the things that were occurring in the Church elsewhere in Polynesia. In one of my letters home, I wrote, "I hear the work is going very well in the Cook Islands. They have another good Idaho boy serving there." At the time I wrote those words, the Idaho missionary serving in Rarotonga was Elder Norm Thuesson who coincidentally was serving a second mission there during the filming of *The Other Side of Heaven*. —*John Groberg*

CHRIS KNEW VERY LITTLE ABOUT MORMONISM or missionary work when he accepted the role of Elder Groberg. He took a crash course in both topics by spending time working with the two LDS missionaries who were assigned to the island of Rarotonga. I'll never forget them. Elders Gardner and Gardner. —*Jerry Molen*

*John Paekau ("The Governor")*

I HAD JUST DIRECTED MY LAST SHOT ON THE ISLAND OF RAROTONGA and was packing up my office so I could fly out to New Zealand that same night. Suddenly, one of our extras burst into the room and told me that one of our actors, John Paekau, had collapsed in the hotel lobby and was being rushed to the hospital.

"All I can think is that you have to give him a blessing," she said. We had shot the "blessing of Nuku" scene a few days earlier, and this island local, along with others, had been touched by it.

Realizing I had no oil with me, I jumped into my car and rushed home to get some. I then jumped back into my car and headed for the missionaries' apartment, since I couldn't find John, Jerry or Steve.

Elder Thuesson and I hurried to the hospital but we were too late. John was declared dead as we stood outside the door. A few of the Polynesian actors and crew members were already there, comforting John's wife and young grandson.

I headed back home and told my family what had happened. I packed my bags, hugged my wife and kids, then returned to the hospital on my way to the airport. Many of the cast and crew had already gathered and, true to Polynesian custom, had set up blankets and mats for an all-night vigil. I spoke with them briefly, then went inside.

I found our first assistant director, Carey Carter, a massive Maori man, and his wife, Vanessa Rare, sitting in the room with John and his wife, Lovey. She was holding his right hand to her breast, stroking his arm, weeping gently. She talked about their life together, how it had not always been easy, but how it had been good ever since John had "found the Lord." She talked about how he had hidden his heart ailment from her until quite recently, not wanting to upset her.

After some time, I headed back outside and sat down on one of the mats with the growing number of mourners. I felt very bad about leaving this situation behind to continue to New Zealand, but knew my immediate departure was absolutely essential to the movie. I was grateful that John and Jerry were remaining in Rarotonga for a few more days.

Suddenly, Lovey came out and explained that the orderlies were anxious to dress her husband for burial before rigor mortis set in. Someone had delivered his suit from the hotel, but they had forgotten to bring his socks. I remembered that I had put on brand new socks for the flight to New Zealand. I offered them to Lovey and she took them graciously, returning back inside to dress her husband one last time.

The next day the cast and crew held a memorial service for John in the hospital parking lot. It was a traditional Polynesian "tangi" where those who wanted to could stand and share their remembrances of the departed. My son, Christian, was the only "pakeha" to speak. He read a brief tribute I had faxed him upon landing in New Zealand: "The gentle giant is gone, but he has left not merely footsteps; rather, a path that we may walk on our way back to Him. Go to the light, John. Greet the light! It lives in you."

After the tribute there was a moment or two of silence before two of our actresses, Miriama Smith and Apii McKinley, jumped up and spontaneously began singing a tearful rendition of a hymn they had learned a few weeks earlier for a scene in the movie: "God Be With You Till We Meet Again." The entire cast and crew joined in. —*Mitch Davis*

AFTER 45 LONG DAYS OF SHOOTING IN THE HEAT OF THE TROPICS, we moved our entire production down to New Zealand, where it was the dead of winter. Everyone went from shorts and tee shirts to several layers of warm clothing. Well, almost everyone. —*Mitch Davis*

WE HAD TO START SHOOTING IN RAROTONGA before we were able to cast the part of Jean Sabin Groberg. Our U.S. casting director continued auditioning in Los Angeles and sent videotapes to us down in the Cook Islands. As soon as we saw Anne Hathaway's tape, we knew we had our Jean. —*John Garbett*

ANNE JOINED US IN NEW ZEALAND after we'd been shooting in the Cook Islands for almost two months. We were all pretty worn out by the time this 18 year-old gal bounced off her plane, bursting with energy.

A few days later Anne raced onto the set. "Mr. Davis, Mr. Davis! I got my next part! It's this little Disney movie called *The Princess Diaries*!" I immediately knew that our up-and-coming actress was about to become a bona fide movie star. —*Mitch Davis*

ONE OF JERRY'S MANY CREATIVE CONTRIBUTIONS to the movie was encouraging me to enhance the love story between John and Jean. Jerry understood better than I the emotional power of two young lovers pulled apart by life's circumstances. He wisely suggested I spend more time on their conversations "across the sky" with each other. —*Mitch Davis*

I HAVE HAD SOME TEASING FROM THE FAMILY about the kissing scene on the swing set. It is true that John and I spent some time talking and swinging on an old swing near the BYU campus. We did talk about sending messages to each other via the moon. But our first kiss was saved for that special night, after he had been home from his mission for a while, when I accepted his proposal to become his wife and eternal companion. —*Jean Groberg*

THIS MOVIE IS A LOVE STORY between the guy and the girl, how he's waiting for her and she's waiting for him. It's also a love story between John Groberg and the island itself, the people he comes to love as his family. It's a movie about loving everything around you, and I think that's a beautiful message. —*Anne Hathaway*

I have often had the feeling that you probably have learned these valuable lessons much before and much better than I have - I do think you have some wonderful philosophy Jean - Keep it up. Keep up the faith - everything that is right will work out. The Lord has his hands in both of our lives and I don't worry about anything. Just do what we are called to do, and leave the rest up to the Lord. I'm so grateful for peace of mind in these matters and I'm so grateful to know that you have the same (or stronger) faith that I do and that you will always be perfectly honest and frank as I have always tried to be. There's still over a year, and maybe longer - but it's all in the Lord's hands - Jean, thanks for the letters - the expressions of love and faith - I hope you receive as much benefit from my letters as I do from yours - Love John.

*Letter from John to Jean, 1956*

I TOLD JOHN THAT I AGREED WITH HIM that the filmmakers had done a great job of accurately depicting the spirit of our relationship, with one exception: He was not nearly that good of a dancer. —*Jean Groberg*

*Elder Groberg with his musical siblings, circa 1949*

ELDER GROBERG WAS KIND ENOUGH TO ALLOW US to use the actual trumpet he took on his mission as a prop in the movie. It was fun watching the prop guys fawn over the instrument. It was, as they say, the genuine article. —*Jerry Molen*

THE STORM-AT-SEA SEQUENCE WAS PROBABLY THE FILM'S MOST logistically ambitious undertaking. We had to create the appearance of three men in an open boat in fifty-foot waves during a tropical storm, including fierce lightning, and we had to do so safely.

We took over the Auckland dry dock for several days and built a stunt-set inside it. We put our boat at the bottom of the reservoir on a sort of train track with a remote joystick that allowed us to control it like an amusement park ride. Then, on one side of the dry dock, we built a huge wave chute with tanks of water that would dump into it on cue.

Above the set, we hung a helium balloon with a light inside it that gave the entire area a moonlit look. We also hung rain towers and a special lightning striker above the boat. We had four cameras rolling on every shot, including one on what is called a "giraffe" crane. There was a safety boat in the water at all times with three rescue divers ready in case of emergency.

Whenever Mitch called "action," we'd turn on the rain towers, the lightning strikers would start firing, and the safety boat would take a few spins around our actors' boat to churn up the water. Then the cameras would start rolling and the effects technicians would run the boat toward the chute as other technicians dumped the tanks of water onto it, creating the waves.

It was a very big night for us. The special-effects house in Canada took all the live images we created and added computer-generated effects. It's been gratifying to see how many reviews of the movie have applauded this scene for its power and believability. —*John Garbett*

THERE WERE MANY TIMES IN THE MAKING OF *THE OTHER SIDE OF HEAVEN* when I felt extreme gratitude for the tools John and Jerry gave me to make the movie, but I never felt better-served than the night we shot the storm sequence. When I got out of the car and saw the army of filmmakers assembled and the incredible stunt-set they had built, I felt like they had snuck me onto the set of a Steven Spielberg movie. —*Mitch Davis*

...3, 1955

Thursday, March 3, 1955 - I worked on the language
and read the O.T. in the Morning. After a great blessing & good prayer
I was blessed with these feelings: My friend - my bosoom friend - The battle
was thick - the waves beat furiously - I was almost
downed - My lungs full of water - I could hardly breath
desparately I grabbed and held. Hardly knowing
what to do - My friend by my side - The battle was
almost too much for me - I began to find - I couldn't
make it - That helping hand - Somehow - someway
I struggled ashore - Helped all of the way - I lay
motionless - silient - quietly I opened my eyes - all
was still - all was motionless - I was alive! Saved -
I looked around - My friend - I cried "My friend"

114

"My friend" Frantically I ran and also raised him
to my knee — My friend, my friend — My, streaming tears
bathed his quiet motionless face — Oh my friend — Oh
my friend — answer me — answer — My friend — my
friend — But all was silent — and then I knew — And
then I knew — He had made the supreme sacrifice for
me — Oh my friend — my friend — How is it that (Break for a
period of tears — one of the few times I have really cried hard
for joy — The joy of Christ — His atonement — and dieing for all of us)
thou wouldst lay down thy life for me — Tears flooded
to the sea — I buried my face in your motionless bosom —
And wept — and wept — and wept — But for joy — For
even Christ laid down His life for all of us — He'll
pull us thru the battle — up to the shore — wash us
in His Blood — To be a friend — To be a friend to Christ.
That spirit above in silent quietness exclaimed. All
is well — I live — I live thru Christ — and thru Him — all
will live — All is well — fear not — Where oh lithaye
Spirit — Where is thy dwelling place? Can I not come?
To be again with my friend — Yes — bear the burdens
of life — and thru Christ — Come and dwell with me
forever — For greater love hath no man than this.
That he lay down his life for another. And forget your
life for the good & service of others — For whosoever
shall lose his life shall find it — and whosoever shall
find his life shall lose it. Oh to lose my self for
the good of others — To sacrifice — to work to labor —
And thru the gift of Christ — My friend — Our friend. ful

JOHN AND JEAN GROBERG HAPPENED TO VISIT OUR SET on the day we were shooting their wedding scene, and we convinced them to appear as extras. This was the first time they met Anne Hathaway, who played Jean. When I introduced them to Anne, Elder Groberg immediately won her over by saying, "So, you're the lucky girl who gets to play my wife." —*Mitch Davis*

*John and Jean Groberg on their wedding day, September 6, 1957*

**To:** Investors
**Date:** Tue, 12 Sep 2000 14:23:56
**Subject:** INVESTOR UPDATE

Dear Investors--

We've been very busy the last few weeks. We are back in the States, editing the film on a very aggressive post-production schedule. Sorry we haven't updated you for a while.

Attached is a thank-you note I wrote to the cast and crew at the conclusion of principal photography. It contains anecdotal history I think you might enjoy.

Please add yourselves to the letter in terms of the people I was extremely grateful for "when I climbed out of the helicopter...having just completed the final shot of the film." Without you, there would have been no final shot, let alone the first one.

All the best to each and every one of you.

Mitch, John and Jerry

*****
CAST AND CREW LETTER

Hello everyone!

It's the day after picture wrap and already I find myself on a plane headed back to the States. My father had a minor stroke this morning so I had to leave New Zealand earlier than expected. I wanted to take a moment to express my gratitude to each of you for your help with our movie.

Twenty-three years ago, I began my missionary service in the tiny village of La Banda, Argentina. Like Elder Groberg, I struggled to learn a foreign language, did my best to reform the town drunk, and worked hard to serve my fellow man. The experience of living among the people of a different land has had a deep and lasting impact on me.

About halfway through my mission, I decided that someday I would make a movie about the Mormon missionary experience. I was convinced that this rigorous rite of passage could be appreciated universally, rather than merely within the confines of Mormonism.

In the ensuing years I finished my mission, finished university, married the girl of my dreams, worked to pay off my student loans, went back to school to study filmmaking, worked at a couple of studios to pay off my new student loans, wrote several scripts, sold one of them, and fathered five children. All the while, for 22 years, I continued inching toward my goal of making a missionary movie.

So it was that, when I climbed out of the helicopter yesterday afternoon, having just completed the final shot of our film, I was overcome with gratitude.

I was grateful for my dear wife, Michelle, who has consistently and selflessly encouraged me to pursue my dream, even when that pursuit involved significant sacrifice for her and our family. I was grateful for my five children who encouraged and supported me as well.

I was grateful for John and Jerry, who put their arms around me a year-and-a-half ago and helped make our movie a reality. I was grateful for their seasoned leadership as we dealt with the harsh realities of making a movie on a remote island.

I was grateful for sensitive, wise performances by our skilled and generous actors. I was grateful for the relentless casting directors who helped us find them.

I was grateful for Chris Gorham, who carried so much of our film's burden on his capable shoulders. I was grateful for his wife Anel's bright and happy spirit. I was grateful for the Polynesian actors' "katoko" for one another, and the degree to which it affected our entire cast and crew. I was grateful that Anne Hathaway showed up just in time to reenergize our exhausted director.

I was grateful for beautiful and well-managed locations, dazzling and authentic costumes, and visually rich sets. I was grateful for thoughtful compositions, magnificent lighting and graceful camera moves. I was grateful for a diligent and skilled sound department.

I was grateful for the beautiful people of Rarotonga, especially the loving mamas, the happy elders and the playful children who worked as our extras. I was grateful for the casting assistants who supervised them, and the assistant directors who directed them.

I was grateful for the production office workers who often toiled into the wee hours of the morning. I was grateful for many of you, starting the next day's work during those same wee hours. I was grateful for the unit personnel who kept my chilly bin full and the portaloos empty.

I was grateful for Sarah's broken hand, wardrobe Chris's broken foot, actor Chris's cut finger, Sidey's smashed finger, Dean's broken collar bone, M.J.'s strained elbow, and Mark's scraped-up face.

"EYE OF THE STORM"

| ROLL | SCENE | TAKE |
|------|-------|------|
| B27 | X 72 A | 7 |

I was grateful for the car and motorcycle accidents that were never as serious as they could have been. I was grateful for the runaway trailer that narrowly missed the group of schoolkids.

I was grateful for the many islanders of various faiths who prayed for our film's success. I was grateful that, whenever absolutely necessary, the clouds parted, the sun shone, the rain stopped and the fog lifted. I was grateful for the several days of heavy rain that did not fall until the day after we left Rarotonga.

I was grateful for the foul language that wasn't often heard on our set. I was grateful for the theological discussions that often were.

I was grateful for great stunts, amazing special effects, perfect props, and accountants who delivered per deims with a smile. I was grateful for thirty hard-working carpenters who never said no, and who made the rich man's yacht look like it really belonged.

I was grateful for a cheerful, skilled editor, for a proactive video-effects supervisor and a scrappy second unit. I was grateful for two amazing assistants, and fresh crayfish delivered by Seth.

I was grateful for the life of John Paekau, for Carey, Vanessa and Alvin, comforting John's wife at the hospital while Pua, Whetu and Glynnis comforted his grandson. I was grateful for Apii and Miriama singing at John's memorial after my son, Christian, spoke.

Most of all, I was grateful for each and every one of you, for your hard work, your kind encouragement, your friendship and support. I hope that support will continue, that you will keep us in your thoughts and prayers as we strive to craft a finished film worthy of your collective efforts.

I love and appreciate all of you. My family and I will miss you dearly. Please keep in touch with us.

Hurrah for Israel!

Mitch

I was a little unprepared for the letdown that occurs when principal photography is over. You go from being the general of a small army to sitting in a dark room with one guy and a bunch of computer monitors. I was totally exhausted, so sitting around didn't seem like such a bad thing, but I did miss all the beautiful people with whom I had made the movie.—*Mitch Davis*

Most moviegoers aren't aware of how important the post-production process is. There are 24 frames of film per second of screen time, and every frame gets examined and reexamined by the editor. Every piece of sound gets created or treated by the sound designers. Every special effect gets implemented, and every musical cue perfectly-timed. You can make or break a movie in post-production, and Steve Ramirez did a fabulous job of shepherding us through that part of the filmmaking process.—*Jerry Molen*

We were on a pretty tight post-production schedule, so Steve and I often turned to prayer when we got stuck editorially. It was quite remarkable how often we got off our knees having decided to make the exact same changes. Sometimes, without even saying a word, we'd just sit back down at the edit console and make the crucial cuts.

It was the same way with our composer, Kevin Kiner. I'd drive up to his house after editing with Steve all day and he'd take me out back to his studio to play me the new pieces he'd written. More than once he had to nudge me to make sure I was awake. Kevin calls the score for our movie 'a miracle.' We had so little time to create it ourselves, we really relied heavily on prayer. I know this made the difference.—*Mitch Davis*

# THEME IDEA

MITCH AND I HAVE BEEN FRIENDS SINCE WE WERE SEVEN OR EIGHT YEARS OLD. He taught me my first chords on the guitar, and we were in a garage band together in the sixth grade.

In spite of Mitch's best efforts, I am a devout Catholic, but I'm not one of those composers who usually has spiritual experiences while writing my music. I just sort of sit down and bang it out. Writing the score for this movie was very different.

Mitch had just asked me to do the score for *The Other Side of Heaven*, and I was pretty stressed out because I was coming into the project a little late. I was lying on my bed one night while my wife, Mercy, read to me from the Bible. She was reading the story of the Annunciation when, all of a sudden, I just heard this tune playing in my head.

I jumped up and told Mercy to go to sleep without me. I ran downstairs to the piano and wrote down this melody that seemed to have come from out of nowhere. All at once, I had the theme for *The Other Side of Heaven*.

I've told Mitch many times that there is something very special about the spirit of this movie. Receiving musical inspiration like I did that night… it's never happened to me before, and I'm not sure it ever will again.—*Kevin Kiner*

# EYE OF THE STORM
# 1M1 MAIN TITLE

KEVIN KINER

THE RECORDING OF THE ORCHESTRAL SCORE TOOK PLACE in the city of Prague, the Czech Republic. As I sat there watching these incredibly talented Eastern European musicians playing music composed by a Catholic man from Los Angeles for a movie about a Mormon boy from Idaho and the eternal friends he made in Tonga, I remembered the charge given me by Elder Groberg: "Make a movie that will touch the light of Christ that is found in all men, regardless of their creed or color or nationality." —*Mitch Davis*

*The following excerpts are from a letter Mitch Davis wrote at an early stage of the filmmaking journey. He had visited Tonga to do some research in preparation for the movie. Deeply touched by what he experienced, he wrote to Elder Groberg to share his impressions of that memorable visit.*

Dear Elder Groberg,

I wanted to take a moment to describe a few of the experiences I had during my brief stay in Tonga. Notwithstanding the passage of more than forty years since your mission there, I clearly found vestiges of the magic you so vividly described in your book and in your visits with me.

I was amazed at the lingering impact of your personal ministry there. One great missionary, one great man, can make a difference, and you certainly have done so in the Kingdom of Tonga. I was reminded of the scripture: "Thus God has provided a means that man, through faith, might work mighty miracles; therefore he becometh a great benefit to his fellow beings."

My Tongan experience began as I arrived in Nuku'alofa at 2:30 A.M. on a Friday night. I was amazed to find hundreds of Tongans—mothers, fathers, little children—standing on the outdoor balcony of the airport, waiting to greet their loved ones home. I was reminded of your stories of families waiting at the harbor for the sea to return their loved ones. I remembered you saying that, in Tonga, there is little difference between two in the morning and two in the afternoon.

While going through customs I made the acquaintance of a man named William. He offered me a ride to town and I accepted.

Once inside his car, I explained the nature of my visit to Nuku'alofa. He smiled when I mentioned your name. "Ah, yes. Groberg. A very good-looking man," he said. He went on to explain that although he was Catholic, he had heard you speak at some civic events during your term as mission president.

He took me to a hotel and talked the desk clerk into giving me a room even though I had no reservation. It was almost 4:00 A.M. when he left me there.

The next morning I rented a car and began driving around the island. I was impressed at how many Mormon churches I saw—as if I were somewhere in Idaho or Utah. I stopped at the temple to ask directions to my planned destination. I saw many beautiful people entering the Lord's house. They were all very friendly and humble, yet proud to be doing the Lord's work.

Leaving there, I soon found myself on a bumpy dirt road. I had gone a few miles when I hit a rock and blew out a front tire. I went to the trunk and found a jack, but there was no jack handle or lug wrench. The sun was setting and I realized it would be dark soon. I turned the car around and tried to drive on the flat tire.

I quit driving after a short distance, afraid I might ruin the rim. Then, gratefully, I saw a truck coming in my rear view mirror. I got out of the car to flag the man down, but I didn't need to. He pulled right up alongside me, and asked in perfect English, "What's going on, man?"

I explained my situation and he immediately got out to help. We talked as we worked, and I learned that he had been raised in the United States in the San Francisco area. As a young man, he had gotten into some trouble, and even spent time in prison. His father suggested that he go to Tonga to straighten out his life. He arrived in Nuku'alofa with little to call his own, but soon met a Mormon girl who converted him to the gospel. After a time he was sealed to her in the temple. Eventually he became a bishop.

His wife and children walked out of the fields just as we were finishing the tire together.

"Me, a bishop," my new friend mused. "Who would believe it?" I looked at his beautiful family and considered how kind he had been to stop and help me.

"Heavenly Father would," I thought with all the conviction of my heart.

I got back into my car and headed for town. By then it was dark, and I was just turning back toward Nuku'alofa when I noticed a funeral procession turning onto the road ahead of me.

I had been anxious to witness a Tongan funeral, so I fell in line and followed the caravan for many miles. Finally, the procession stopped in front of a small home. Preparations for an all-night party were in full swing. Lights were being set up in the yard. Large tarps had been stretched out between trees in case of rain. Palm fronds were spread out on the ground.

I parked my car and stood a safe distance away as the casket was carried inside and most of the crowd filtered in. Several individuals stayed outside so I joined them. They took my presence in stride, and seemed glad, even honored, to have me there.

There was a loud speech coming from inside the house, and I made my way to a louvered window for a better look. A middle-aged son was giving some sort of oration from the far room where his mother lay in her casket. The speech was fiery and flowery, more impassioned than emotional. After some time, he finished and left the room. It seemed as if now was the women's turn.

A couple of middle-aged women whom I guessed to be the deceased's daughters made their way over to the casket and began to sob. The larger of the two began to wail, and her cries grew increasingly overwrought. She began slapping the floor with her hands, wailing louder and louder with her face only inches from that of her deceased mother, as if scolding her for dying. One refrain repeated itself over and over: "O ia ue! O ia ue!"

I was intrigued to watch the other mourners reacting to this one woman. It was almost as if she did all the mourning for them. Several other women made themselves busy preparing the feast. They scurried right past the wailing woman, stepping over or around her.

Eventually, either the exertion or the emotion got the best of the obese mourner, and she passed out on the floor mid-wail. "O ia..." then silence. Everyone sprang into action as they saw the motionless woman on the floor.

Several men—big, strong men—squeezed inside the room and strained to lift the extremely robust body of this woman so that they could carry her out onto the porch. Several women and young people crowded around her on the porch, and I could see someone's hands pumping up and down, as if performing CPR.

A larger crowd gathered, some murmuring to each other about the possibility of a second death and a second funeral. Apprehension grew on the faces of those watching from afar.

Suddenly the large woman awakened, picking up her wail right where she left off: "...Ue! O ia ue!" She jumped to her feet and bustled back inside the house, where another woman had taken advantage of her absence and knelt by the casket. As both women started wailing again, a little toddler sat between them looking perplexed.

The lights came on outside where I stood, and I felt suddenly conspicuous in my palangi skin. I turned and headed for my car. As I left, the men were all sitting in a circle under one of the canopies, laughing and sharing stories, waiting for the food.

The next day I went to church with Tonga Totai Pale'tua—the man you suggested I visit—and his family. He sat next to me with his arm around my shoulder during most of the meeting. Finally he asked, "Do you want to bear your testimony?" He kindly encouraged me: "I go. My wife go. You come. Is good."

We walked to the stand together and a slight murmur was heard among the congregation. When it came our turn, Tonga's wife stood first. She bore a sweet, fervent testimony. Then it was Tonga's turn, and he strode to the pulpit.

Tonga was wearing a light blue polyester leisure suit he must have bought in the 1970s in Salt Lake City, along with some suede leather Wallabees probably purchased that same year. He was not a big man, and all of his conversations with me had been held in broken English. But when he took the pulpit, when he began to speak in his own tongue, he grew in stature five-fold.

I could not discern Tonga's words, but it was clear that he was teaching this congregation. They laughed with him, smiled up at him fondly, nodded their heads in agreement and understanding. Then he was done, and it was my turn.

There was no way I could be anything but a letdown following Tonga. I shared a brief testimony of missionary work, told the congregation how honored I was to be in their presence, then sat down. How I wished I could speak to these people in their language! That I could show them I loved them enough to use their own words!

But I was just a palangi, and did sin in my wish. I took Tonga Totai and his wife home where they gave me my first good taste of real Tongan food.

The next morning I left for the airport. It didn't take long for me to learn that my taxi driver was LDS. I told him of my reason for being in Nuku'alofa. He nodded fondly when I mentioned your name.

"I met him once, when I was little," he said. "In Pangai, 1956." I marveled at the fact that, once again I was sitting with someone who had personal knowledge or you and your ministry. When we arrived at the airport, he jumped out to help me check my bags. I thanked him for his help and asked his name.

"Sione," came the answer. "Sione Tukinoa."

I mentioned that one of your counselors in Pangai had been named Sione. He smiled proudly.

"I know," he said. "He was my uncle."

When I got over my shock, I held the taxi driver at arms' length and just looked at him. For a moment it seemed Sione Vea stood before me. But it was time for me to leave, and all I could say was, "God bless you, my brother."

I checked in for my flight, then headed to a waiting area, where I sat watching the people coming and going. I marveled at how noisy and happy a scene it was. Everyone, it seemed, was either talking or laughing or hugging or waving or wiping tears. The entire airport felt like a joyous family reunion.

Finally it was time for me to leave Tonga, and I walked out onto the tarmac with a humid breeze blowing. It was 9:30 at night. Again, the airport balcony was full of people. They would call out to each person who was departing by name. The departing traveler would turn and wave to their many loved ones on the balcony. It was clear when they did so that they knew how beloved they were. I was jealous of those whose names were called and had to squelch the urge to turn around and wave to the crowd, pretending to be a part of it all.

I have seen many beautiful sites on this trip, which has included stops in Fiji, Rarotonga and New Zealand, but nothing I have seen can compare to what I felt in the isles of the Kingdom of Tonga.

There is something exceptionally sacred about that place. During my time there, Heavenly Father repeatedly moved people in and out of my path quite purposefully. I thank you again for your powerful ministry there, and for allowing me to experience a bit of it vicariously. It fills me with hope to know that every faithful missionary will leave such a lasting impact for good on the souls of men. I pray that in some small way our film can leave a similar impression.

"There is a connection between heaven and earth." There is. Yes, there really is.—*Mitch Davis*

*Anita Schiller*

*Ken George*

*Hugh Hogle*

PHOTO CREDITS

| | |
|---|---|
| 1 | Anita Schiller |
| 2 | Ken George |
| 3 | Portraits courtesy of John and Jean Groberg |
| 4 | Ken George |
| 10 | Anita Schiller; 2nd from left Hugh Hogle; 2nd from right unknown |
| 13-17 | Anita Schiller |
| 18-20 | Ken George |
| 21 | Anita Schiller |
| 22 | Anita Schiller; far right unknown |
| 24 | Ken George |
| 26-28 | Courtesy of John and Jean Groberg |
| 30 | Anita Schiller; 2nd from left Ken George |
| 31-33 | Anita Schiller |
| 34 | Digita Stock |
| 35 | Anita Schiller |
| 36 | Ken George |
| 38 | Anita Schiller |
| 41 | Ken George |
| 42-43 | Anita Schiller |

| | |
|---|---|
| 45-46 | Ken George |
| 48 | Hugh Hogle |
| 51 | Anita Schiller |
| 52-56 | Ken George |
| 58 | Left Ken George; right courtesy of John and Jean Groberg |
| 61 | Ken George |
| 62-67 | Courtesy of John and Jean Groberg |
| 68-71 | Ken George |
| 72-77 | Anita Schiller |
| 79-81 | Ken George |
| 82 | Courtesy of John and Jean Groberg |
| 83-85 | Ken George |
| 86-89 | Courtesy of John and Jean Groberg |
| 90-91 | Ken George |
| 92 | Left Ken George; right Hugh Hogle |
| 93 | Anita Schiller |
| 94-95 | Ken George |
| 96-97 | Courtesy of John and Jean Groberg |
| 98 | Left Anita Schiller; right Ken George |
| 99 | Left Anita Schiller; right courtesy of Nuku Fonua |
| 100 | Anita Schiller |
| 101 | Ken George |

102     Hugh Hogle

103-108 Ken George

110     Courtesy of John and Jean Groberg

111-112 Ken George

113     Left Anita Schiller; right courtesy of
          Sione and Simaima Tulua

115-123 Anita Schiller

124-129 Ken George

130     Left Anita Schiller; right Ken George

131-132 Ken George

133     Left Ken George; right Anita Schiller

134     Storyboard courtesy of Threemark Entertainment, LLC

136-143 Ken George

144     Anita Schiller

145     Courtesy of John and Jean Groberg

146-149 Ken George

150     Anita Schiller

151     Ken George

153     Anita Schiller

154     Ken George

155-157 Anita Schiller

158-159 Photos, circa 1955-56, and letter courtesy of John and Jean
          Groberg: a. Elder Groberg (right, holding trumpet) with scout
          in Pangai, b. Feki and Simaima c. Family in Hihifo,
          d. Feki on horseback e. Elder Groberg (4th row back, far
          right) with school children.

160     Anita Schiller

161     Ken George

162-163 Anita Schiller

164-168 Ken George

170-171 Photos of Pangai, circa 1956, courtesy of John and Jean Groberg

172-175 Anita Schiller

176     Ken George; right Anita Schiller

179-180 Ken George

181     Courtesy of John and Jean Groberg

182     Anita Schiller; 2nd row from bottom, far right Ken George

183     Ken George; middle row, far left Anita Schiller

185     Anita Schiller

186     Courtesy of John and Jean Groberg

187     Ken George

188     Anita Schiller

190     Anita Schiller; bottom Ken George

191     Anita Schiller

192     Courtesy of John and Jean Groberg

194-195 Ken George

196     Courtesy of John and Jean Groberg

197     Ken George

198     Anita Schiller; top left Ken George

199-202 Ken George

205     Anita Schiller; top row, far left and bottom row, far right
          Ken George

206     Anita Schiller

210     Mitch Davis

211     Courtesy of Kevin Kiner

212     Musical score courtesy of Kevin Kiner

213     Mitch Davis

219     Anita Schiller

220     Left, Joan Schreiner; center and right unknown

222     Anita Schiller

224     Anita Schiller

AS FAR OUT IN THE OCEAN AS WE WERE, I never felt like we were alone on the island. I felt like there was a Divine hand guiding and protecting the whole shoot. We were on an incredibly tight shooting schedule and any small problem would have had big ramifications, but I always felt like we were being protected, and we were. —*Jerry Molen*

# TAPESTRY

## MODERN
## IMPRESSIONS

*Writing in Our Times*

# TAPESTRY

The **Tapestry** program of language materials is based on the concepts presented in *The Tapestry of Language Learning: The Individual in the Communicative Classroom* by Robin C. Scarcella & Rebecca L. Oxford.

❖

Each title in this program focuses on:

❖

Individual learner strategies and instruction

❖

The relatedness of skills

❖

Ongoing self-assessment

❖

Authentic material as input

❖

Theme-based learning linked to task-based instruction

❖

Attention to all aspects of communicative competence

# TAPESTRY

# MODERN IMPRESSIONS

## Writing in Our Times

### Marie Hutchison Weidauer

Heinle & Heinle Publishers
A Division of Wadsworth, Inc.
Boston, Massachusetts, 02116, USA

The publication of *Modern Impressions* was directed by the members of the Heinle & Heinle ESL Publishing Team:

David C. Lee, Editorial Director
John McHugh, Market Development Director
Lisa McLaughlin, Production Editor

Also participating in the publication of this program were:

Publisher: Stanley J. Galek
Editorial Production Manager: Elizabeth Holthaus
Assistant Editor: Kenneth Mattsson
Manufacturing Coordinator: Mary Beth Lynch
Full Service Project Manager/Compositor: PC&F, Inc.
Interior Design: Maureen Lauran
Cover Design: Maureen Lauran

Manufactured in the United States of America

ISBN 0-8384-4084-3

Heinle & Heinle Publishers is a division of Wadsworth, Inc.

10 9 8 7 6 5 4

*to my M.D.*

## PHOTO CREDITS

## ACKNOWLEDGMENTS

44, The Covert Curriculum, Alvin Toffler.

47, Chapter 21 from Kaffir Boy. Reprinted with the permission of Macmillan Publishing Company from KAFFIR BOY by Mark Mathabane. Copyright © 1986 by Mark Mathabane.

56, Private Education with a Conscience, Jean Merl. Copyright holder: Los Angeles Times.

80, My Father Worked Late, Jim Daniels. Copyright holder: University of Wisconsin Press.

85, Helen, Mr. Mellow, and the Briefcase, Kyle D. Pruett. Copyright holder: Kyle D. Pruett.

91, Fatherhood: The Second Round. Copyright © 1991 by the New York Times Company. Reprinted with permission.

97, Life without Father, Nina J. Easton. Copyright holder: Los Angeles Times Magazine.

127, Who Are the Poor? Richard H. Ropers. Copyright holder: Plenum Publishing, New York.

139, A Killer in the Deep South. Reprinted with the permission of Macmillan Publishing Company from LIVING HUNGRY IN AMERICA by Dr. J. Larry Brown, Ph.D. and H.F. Pizer, P.A.-C.

162, Some Conclusions about Successful Coping Responses. *Coping with Life Challenges,* Chris L. Kleinke, Brooks/Cole Publishing Company, 1991.

165, Breaking the Bonds of Hate, Virak Khiev. Copyright holder: Virak Khiev.

170, Choosing Not to Die Alone, Pamela Warrick. Copyright holder: Los Angeles Times.

182, A Little Push from Big Brother Goes a Long Way, Bob Poole. Copyright holder: Los Angeles Times.

# WELCOME TO TAPESTRY

*E*nter the world of Tapestry! Language learning can be seen as an ever-developing tapestry woven with many threads and colors. The elements of the tapestry are related to different language skills like listening and speaking, reading and writing; the characteristics of the teachers; the desires, needs, and backgrounds of the students; and the general second language development process. When all these elements are working together harmoniously, the result is a colorful, continuously growing tapestry of language competence of which the student and the teacher can be proud.

This volume is part of the Tapestry program for students of English as a second language (ESL) at levels from beginning to "bridge" (which follows the advanced level and prepares students to enter regular postsecondary programs along with native English speakers). Tapestry levels include:

Beginning
Low Intermediate
High Intermediate
Low Advanced
High Advanced
Bridge

Because the Tapestry Program provides a unified theoretical and pedagogical foundation for all its components, you can optimally use all the Tapestry student books in a coordinated fashion as an entire curriculum of materials. (They will be published from 1993 to 1995 with further editions likely thereafter.) Alternatively, you can decide to use just certain Tapestry volumes, depending on your specific needs.

Tapestry is primarily designed for ESL students at postsecondary institutions in North America. Some want to learn ESL for academic or career advancement, others for social and personal reasons. Tapestry builds directly on all these motivations. Tapestry stimulates learners to do their best. It enables learners to use English naturally and to develop fluency as well as accuracy.

## Tapestry Principles

The following principles underlie the instruction provided in all of the components of the Tapestry program.

### EMPOWERING LEARNERS

Language learners in Tapestry classrooms are active and increasingly responsible for developing their English language skills and related cultural abilities. This self direction leads to better, more rapid learning. Some cultures virtually train their students to be passive in the classroom, but Tapestry weans them from passivity by providing exceptionally high interest materials, colorful and motivating activities, personalized self-reflection tasks, peer tutoring and other forms of cooperative learning, and powerful learning strategies to boost self direction in learning.

The empowerment of learners creates refreshing new roles for teachers, too. The teacher serves as facilitator, co-communicator, diagnostician, guide, and helper. Teachers are set free to be more creative at the same time their students become more autonomous learners.

### HELPING STUDENTS IMPROVE THEIR LEARNING STRATEGIES

Learning strategies are the behaviors or steps an individual uses to enhance his or her learning. Examples are taking notes, practicing, finding a conversation partner, analyzing words, using background knowledge, and controlling anxiety. Hundreds of such strategies have been identified. Successful language learners use language learning strategies that are most effective for them given their particular learning style, and they put them together smoothly to fit the needs of a given language task. On the other hand, the learning strategies of less successful learners are a desperate grab-bag of ill-matched techniques.

All learners need to know a wide range of learning strategies. All learners need systematic practice in choosing and applying strategies that are relevant for various learning needs. Tapestry is one of the only ESL programs that overtly weaves a comprehensive set of learning strategies into language activities in all its volumes. These learning strategies are arranged in six broad categories throughout the Tapestry books:

Forming concepts
Personalizing
Remembering new material
Managing your learning
Understanding and using emotions
Overcoming limitations

The most useful strategies are sometimes repeated and flagged with a note, "It Works! Learning Strategy . . ." to remind students to use a learning strategy they have already encountered. This recycling reinforces the value of learning strategies and provides greater practice.

### RECOGNIZING AND HANDLING LEARNING STYLES EFFECTIVELY

Learners have different learning styles (for instance, visual, auditory, hands-on; reflective, impulsive; analytic, global; extroverted, introverted; closure-oriented, open). Particularly in an ESL setting, where students come from vastly different cultural backgrounds, learning styles differences abound and can cause "style conflicts."

Unlike most language instruction materials, Tapestry provides exciting activities specifically tailored to the needs of students with a large range of learning styles. You can use any Tapestry volume with the confidence that the activities and materials are intentionally geared for many different styles. Insights from the latest educational and psychological research undergird this style-nourishing variety.

## OFFERING AUTHENTIC, MEANINGFUL COMMUNICATION

Students need to encounter language that provides authentic, meaningful communication. They must be involved in real-life communication tasks that cause them to *want* and *need* to read, write, speak, and listen to English. Moreover, the tasks—to be most effective—must be arranged around themes relevant to learners.

Themes like family relationships, survival in the educational system, personal health, friendships in a new country, political changes, and protection of the environment are all valuable to ESL learners. Tapestry focuses on topics like these. In every Tapestry volume, you will see specific content drawn from very broad areas such as home life, science and technology, business, humanities, social sciences, global issues, and multiculturalism. All the themes are real and important, and they are fashioned into language tasks that students enjoy.

At the advanced level, Tapestry also includes special books each focused on a single broad theme. For instance, there are two books on business English, two on English for science and technology, and two on academic communication and study skills.

## UNDERSTANDING AND VALUING DIFFERENT CULTURES

Many ESL books and programs focus completely on the "new" culture, that is, the culture which the students are entering. The implicit message is that ESL students should just learn about this target culture, and there is no need to understand their own culture better or to find out about the cultures of their international classmates. To some ESL students, this makes them feel their own culture is not valued in the new country.

Tapestry is designed to provide a clear and understandable entry into North American culture. Nevertheless, the Tapestry Program values *all* the cultures found in the ESL classroom. Tapestry students have constant opportunities to become "culturally fluent" in North American culture while they are learning English, but they also have the chance to think about the cultures of their classmates and even understand their home culture from different perspectives.

## INTEGRATING THE LANGUAGE SKILLS

Communication in a language is not restricted to one skill or another. ESL students are typically expected to learn (to a greater or lesser degree) all four language skills: reading, writing, speaking. and listening. They are also expected to develop strong grammatical competence, as well as becoming socioculturally sensitive and knowing what to do when they encounter a "language barrier."

Research shows that multi-skill learning is more effective than isolated-skill learning, because related activities in several skills provide reinforcement and refresh the learner's memory. Therefore, Tapestry integrates all the skills. A given

Tapestry volume might highlight one skill, such as reading, but all other skills are also included to support and strengthen overall language development.

However, many intensive ESL programs are divided into classes labeled according to one skill (Reading Comprehension Class) or at most two skills (Listening/Speaking Class or Oral Communication Class). The volumes in the Tapestry Program can easily be used to fit this traditional format, because each volume clearly identifies its highlighted or central skill(s).

Grammar is interwoven into all Tapestry volumes. However, there is also a separate reference book for students, *The Tapestry Grammar,* and a Grammar Strand composed of grammar "work-out" books at each of the levels in the Tapestry Program.

## Other Features of the Tapestry Program

### PILOT SITES

It is not enough to provide volumes full of appealing tasks and beautiful pictures. Users deserve to know that the materials have been pilot-tested. In many ESL series, pilot testing takes place at only a few sites or even just in the classroom of the author. In contrast, Heinle & Heinle Publishers have developed a network of Tapestry Pilot Test Sites throughout North America. At this time, there are approximately 40 such sites, although the number grows weekly. These sites try out the materials and provide suggestions for revisions. They are all actively engaged in making Tapestry the best program possible.

### AN OVERALL GUIDEBOOK

To offer coherence to the entire Tapestry Program and especially to offer support for teachers who want to understand the principles and practice of Tapestry, we have written a book entitled, *The Tapestry of Language Learning. The Individual in the Communicative Classroom* (Scarcella and Oxford, published in 1992 by Heinle & Heinle).

## A Last Word

We are pleased to welcome you to Tapestry! We use the Tapestry principles every day, and we hope these principles—and all the books in the Tapestry Program—provide you the same strength, confidence, and joy that they give us. We look forward to comments from both teachers and students who use any part of the Tapestry Program.

Rebecca L. Oxford
University of Alabama
Tuscaloosa, Alabama

Robin C. Scarcella
University of California at Irvine
Irvine, California

# PREFACE

$M$*odern Impressions: Writing in Our Times* has been designed to guide the low-advanced ESL student into developing his capacity as an English writer as he comes to understand his beliefs about several institutions in society. While the social issues the student works with are presented in the U.S. context, they are applicable to other societies as well, as chapter exercises based on multicultural information and student writings attest to.

Just as any writer's purpose is to communicate a message, the students' purpose in the text is to find a message and succeed in communicating it. The chapters are very much content-driven; the more students learn about the topic and learn to recognize their own opinions on the topic, the more they have to say in their writing and the more they will care about saying it in a way which accurately reflects their opinions. As writing is a recursive process of discovery, the text gives students opportunities to discover knowledge and feelings about their topics and to craft, and re-craft, their writings. The text brings all of the students language skills together by encouraging them to receive input from reading and interactions with native speakers and each other while encouraging output not only through writing but speaking as well.

*Modern Impressions* has seven chapters, arranged in such a way that the major topic chapters (4, 5, 6, and 7) can be done in any order.

## CHAPTERS 1, 2, AND 3

- Chapter 1 is designed as a "first day" group of activities to increase students' awareness of their preferred learning styles and their writing goals and acquaint them with other possibilities for both.
- Chapter 2 acquaints students with the basics of organizing essays. It may be done all at once or in conjunction with any of the major chapters.
- Chapter 3 gives students information about writing persuasive essays. In the major chapters, students are repeatedly given choices of essay topics reflecting

narrative, descriptive, analytic or persuasive modes of writing. Chapter 3 may be done early by students who want to launch into persuasive writing early; it may be done by the class as a whole when the teacher desires.

## CHAPTERS 4, 5, 6, AND 7

There are four major topic chapters in *Modern Impressions.* They are conceived to constitute 12–15 hours of instruction spread out over approximately three weeks. Each chapter contains a choice of major essay assignments, several readings on the topic, writing skills instruction, language skills instruction, an editing strategy, a punctuation note, assessment of writing, sample student writings, and a writer's notebook. The skills are spiraled among each other in each chapter so that classes may work in the chapters in order of presentation of the materials. The chapters are designed in such a way that they support the revision process as students work their way through three drafts of a major essay and are referred back to these drafts to make changes using what they have just learned.

### The Major Essay Assignments

Each major chapter offers students several choices for a major essay assignment (750–1000 words): a descriptive and/or narrative assignment, an analytic assignment, or a persuasive assignment. Students are encouraged to challenge themselves by choosing a topic which is a little bit harder than they are used to. Students continually work on drafts of this essay during the chapter and are repeatedly urged to revise or edit their drafts when they have learned a new writing or language skill.

### The Readings

Each major chapter has one main topic centered on three or four readings. Each chapter begins with a short "Introductory Reading," which serves to orient students toward the topic, and continues with "In-Depth Readings" and "Further Readings" which are longer, provide many more details about the topic, and raise some of the most important issues associated with the topic. Teachers who prefer to assign less reading can choose from the readings or have students choose the reading(s) they prefer to read. Teachers who prefer to include more reading can send students to the library to find additional articles, an activity which has been found to be very successful in pilot use of this text. Each reading has several activities to support it and develop students' knowledge of the topic:

- Vocabulary Enrichment exercises help students learn new vocabulary, and a Vocabulary Checklist at the end of each chapter lets students record words they wish to remember for future use.
- Elaborating on the Reading helps students understand the points raised in the readings and come to grips with their own opinions on the topic. The exercises include question–answer, roleplay, simulation, and interviews in the community and may be written or oral.
- Short Writings of 150 to 200 words are designed to further students' knowledge of the topic and develop their writing skills. Short writings are often preceded by information about writing style, organization, or the writer's process. They may be assigned for homework or under time pressure in class as "quick writings."

### The Writing Skills

Each major chapter also contains information and exercises to improve students' writing skills. These skills acquaint students with the process of writing, clear organization of writing, and techniques for clarifying or strengthening their writing. The organizational techniques that are introduced coordinate with the analytic major essay assignment for each chapter.

### The Language Skills

Two types of language skills are developed in *Modern Impressions:* the skill to control or correct errors and the skill to write syntactically complex sentences. Most exercises are in context, consisting of paragraph-level discourse, in some cases essay level, for students to edit or manipulate in some way. Care has been taken to design exercises which approximate the actual process of revising or editing whenever possible. Students are continually referred back to their drafts to make changes based on the new language skills they have learned.

### The Editing Strategy

Each major chapter contains one editing strategy which is independent of any particular topic or grammar point, one which they can use again and again in their writing in the future.

### The Punctuation Note

Major chapters also contain a brief punctuation note coordinated with a teaching point raised with one of the language or writing skills.

### The Assessment

In order for students to revise their drafts, the text promotes two types of assessment. Students assess their own work through Reflections on drafts one and three. Students assess each other's work in the Peer Responses for draft two. Both Reflections and Peer Responses are guided by a set of five questions. By using the Reflection and Peer Response techniques, students become more empowered writers because they improve their ability to read critically and depend more on themselves as they revise.

It is expected that a third mode of assessment includes teacher assessment. One successful technique for teacher assessment of ESL essays at the University of California, Irvine, has been to provide reactions to content and organization on the first draft, delay marking language problems until the second draft, and respond to the overall success of the essay and its revisions on the third draft. This gives students time to come to grips with the topic and their message while providing the guidance on language skill that they need at a time when it will not interfere with their writing processes.

The final mode of assessment is the Writer's Notebook, which gives students an opportunity to evaluate more broadly what they have been learning about writing and what they would still like to accomplish during this course. It is a type of "journal" of their writing development.

### The Student Writings

Student writings are generally used twice per chapter: once as the basis for practicing the Peer Response of draft two, and once for further discussion or workshopping as students work on draft three. These writings have been chosen for the most part because they are good and because they provide interesting points of view on the chapter's topic, but they are not perfect. In addition, they have been *lightly* edited to remove grammatical errors.

## ACKNOWLEDGMENTS

I would like to acknowledge Rebecca Oxford, David Lee, and Ken Mattsson for their fine input into this text and their patience. I am most especially grateful to two special people who have devoted a great amount of time to helping me develop this text. Robin Scarcella has been a wonderful sounding board for ideas, provided very helpful suggestions as she read the manuscript and was a continuing source of encouragement. Colleen Hildebrand, who taught with the text, was also a bountiful source of creative ideas and newspaper clippings and a perpetual inspiration to me.

I would also like to thank the following reviewers, whose suggestions and encouragement were much appreciated while the manuscript was being developed:

Debra Dean, University of Akron
John Dumacich, New York University
Robert Fox, St. Michael's College
Judith Graves, Eurocenters Alexandria
Karl Krahnke, Colorado State University
Carol Moder, Oklahoma State University
Guillermo Perez, Miami-Dade Community College
Lawrence Udry, University of Tennessee at Martin
Elizabeth Xiezopolski, Contra Costa College
Fran Korenman Yoshida, New York University

And finally, I thank the following instructors and their students for field testing early versions of the manuscript in their classes and providing helpful comments:

Barbara Campbell, State University of New York at Buffalo
Ellen Kohn, George Mason University
Lynn Patterson, University of Tennessee at Martin
Hugh Rutledge, Northeastern University

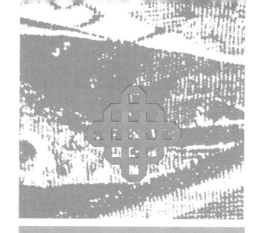

# CONTENTS

# 5 Fathers: Are They Central or Peripheral?   75

# *Your Learning Style and Writing Goals*

## 1

### CHAPTER

In this chapter, you will come to recognize some of the ways you prefer to learn as well as set some goals for yourself as a writer and English learner in this course.

By learning style, we mean the collection of behaviors you use in order to learn. You have studied English writing for a period of time now, and you have probably developed your own, individual, learning style for learning to write well. While you may not be able to change, or even want to change, your style, you may soon discover that some characteristics of your language learning style do not permit you to write as easily or as much as you might like.

This chapter will also give you a chance to consider various types of writing, those for academic life and personal life, and determine which of these most interest you. It will also provide an opportunity for you to consider aspects of writing which you may not have considered before and will give you a chance to reflect on your feelings about writing.

The purpose of this chapter, then, is for you to become more conscious of the language learning style that you have and the goals that you want to achieve.

# PART II: YOUR LEARNING STYLE

In this section, you will be presented with several situations. Try to imagine yourself in each situation, and answer the questions given. In many cases, you may already have found yourself in the situation described and can answer from your experience. In doing this, you should begin to understand more about yourself as a learner.

## QUESTIONNAIRE

### Situation 1

In your English class, your teacher does not believe in giving you rules to study. Instead he presents sample sentences for you to read and study and asks you to interact with your classmates using what you have just seen. Do you . . .

    **a.** enjoy this as a game?
    **b.** become very nervous and wish you were in a different class?

### Situation 2

Your teacher often asks students to do exercises or activities from the textbooks in small groups while she moves around the room and listens, occasionally answering questions. She does not go over the answers. Do you . . .

    **a.** enjoy the freedom this gives you to use the language?
    **b.** resent your teacher for being too lazy to teach?

### Situation 3

Your teacher occasionally invites members of your class to read their essays aloud to the class. Do you . . .

a. have a more rapid heartbeat and sweaty hands when you know your turn is coming soon?
b. read yours quite freely with few or no feelings of discomfort?

### Situation 4

When you are preparing for an examination, do you usually . . .

a. study information that is on paper?
b. listen to audiotapes of the lecture or exercises?

### Situation 5

When you are learning how to create a good piece of writing, do you . . .

a. like somebody to tell you specific rules?
b. like to figure out how good writing works yourself and try different things?

### Situation 6

When you are among people who speak English much better than you do, do you . . .

a. generally stay quiet?
b. participate in the conversation anyway?

### Situation 7

The end of the school year is coming in your country, and you would like to do something special for everybody in your English class, including your teacher. Do you . . .

a. make a card with a poem in your native language for all to enjoy?
b. make a card with a poem in English for all to enjoy, even though it will probably have errors?

### Situation 8

You have been studying English for a few months when your school or institute announces a writing contest. Do you . . .

a. forget about it because you know your English isn't good enough?
b. try to write a piece in English for the contest anyway?

### Situation 9

You have been assigned to read a magazine article and write a paper about it. Do you . . .

a. prefer to figure out your own way to understand the article and write your paper?
b. prefer to have the teacher provide a more specific assignment with questions to answer and guidelines to follow?

**Situation 10**
When you are learning English grammar, are you more likely to . . .

**a.** remember better from charts in your textbook?
**b.** remember better by hearing and learning a popular song using that particular grammar?

## EXPLANATION

The situations above serve to illustrate five basic differences in learning styles from one person to another. In some cases, you may discover that you like a combination of two styles.

## 1. Analytic and Nonanalytic Learners

Some people are very detail oriented. They like to study each aspect of whatever they are learning, memorize "rules," and apply these rules very carefully. They are also often very annoyed by exceptions to rules. When they are writing, they may be so aware of the form of their sentences and text that they may be unable to write at all. This is one type of "writer's block."

Other people don't care very much about details. To them, the important thing is *doing* rather than *studying*. These people expect the language to come to them naturally, perhaps through practice in real life, not by studying books. When writing, they are not very worried about the structure of their writing or language. They are more concerned about getting their ideas across. Such people are often able to fill many pages quickly.

Which one describes you better? If you look at the 10 situations above, which describe analytic and nonanalytic learners? How did you answer these questions?

### CONSIDER

• Can you think of both advantages and disadvantages of each learning style in learning English writing?
• Is there a reason for you to alter your style?
• Do you think you can?

## 2. Visual and Auditory Learners

Visual learners (as you can probably guess) like to have things written down. They like textbooks with charts, graphs, and pictures. They like their teachers to give out handouts which summarize what has been studied in class. They also like their teachers to write on the chalkboard often. When they remember things, they may even see these things in their "mind's eye." When they are writing, they may prefer to prepare *outlines* (lists of points to discuss) to follow. Sometimes, these outlines can be in the form of drawings or illustrations rather than lists of phrases.

Auditory learners depend more on the sense of hearing than sight. They remember more easily when somebody tells them how to do something than when somebody shows them. These people would find it easier to memorize poetry if they could listen to a tape of the poem several times rather than studying the poem on a piece of paper. When they are writing, they may find it helpful to discuss the topic with others before writing, rather than writing an outline.

Which one describes you better? If you look at the 10 situations above, which describe visual and auditory learners? How did you answer these questions?

## CONSIDER

- Can you think of both advantages and disadvantages of each learning style in learning English writing?
- Is there a reason for you to alter your style?
- Do you think you can?

## 3. Extroverted and Introverted Learners

Extroverted people are very sociable. They love to interact with other people, to talk. They enjoy being in crowds and may, in fact, feel lonely when there aren't many or any people around. Some extroverts are so outgoing that it is hard for anyone else to speak! Extroverted people might find it hard to spend long periods of time writing, which tends to be a solitary activity once the preparation is done. But they are very happy in the preparation when it involves discussion with others.

Introverted people *may* be afraid to be among people, or they may simply prefer their own company to anyone else's company. When asked to speak in front of a crowd, introverted people may become very anxious or may say that they have nothing to say. It is too simple to say that introverts like to be alone; some introverts like to *watch* a crowd but do not like to participate in the conversation. When they are writing, introverts might be very happy to find information in written materials but less happy to go out and interview people for the information.

Which one describes you better? If you look at the 10 situations above, which describe extroverted and introverted learners? How did you answer these questions?

## CONSIDER

- Can you think of both advantages and disadvantages of each learning style in learning English writing?
- Is there a reason for you to alter your style?
- Do you think you can?

## 4. Learners Who Are Tolerant and Intolerant of Ambiguity

People who are tolerant of ambiguity don't need to know exactly what they are doing and why. They are willing, perhaps, to drive across the country with only a vague idea of which highways to follow—they'll figure it out on the way. They enjoy surprises and are generally not frustrated by "not knowing." They try it anyway. Writers who are tolerant of ambiguity are happy to start writing without knowing what they plan to say. They enjoy the *discovery* aspect of writing. Professional fiction writers often say that their characters come alive and direct the plot, not the writers themselves.

People who are intolerant of ambiguity feel more comfortable with a plan. They like to know what they are doing, how they will do it, and why they are doing it that way. If they were to drive across the country, they would have a map for every state with the exact route drawn on the maps (and perhaps also a list of the gas stations, restaurants, hotels, and the weather reports!). These people like to know what's around the corner. If they don't know how to do something, they avoid doing it. Writers who are intolerant of ambiguity prepare complete outlines and follow them item by item. As a result, they discover no surprises about the topic while they are writing.

Which one describes you better? If you look at the 10 situations above, which describe learners who are tolerant and intolerant of ambiguity? How did you answer these questions?

### CONSIDER

- Can you think of both advantages and disadvantages of each learning style in learning English writing?
- Is there a reason for you to alter your style?
- Do you think you can?

## 5. Inductive and Deductive Learners

Inductive learners like to figure things out for themselves. It's like a game to them. When they were children (perhaps even as adults) they liked to pull things apart to see how they worked. Inductive learners are capable of learning and following rules, but they more often enjoy more making a game of figuring out how things like languages work rather than studying rules in books. Sometimes they seem to do it by instinct. Inductive learners can be very tolerant of ambiguity since they often must wait until they've seen enough data to figure things out. Writers who follow the inductive style don't want to be told how to write well; they prefer to try things and see how they work or look at interesting readings and try to imitate them.

Deductive learners are frustrated by not having rules to follow. They prefer to see rules, perhaps in very great detail, study them, and then apply them in situations where they work. Deductive learners are not very happy when they discover that their rules don't work in all situations. In fact, deductive learners are generally not very tolerant of ambiguity. Rules make them feel more secure because these learners are very concerned with being "right." Writers who prefer the deductive style tend to produce technically correct but not very exciting writing.

Which one describes you better? If you look at the 10 situations above, which describe extroverted and introverted persons? How did you answer these questions?

## CONSIDER

- Can you think of both advantages and disadvantages of each learning style in learning English writing?
- Is there a reason for you to alter your style?
- Do you think you can?

**QUIZ:** To be sure that you understand the information about learning styles above, answer the following questions T (True) or F (False).

1. _____ Someone who is very introverted might not develop his speaking skills well because he doesn't give himself opportunities to speak.

2. _____ An extrovert might have trouble showing her writing to others.

3. _____ Someone who learns inductively might not develop strong language skills because he may only learn what his books tell him.

4. _____ Someone who is intolerant of ambiguity would do very well living in a second language culture before she has learned the language well.

5. _____ Someone who is visually oriented would not do well in a large lecture class.

6. _____ Someone who is analytical would feel comfortable producing language without knowing whether its form was correct or not.

*(Key: 1 T, 2 F, 3 F, 4 F, 5 T, 6 F.)*

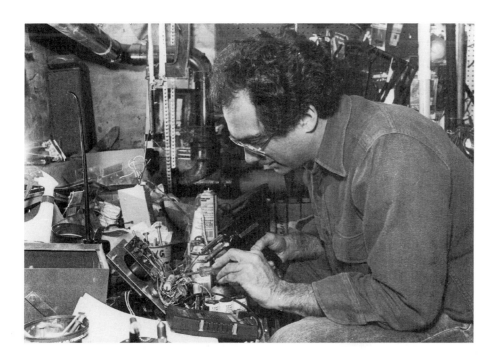

## Some Final Questions

Of the five learning styles described above, who are the risk takers?
What role might risk taking play in successful language learning?
Which learning styles do you think will help you achieve your own language and writing goals in this class?

### SHORT WRITING (100–150 WORDS)

Using the information you have studied in this chapter about different learning styles, summarize the learning styles that you most often employ when learning a new language. Do the styles you have adopted in the past satisfy you? Is there a new style you would be interested in trying? Why or why not?

# PART III: YOUR WRITING GOALS

In this part of the chapter, you will think about what your relationship with writing has been and what you would like it to be in the future. This will help you set some goals for yourself in this course.

### QUESTIONNAIRE

**1.** Mark the kinds of writing you have done most commonly in your adult life.

_____ personal letters

_____ diary/journal

_____ poetry

_____ essays

_____ reports/research papers

_____ other _____

**2.** Rate each type of writing below for how confident you feel doing it. Write a number from 1 to 5 in the space provided.

Least Confident = 1    2    3    4    5 = Most Confident

_____ personal letters

_____ diary/journal

_____ poetry

_____ essays

_____ reports/research papers

_____ other _____

3. Writing well actually involves a number of skills and activities. Rate your following abilities. Write a number from 1 to 5 in the space provided.

    Least Able = 1      2      3      4      5 = Most Able

    _____ to write interesting content

    _____ to be willing to make substantial changes in my work

    _____ to know enough grammatical structures to say what I want to say the way I want to say it

    _____ to control grammatical errors

    _____ to have a broad enough vocabulary to say what I want to say

    _____ to show my writing to others and accept critical feedback

    _____ to examine my own work and find ways to improve it

    _____ to read texts related to my work, understand them, and use their ideas in my work

    _____ to understand my readers' needs and meet these needs

    Which of the skills named above would you like to improve? Which learning styles can help you do this?

4. Are you a good writer or not? How do you know?_____

    _____

5. In which area(s) would you like to improve your English writing skills in this course?

    _____ personal (letters, diary/journal, poetry/stories)

    _____ academic (reports, research papers, essays)

    _____ professional (letters, reports)

6. Specifically, what are you interested in improving in your writing? Write a number from 1 to 5 in the space provided.

    Least Interested = 1      2      3      4      5 = Most Interested

    _____ your individual writing style

    _____ your grammatical abilities

    _____ your vocabulary

    _____ your confidence in writing

    _____ the quality of your work's content

    _____ the quality of your work's organization

7. Which learning styles do you believe will help you meet the goals you have chosen? Why?

    _____

    _____

## SHORT WRITING (100–150 WORDS)

Having reviewed many possibilities for developing your writing skills in this chapter, write a letter to your teacher explaining what you would like to learn in this course about writing well. What might your teacher include in the course in order to make the course more valuable for you?

# The Rudiments of Organizing an Essay

# PART I: INTRODUCTION

In this segment of the text, you will learn some general principles for presenting written information in English. Later, in Chapters 4, 5, 6, and 7, you will learn more specific variations appropriate for different kinds of writing.

# PART II: YOUR AUDIENCE

Who will your readers be? How does your writing change when your reader changes? Should you write to please your readers or to please yourself? These are some of the basic questions writers ask when they begin a new piece of writing. Sometimes we are lucky enough to know exactly who our readers will be and what they will be looking for. More often, this is not the case.

In order to begin understanding the issue of "audience," try to imagine what kinds of writing the following potential audiences might expect from you. The first one is done for you.

**1.** a history teacher ___*term papers, essay tests, short test answers, summaries*___

**2.** an English teacher _____

**3.** your best friend _____

**4.** your employer _____

**5.** your landlord _____

**6.** yourself _____

While you were doing this exercise, you should have discovered that there are many different types of writing, each appropriate in a different situation. Research papers, essays, tests, letters, resumes, diaries, poems—all have different purposes and different requirements.

Now let's take a few examples from the exercise above and make it more specific. In the following types of writing, what is the reader on the right looking for in the type of writing on the left? The first one is begun for you.

**1.** school essay / teacher ___*interesting and informative material about the topic,*___
___*clear presentation of the material, correct grammar, good use of vocabulary*___

**2.** letter / friend _____

_____

**3.** letter / newspaper _____

_____

4. school essay / your classmate _____

_____

5. school essay / yourself _____

_____

In this text, you will be asked to write in several forms: essays, letters, short answers, even a poem, if you like in Chapter 5. Your audience will also be varied and will include at least three people:

- your teacher, who will provide you with feedback and may also decide to grade your work;
- your classmates, who will give you feedback that is most likely different from a teacher's comments; and
- you, yourself, who will give feedback in the form of personal reflections on each major essay.

Your teacher may also decide to expand your audience and, thus, the feedback you receive, by copying your essay and distributing it to your class for discussion or by reading it aloud and discussing it with your class. In all cases, this feedback will help you to develop the skill a writer needs to "read" (or understand) his or her audience and predict what the audience needs. But you will balance this with your own needs as a writer, also, because in order for you to enjoy writing, you must receive personal satisfaction from what you write.

Try to predict what the different audiences mentioned above might want to see in the essays you will write for this course.

1. your teacher _____

_____

2. your classmates _____

_____

3. yourself _____

_____

# PART III: UNITY AND THE PARAGRAPH

In 1965 Robert Kaplan, a linguist at the University of Southern California, looked into a very interesting question regarding writing styles in different cultures: Are they different? He found that they were. In order to see just how they might be different, discuss how you would deal with the following situation with some of your classmates. This will give you a "window" onto the topic of culture and will be the beginning of our discussion of unity. If you can work with classmates from cultures other than your own, all the better!

**Forming Concepts: Learning by analogy gives you an opportunity to take advantage of knowledge you already possess to learn faster.**

### Situation

Imagine that you work in a company in your native country. One day, while you are working, you suddenly have a brilliant idea. You have found a way to change one of the procedures in your company in such a way that the new procedure will save your company a great deal of time and money. How do you let the company know about the new procedure?

Jot down the suggestions of your group below:

_____

_____

_____

_____

In the United States, it is quite likely that you would immediately rush to your boss's office, knock on the door, and say, "Do you have a minute? I've just had a brainstorm!" People in the United States tend to be very direct and perhaps not very patient. In addition, they are often very interested in getting credit for their ideas. In some countries the correct thing to do in the above situation may be to invite the boss out after work and make him or her think the idea was his or hers or invite several coworkers out and make the idea everybody's, perhaps even over a period of time. However, in the United States, it is still probably most common to be more direct.

Related to this is the directness people from the United States show in areas which we call nonverbal communication. They look others directly in the eye (in fact, they think someone who doesn't look in their eyes may be lying), they walk fast on the street without looking at anybody or smiling (although, in fact, they have seen you half a block away and ignore you only when they get closer), and, if you speak slowly, they interrupt you to finish your sentences.

What does this have to do with writing? Plenty! "Culture" is composed of many components, only one of which is writing. It isn't likely that a culture which practices directness everywhere else would tolerate much indirectness in writing. And in fact that is true in the United States where good writing, at least most nonfiction writing, is generally thought to "get to the point." (Always remember that famous writers are allowed to break the rules.)

# Unity

One way you can remind yourself of the typical writing style of the United States is to remind yourself of one of the most common U.S. stereotypes—"Time is money."* In many cultures' writing styles, it is permissible to postpone naming the topic of the writing (or never to name it) or to deviate from the topic temporarily. However, the style of the United States requires a specific set of characteristics which we will refer to as *unity*. The principle of unity in the United States involves three characteristics:

- that you very early make clear the topic and the aspect of this topic that you plan to discuss;
- that you give only information and examples which are directly related to the topic and the point of view you have chosen; and
- that you *not* discuss anything that is not directly related to the topic and point of view.

These characteristics are true on two levels: for the *whole writing* and its topics and for the *individual paragraphs* and their subtopics.

**EXERCISE:**    Read the following topics and their aspects to discuss. Then determine which piece of information or example cannot be used in the writing because it violates the principle of unity.

1. *topic = education*                     *aspect to discuss = determines a child's*
                                                                        *future*

   - Literacy is important for full participation in society.
 ➥ - Teachers may not always be competent.
   - Children become fully socialized in classrooms with other children.
   - Children may find their talents when they are in school.

2. *topic = fatherless children*       *aspect to discuss = have more problems*
                                                                          *than other children*

   - Fatherless children are more often involved in crime as teenagers.
   - Fatherless children have more difficulty as adults relating appropriately to men.
   - Fatherless children more often suffer from poverty.
 ➥ - Fatherless children may learn to be more independent and self-sufficient.

3. *topic = poor people*                   *aspect to discuss = need more help from*
                                                                          *the government*

   - The government ought to stimulate job growth for the unemployed.
   - The government should provide more day care for children so that single mothers can go to work.
   - There should be more places for homeless people to stay until they can find a home of their own.
 ➥ - Financial assistance from the government to poor people encourages these people not to help themselves.

---

*People in the United States are often stereotyped as overly concerned with money and unwilling to spend time on anything which won't result in the accumulation of more money. Hence, "Time is money."

# The Topic Sentence

Another part of the "time is money" paragraph is the topic sentence, which usually appears early in the paragraph but may actually also appear elsewhere in the paragraph. Many highly experienced writers write paragraphs with such strong unity that a topic sentence is unnecessary. We say that the topic sentence is *implied*. However, most writers do construct topic sentences because these sentences are helpful to readers, who are constantly trying to understand the written text.

You are already familiar with topic sentences from the previous exercise. They typically contain a topic (such as "education") and an aspect to discuss (such as "determines a child's future"). Examine the following paragraphs. Underline the topic sentence for each. Don't expect all to be at the beginning.

**A.** "Academically, Poly students are standouts. On the Scholastic Aptitude Test, a widely used college entrance examination, the class of 1991 scored an average of 615 out of a possible 800 in the verbal part of the test and 675 in math. The national averages for public high school students were 419 and 473 respectively, according to the college Board, which sponsors the exam. . . . Last year, 38 students, or 51% of the class of 1991, were National Merit or National Achievement honorees." (Merl, 1992, Sec. A p. 30)

**B.** "For minority-group children the poverty situation is even more drastic. An astonishing 43 percent of black and 37 percent of Hispanic children live below the poverty threshold. Eighteen and a half million children live in the central cities; 29 percent of them live in poverty. The majority (71 percent) of poor children live in families with two parents present, and with one or both parents working." (Ropers, 1991, p. 45)

**C.** "As work shifted out of the fields and the home, children had to be prepared for factory life. The early mine, mill, and factory owners of industrializing England discovered, as Andrew Ure wrote in 1835, that it was 'nearly impossible to convert persons past the age of puberty, whether drawn from rural or from handicraft occupations, into useful factory hands.' If young people could be prefitted* to the industrial system, it would vastly ease the problems of industrial discipline later on. The result was another central structure of all Second Wave societies: mass education." (Toffler, 1980, p. 29)

**D.** "Most Americans believe the stereotype that immigrants work hard, get a good education and have a very good life. Maybe it used to be like that, but immigrants can't play by the rules anymore. You have to be deceptive and unscrupulous in order to make it. If you are not, then you will end up like most immigrants I've known. Living in the ghetto in a cockroach-infested house. Working on the assembly line or in the chicken factory to support your family. Getting up at 3 o'clock in the morning to take the bus to work and not getting home until 5 p.m." (Khiev, 1992, p. 8)

---

*Trained ahead of time.

E.    "Throughout history, men have been torn from their families by war, disease and death. But in '90s America,' men are choosing to disconnect from family life on a massive scale, and at far higher rates than other industrialized countries. 'Men are drifting away from family life,' says Blankenhorn. 'We are in danger of becoming a fatherless society.'" (Easton, 1992, p. 15)

## The Body of the Paragraph

In addition to a topic sentence, a paragraph must have other sentences which support and explain the topic sentence. (Newspapers often have one-sentence paragraphs because the columns are so narrow that multisentence paragraphs would be very long and difficult to read.) There are many styles for developing a paragraph. You will discover your own preferred style as you gain experience in writing. For now, you might consider the following basics as a starting point.

- topic sentence;
- one or more sentences of explanation of the topic sentence;
- evidence, in the form of examples, statistics, or quotes perhaps, to support your topic sentence; and
- a summary of how your evidence supports your topic sentence if it is not immediately obvious.

Let's see how this basic method works in a paragraph. Examine the paragraph below noticing the parts described above.

**"I hated America because to me, it was not the place of opportunities or the land of 'the melting pot' as I had been told.** [topic sentence] *All I had seen were broken beer bottles on the street and homeless people and drunks using the sky as their roof. I couldn't walk down the street without someone yelling out, 'You —— gook' from his car.* [evidence] Once again I was caught in the web of hatred. I'd become a mad dog with the mind-set of the past: 'When trapped in the corner, just bite.' The war mentality of Cambodia came back: get what you can and leave. I thought I had come to America to escape war, poverty, fighting, to escape the violence, but I wasn't escaping; I was being introduced to a newer version of war—the war of hatred." [explanation] (Khiev, 1992, p. 8)

Analyze paragraphs A, B, and C below in the same way.

A.    One new strategy for involving students more in their educations is youth apprenticeships, where the students get job training by working alongside professionals who are already on the job. The problem is that youth apprenticeships don't work very well for several reasons. First, youth apprentices are often used for the kinds of work that nobody else in the company wants to do: delivering messages, making photocopies, answering phones. Second they are rarely given a chance to see the real business of the company in action; they may spend a good deal of time simply sitting alone. Says Hannah Finan Roditi, who used to be a consultant for youth apprentice programs, "Students in work/study programs learn few academic or technical

skills and almost nothing at all about independent thinking." (Rebeck, 1992, p. 34-35)

**B.** Research has found that children don't dream in quite the same ways as adults do. For one thing, their dreams are much more frightening than adults' dreams are. For example, they often dream about being chased by animals or monsters. In fact, according to Dr. Robert Van de Castle at the University of Virginia, children dream about animals much more often than adults do. In addition, children often dream that they are the victims of physical attack, perhaps because they feel so small and defenseless in the face of the large world around them. (Keough, 1990, p. 17)

**C.** "Money is a language; further, there are different money languages in different cultures. In Japan, wedding guests are given money in an envelope, but children don't get allowances.* Wealthy people can expect less wealthy social climbers to pick up the tab for a meal in the United States, but not in Mexico or Ghana. In Sweden a taxi driver will give you back a tip; in New York you may get physically assaulted for not giving the driver a sufficiently large tip." (Phillips, 1992, p. 73)

**EXERCISE:** Practice writing unified paragraphs by reading the following topic sentences and completing each paragraph with your own ideas. Try to include some explanation and an example for each.

1. One topic that should be taught by a child's family at home rather than by a teacher at school is _____

_____

_____

_____

2. The best thing for a visitor to see in my country is _____

_____

_____

_____

3. Television has had a(n) _____ effect on education. _____

_____

_____

_____

_____

---

*An allowance is money parents give their children for personal spending. It is called "pocket money" in other countries where English is spoken.

Just as the *topic sentence* guides your readers' understanding of the paragraph, the *thesis statement* guides your readers' understanding of a longer piece of writing. It is a writer's promise to his or her readers: This is what my paper is about. The thesis statement is similar to the topic sentence in other ways as well:

- It appears near the beginning of the writing, either at the end of the introduction or as the first sentence of the writing if there is no introduction.
- It has a topic and an aspect to discuss.
- All information and evidence in the entire writing must be *unified* with the thesis statement.
- Highly experienced writers may not include thesis statements in their writing.

**EXERCISE:**   Practice identifying the topic and aspect to discuss in each of the following thesis statements. Then discuss possible paragraph topics for the rest of the essay for each.

1. Various societal, political, and cultural factors have made the American welfare state a reluctant one. (Jansson, 1993, p. 319)
2. Four factors are crucial to understanding variations in the degree of paternal involvement in the family. (Lamb, 1987, p. 17.)
3. The liberal tradition of the U.S. welfare policy has been an ambiguous one. (Jansson, 1993, p. 341)
4. If reading is the cornerstone of learning, then the best foundations are built in New Zealand. (Burns, 1991, p. 53)
5. Three skills that help improve assertiveness are owning our feelings, being empathic, and being tactful. (Kleinke, 1987, pp. 107–108)

## Poor Thesis Statements

There are some characteristics that you will want to avoid in your thesis statements.

- A thesis statement must not have *only* a topic or *only* an aspect to discuss; it must have both.
- A *fact* cannot be a thesis statement. What could you possibly say to support it if it is obviously true? Thesis statements express *opinions,* which must be supported in the body of the paper and about which there is a lot to say.
- A thesis statement is given in a complete sentence. It is not a title; it's a sentence.
- A thesis statement expresses one opinion about one topic, although it may mention several reasons for that opinion. Thesis statements that have several topics or several opinions lead to unclear, incoherent papers.
- Related to the previous quality, thesis statements must not be too broad. Remember, it is the writer's promise to the reader. If a thesis statement is too broad, it promises too much, and the paper won't be able to keep that promise.

**Forming Concepts: Working with classmates helps you understand more as you discuss the work with each other.**

*whole class*

**EXERCISE:** With some of your classmates, determine which of the following could be good thesis statements. Be prepared to explain your answers. How would you improve the poor ones?

1. Coping can be defined as the efforts we make to manage situations we have analyzed as potentially harmful or stressful. (Kleinke, 1991, p. 3)
— 2. Mothers and fathers engage in different types of interactions with their children.
3. Since aging presents challenges and adjustments for all people, it stands to reason that we would want to understand as much about this process as we could. (Kleinke, 1991, p. 143)
— 4. In this essay I will explain about the poverty of children.
— 5. To understand how Americans have addressed social problems in the past, various methods for establishing social welfare policies must be identified.
— 6. Prejudice against low-income persons exists in any society. (Jansson, 1993, p. 332)
— 7. The relationship a father has with his son.
— 8. It would be nice (but boring) if everything in life were easy.

# PART V: INTRODUCTIONS AND CONCLUSIONS

You now have enough information to create unified, clear short papers or essay examinations. In order to write a longer essay, however, you will also need to write an introduction and conclusion.

## Introductions

*52*

By necessity, introductions are more general than the paragraphs that follow them. The reader is just starting to figure out what the essay is about when reading the introduction. Therefore, the purpose of an introduction is to acquaint the reader gradually with the topic of the essay. Although there are many types of introductions possible, below are some characteristics which are common to successful introductions:

• **They catch the reader's attention quickly.** There are a number of ways to do this. Using a quotation from a famous person is one way. Telling a story or anecdote related to the topic is also attention-getting. Asking a question of the reader (called a "rhetorical question") is another way, although it may sometimes appear immature to do so when this is the only type of introductory sentence the writer appears to know how to write.

By far, the best way to catch a reader's attention is to make clear how the topic relates to him or her personally. This means understanding the audience very well.

*PITFALL!*   Avoid quoting a definition from a dictionary as the opening sentence. It is boring and can make writing seem immature.

• **They orient the reader toward the topic.** The introduction is the place where writers give the readers any background information they might need to understand the information in the paragraphs later or to understand why the topic is worth reading about. Historical information might be given or the writer might explain why the topic is important in the present day, whether it has been in the news, perhaps what the different opinions on the topic are.

• **They gradually but obviously lead the reader into the thesis.** Unity applies to introductions too, even though introductions are more general than body paragraphs. Although the writer's *point of view* about the topic is not likely to be clear until the thesis, the *topic* should be clear from the first sentence.

*PITFALL!*   Inexperienced writers sometimes make the introduction so general that it bears little or no relation to the specific topic of the paper. Always remember that the introduction is not simply a placeholder or a required part of a formula; it has a purpose: It orients the reader toward the specific topic of the paper.

## LEARNING STRATEGY

Overcoming Limitations: **When you are unable to write a satisfactory opening for your essay, skip it for a while, work on another part of your essay, then come back to the opening later. You will find it easier to write the opening when you know more about the body of the essay.**

**EXERCISE:**   Evaluate the following introductions using the criteria above. How good are they in your opinion? How does each catch the reader's attention? Where's the thesis statement in each? What do you expect the rest of each paper to be about?

**A.**   "Rose Kennedy (John F. Kennedy's mother) was once asked about her reaction to the many tragedies that had befallen her family. She replied, 'I cope.' Coping can be defined as the efforts we make to manage situations we have appraised as potentially harmful or stressful. These features are important in a definition of coping because they allow us to study different styles and strategies of coping and to evaluate which ones work best in different situations. The goal of researchers has been to find out whether there are personality traits, beliefs, or ways of viewing the world that are more or less adaptive in various situations. In fact, it has been found that certain qualities allow for better coping in stressful or harmful situations." (Kleinke, 1987, p. 3)

**B.** In prewar days it was said that one should fear "earthquakes, thunder, fire, and fathers," but since the war we have seen democracy combined with an overall feminization of society. In contemporary Japan, the father has forfeited his authority. . . . Accordingly, the comic in which "dumb dads" are bringing about the ruin of our schools seems to have become true. So [in December, 1981] the Society of Thunderous Fathers was formed. The founders included a famous actor, a cartoonist, an explorer, a member of the national Diet, and former sumo and boxing champions. (Ohgiya, 1983, p. 960)

"The existence of a group such as the Thunderous Fathers may reflect more than an idle curiosity among the Japanese toward fatherhood. . . . This group rightly notes the confused and controversial nature of the paternal role in modern Japanese culture. . . . The role of the Japanese father is ill-defined [and] devalued." (Lamb, 1991, p. 274)

**C.** In the Diana School in Reggio Emilia, northern Italy, the glass walls are covered with children's art, and more of their art hangs from the ceilings. The children are provided with dressing rooms in case they want to change into a "disguise" for the day and pretend they are someone else. Other imagination-inspiring artwork decorates the classrooms. The school is praised worldwide as a showcase of educational innovations. Says its director, Loris Malaguzzi, "A school needs to be a place for all children, not based on the idea that they're all the same, but that they're all different." (Hinckle, 1991, p. 53–54)

## Conclusions

The function of a conclusion is to bring the essay to a graceful end. That a piece of writing is coming to an end is generally not a surprise to the reader: After all, he or she can see the white space following the last paragraph! Therefore, the function of a good conclusion is *not* to show the reader that the essay is about to end but rather to bring the essay to an end *in such a way that the reader feels satisfied with the essay as a whole.* There are several common methods for doing this. No doubt, as you become a more experienced writer, you will find your own favorite styles.

*PITFALL!* Short writings (under approximately 200 words) do not need elaborate introductions or conclusions. Simply begin with the thesis and end with the last sentence of the last body paragraph, or, at most, a one-sentence summary. On timed writings, such as essay exams, there is no time to write elaborate introductions and conclusions.

Some possible styles for conclusions include:

• **Restating your thesis.** The key is *restating*. If you simply *repeat* your thesis, word for word, your writing will look unsophisticated and immature.

However, stating the ideas of your original thesis using different words can allow you to make your point one last time and add strength to your paper. This is an especially useful method when you are writing a persuasive essay since it allows you to "hit" your reader one more time with your argument.

• **Summarizing your main points.** Related to restating your thesis is restating the main points of your essay. Once again, be careful not to use the same words and phrases that you used in your body paragraphs.

*PITFALL!*   This method does not work on shorter essays because the reader has quite recently read your main points, and they are fresh in his or her mind.

• **Beginning with a quotation from a famous person.** If a well-known person has said something similar to what you have been trying to say in your paper, you may quote him or her as a way of summarizing your points. This can lead you into the conclusion, and you may follow the quote with an explanation of its meaning and a summary of your thesis.

• **Calling your readers to action.** Ask your readers to take action based on the points you raise (particularly useful in persuasive essays), or ask them to learn a lesson from the story you tell. For example, if you write a paper on good education, tell your readers what not to accept in their own educations, or tell them what to look for, based on what you have described in your paper.

*PITFALL!*   Do not include any new major points, evidence, or examples in your conclusion. A new point or evidence requires a new explanation, resulting in a new body paragraph rather than a conclusion.

**EXERCISE:**   Read the following introduction and conclusion pairs. What kind of conclusion is used, based on the types mentioned above? Can you imagine another way of doing each conclusion?

**A.**   When people are asked what is important to them, they invariably mention "education." Everybody wants a good education, and the reason they give is that they want a good job, which generally translates as a job with a high salary. But education is worth more than just a high salary. Probably the most important thing about education is that it gives one power, not just to command a high salary, but to command power in other areas as well.

. . .

Francis Bacon once said, "Knowledge is power." Countless people have discovered the truth of this statement as they have fought to receive equal educations not simply to earn a lot of money but also to command respect from others and to participate in decision making. Without the knowledge that comes from a good education, there is no true power.

**B.**   "In our lives, we often discover the value of precious things when we don't have them. One knows the importance of food better when he is hungry than when he has a full stomach, and he knows the value and power of money better when he is in need of money than when he has plenty. Likewise, a person learns much about what a proper education should provide him when his education fails to provide it. In that sense, coming to

America has been one of the most precious experiences of my life. As an explorer makes his way through an unknown area, I have been a traveler in the 'jungle' called America trying to figure out what it really looks like from outside. Knowing practically nothing about American people or their ways, I have been born again in America learning the new ways from school. In doing so, I have come to realize the difference in teaching styles between two nations, America and Korea, which, in turn, has led me to discover the empowering teaching aspect of American schools, which is what I have been looking for from my education.

. . .

"Living in today's modern society, each person has to deal with all kinds of complex problems everyday. These problems can be about job selection, social life, private life, and mathematical and scientific problems. One may think that we can resolve these problems if the solutions and the answers to each problem have been fed to us previously through education as the teachers in Korea do. However, we have our own personalities, and, in dealing with problems, one has to have his own opinion and an ability to decide what is right for himself to get the best result. In that sense, having an emphasis on developing and empowering one's own way to face problems, the American teaching style is really beneficial to every student, and, studying in America under such a good teaching system with more individual freedom, I feel that I have been really fortunate to have a chance to learn this precious difference in teaching styles between the two countries." (Jay Lee, student)

**C.** "Why do women have a higher chance of being in poverty than any other group that is classified as poor? For one, in present day America, women are being treated unfairly at work. Because of this unfair treatment, they have a higher risk of becoming poor than men do. In order to provide better service to help the American women in poverty, equal participation in the government is needed to change the laws. Although there's no one answer to how to stop poverty, there are ways to alleviate it.

. . .

With all of these barriers women have to cross to be out of poverty, the society has to stop gender-typing in jobs, undervaluing women's work, monopolizing most power systems, and maintaining economic inequality. (Zopf, 1989) In order to increase women's economic opportunities, equal-pay legislation or affirmative action is a step the government can take. A gradual increase of equality for all people can then be seen. The stereotype that a woman's place is at home and a woman is less capable of doing the same work as a man should be perceived as a myth to everyone." (Ronald Chen, student)

## Sample Essays for Discussion

**A.** In this chapter, we have discussed the parts of an essay. The following student-written essays illustrate the principles of writing described in this chapter. The first author arrived in the United States from Korea three years ago and graduated from a U.S. high school.

### COMPARING U.S. SCHOOLS WITH KOREAN SCHOOLS

*Jay Lee*

1    In our lives, we often discover the value of precious things when we don't have them. One knows the importance of food better when he is hungry than when he has a full stomach, and he knows the value and power of money better when he is in need of money than when he has plenty. Likewise, a person learns much about what a proper education should provide him when his education fails to provide it. In that sense, coming to America has been one of the most precious experiences of my life. As an explorer makes his way through an unknown area, I have been a traveler in the 'jungle' called America trying to figure out what it really looks like from outside. Knowing practically nothing about American people or their ways, I have been born again in America learning the new ways from school. In doing so, I have come to realize the difference in teaching styles between two nations, America and Korea, which, in turn, has led me to discover the empowering teaching aspect of American schools, which is what I have been looking for from my education.

2    As soon as I enrolled in Brea-Olinda High School in May of 1990, I recognized the astonishing, visual difference in the American high school and was immediately attracted by it. The advanced features of the school, the number of students in a classroom, and the different characters of the teachers got my attention. The classrooms, so large and well illuminated and equipped, were just the perfect, ideal places to study. The school library was far beyond sophisticated in comparison with the high school libraries in Korea, where, because of a lack of funds, there was no computer system and all we could find were a limited number of ten-year-old books. A soccer field, tennis courts, swimming pools, and indoor basketball courts were things I couldn't even imagine at the high school in Korea.

3    In addition to that, studying with around thirty students in a class even made me feel like people cared for me. Having approximately sixty students in a tiny classroom with extremely poor conditions, high school classrooms in Korea were literally crowded with students, and, studying there, I felt like I was becoming insignificant and just another student being ignored among many.

4    Besides the convenience of studying in a well-equipped, spacious classroom with the small number of students, the teachers were different. Seeming to enjoy teaching students, the teachers were very nice and helpful in comparison to the teachers in Korea, who were very strict and seemed to be teaching just for money. The teachers in America never used physical punishment, which I disliked the most, and that made me feel like they were my friends.

5    In that way, I was really contented with the situations in my new high school, and I thought this was what I was looking for from my education.

However, as I spent enough time with these visual aspects, I realized that they were just giving me materialistic satisfaction, and I knew they were not what I was trying to find from my education. Then, I began to suspect that there was more about American schools, and, soon I was discovering a really surprising and important characteristic in American high schools beyond the dazzling, superficial features and facts, which had been concealed behind the visual appearances. This characteristic was in the empowering teaching style of American high schools, which emphasized leading students to think about problems and develop their own solutions according to the situations. In English classes, especially, I could feel that strongly. There, the ways I thought and expressed my ideas counted more than knowing and memorizing mere facts. This surprised me at first because I was so familiar with memorizing facts and interpretations regarding literature. However, as I began to learn to form my ideas and express them, I knew this was the better and genuine way to study literature. Likewise, I could sense the same teaching style in math and science classes. Instead of directly showing students fast, specific ways of solving problems as Korean teachers do to their students, the teachers in America encouraged students to think creatively, understanding the concepts related to the problems and solving them using students' own ways. After a little difficult transition period to adjust myself to this style, I was so involved in this teaching style and knew this was what I was looking for from a true education.

6    Living in today's modern society, each person has to deal with all kinds of complex problems everyday. These problems can be about job selection, social life, private life, and mathematical and scientific problems. One may think that we can resolve these problems if the solutions and the answers to each problem have been fed to us previously through education as the teachers in Korea do. However, we have our own personalities, and, in dealing with problems, one has to have his own opinion and an ability to decide what is right for himself to get the best result. In that sense, having an emphasis on developing and empowering one's own way to face problems, the American teaching style is really beneficial to every student, and, studying in America under such a good teaching system with more individual freedom, I feel that I have been really fortunate to have a chance to learn this precious difference in teaching styles between the two countries.

Analyze the paragraphs (topic sentences, explanations, evidence), thesis statement, introduction, and conclusion. What makes this piece of writing strong? Who is Jay's audience? Can you find ways to improve the essay?

**B.**    The paper below was written by Tuan Do, a Vietnamese student. In it he describes his complex relationship with his father.

### THE RELATIONSHIP BETWEEN MY FATHER AND ME

*Tuan Do*

1    A typical relationship between a father and a son is what I'm yearning for. A father usually spends time and talks to his son; however, the relationship between my father and me was completely different. My father was a very caring and loving person, but the problem was he never showed any love or affection toward me. In my opinion, society expects fathers to be tough, mean, strict, hot-tempered and stoic. My father was the stereotype of a father.

2    My father often appeared with a monstrous side to his personality. If I did something wrong; he disciplined me by beating or verbally screaming at me; he never told me what I did wrong. He sometimes would say things such as "You idiot, you stupid ——, go clean up or I will kill you!" He sometimes scared me

to death, and most of the time hurt my feelings when he said those things. One thing I always had to do was respect him because he was my father. One time I got angry because he called me a "stupid dog"; I talked back at him. My father immediately slapped me across my face, which made me want to strike back at him, but I

didn't. I just stood there wishing that he was dead, and I never wanted to see him again. Many times I planned to call the police because I thought what he was doing was abusing me.

3      My mother always protected me from my father's hot-tempered actions. Whenever I got into trouble, I went to my mother for help because I knew that she had a way with my father. My father respected my mother and would never say anything to make her mad. One day, I threw a baseball and broke the window in my parents' bedroom. My mother knew about it because I told her. I begged her to help me. She came to my father and said that she had broken the window herself. He didn't say anything but replaced it with a new one. I used my mother as a shield to protect me against my father's spears. I was a bad boy who caused a great deal of trouble when I was young. Things got worse when I began to become a teenager. My father and I were verbally fighting all the time, and we never seemed to agree about anything. My mother said that we were like cats and dogs, constantly on each other's case.

4      With constant fighting, I was never aware that my father's health was slowly declining until one day he got really ill. My mother took him to the hospital; he stayed there for a week and the doctor informed us that he only had ten years to live. He had a disease called lupus, which would slowly destroy his immune system.

5      The relationship between my father and me seemed to change once he was back from the hospital. We stopped the fighting and I began to take care of him because he was sick. We started a whole new relationship. I brought food and water to his bed hoping he would have me sit beside him and teach me something about life or tell me something about himself; however, he didn't. He only said things such as "I'm fine, go study," or "Go help your sister with her homework." With the look on his face, I knew he wanted to hug me and talk to me to make up all the lost time we had. I don't know why I didn't ask him to do that. Probably I was stoic just like he was.

6      On July first of 1991, my father caught pneumonia. My mother drove my father and me to the University of Southern California Hospital. In my mind, I had a feeling that he was not going to make it. I held my father's hand and said, "I love you, Dad." He didn't hear me because he was unconscious. Once we got to the emergency room, my mother and I put him on an emergency bed and rolled him inside. He regained consciousness and began to ask my mother, "Where did you park the car? Be careful or we'll get a parking ticket!" My mother replied,

"Don't worry about it. I have parked in a safe spot. Please lie down and rest." We looked at each other for a few minutes without saying anything. Finally, my mother and I left the room and waited outside. We waited for six long hours thinking nothing was going to happen. We had no idea what was taking the doctors so long because there was no information about my father. At last, a doctor came out and asked if we were the family members of Sang Do. We happily answered, "Yes!" Then the doctor went on and said that my father was very sick and they were in the process of saving his life. Ten minutes later, the doctor informed us that my father "had passed away"! My mother and I were shocked. We thought it was a cruel joke. They showed us the body, and we burst into tears.

7    There are so many things I want to tell my father. He didn't know how much I loved him and how much I cared about him. On the last day of his life, I didn't have a chance to let him know my love. Now it's too late. I can say "I love you" a thousand or a million times, but he will not hear me. I miss him so much.

8    I didn't value my father until I lost him. I regret that I had been living with my father for 18 years and never knew anything about him. I regret that I didn't initiate his talking to me. I would do anything just to bring him back for one minute. For those who have loving parents, please don't take them for granted. You will regret it just like I did.

Because Tuan is story-telling rather than analyzing, we find that the introduction, thesis statement, and conclusion are related in a more relaxed way than they are in analytical essays. However, the essay does have an introduction and thesis which lead us to expect certain information in the essay, and it has a conclusion that follows one of the types mentioned above. Which type? Notice also the paragraph structure with its topic sentences and supporting evidence. Who is his audience? Can you find ways to improve the essay?

## SHORT ESSAY (250–300 WORDS)

Write a short but complete essay describing *one* of the most interesting cultural differences between your culture and another. There are many aspects of culture you might choose to discuss such as a difference in body language, form of dress, a way of showing respect, or a lifestyle difference. Try to write a good introduction, body and conclusion. Use the organizational checklist that follows to help you form your essay.

Organizational Checklist

| **Introductions** | |
| --- | --- |
| *DO* | Catch attention. Stay on the topic of the essay. Gradually but obviously name the topic and the aspect to be discussed. |
| *DON'T* | *Write too generally. Quote the dictionary.* |
| **Thesis Statements** | |
| *DO* | Accurately express the topic of the paper. Promise an essay that you can deliver. Express an opinion about a topic. Form a complete sentence. |
| *DON'T* | *Express a fact. Express several topics. Write very broadly.* |

**Topic Sentences**

*DO*    Express both a topic and an aspect to discuss. Place it anywhere in the paragraph but especially at the beginning. Provide the focus for the entire paragraph.

*DON'T*    *Focus on more than one topic. Name a topic without showing how the topic will be discussed.*

**Body Paragraphs**

*DO*    Write a topic sentence, explanation and, often, evidence and a summary of the importance of the evidence. Directly relate the paragraph to its topic sentence.

*DON'T*    *Write only one sentence in your paragraph, the topic sentence. Omit the explanation. Write information not related to the topic sentence.*

**Conclusions**

*DO*    Bring the essay to a satisfying end. Restate the thesis, summarize main points, use a quotation, or call readers to action.

*DON'T*    *Repeat the thesis word for word. Bring up new points. Summarize the main points of a short essay.*

## Bibliography

Burns, Brendon. "In New Zealand, Good Reading and Writing Come 'Naturally.'" *Newsweek,* 2 Dec. 1991, p. 53.

Hinckle, Pia. "A School Must Rest on the Idea that All Children Are Different." *Newsweek,* 2 Dec. 1991, pp. 53-54

Jansson, Bruce S., 1993. *The Reluctant Welfare State: A History of American Social Welfare.* 2nd ed. Pacific Grove, Cal.: Brooks/Cole.

Keough, Teri. "Night Visions." *New Age Journal.* Nov./Dec. 1990, p. 17.

Kleinke, Chris L. *Coping with Life Challenges.* Pacific Grove, Cal.: Brooks/Cole, 1991.

Lamb, Michael E., 1987. *Fathers: Cross-cultural Studies.* Hillsdale, N.J.: Lawrence Erlbaum Associates, Inc.

Merl, Jean. "Are Private Schools Any Better?" *Los Angeles Times,* 29 Mar. 1992, Sec. A, pp. 1, 30, 31.

Ohgiya, S. "The Society of Thunderous Fathers." In *Basic Information on Current Expressions.* Tokyo: Jukokuminsha, 1983.

Phillips, Michael. *Discourses.* San Francisco: Clear Glass Publishing, 1989. In *Utne Reader,* Sept./Oct. 1992, p. 73.

Rebeck, George. "Is Voc Ed a Dead End?" *Utne Reader,* Sept./Oct. 1992, pp. 34-35.

Schwalb, David W., Nobuo Imaizumi, and Jun Nakazawa. "The Modern Japanese Father: Roles and Problems in a Changing Society." In *The Father's Role: Cross-Cultural Perspectives.* Ed. Michael E. Lamb. Hillsdale, N.J.: Lawrence Erlbaum Associates, 1987.

Zopf, Paul E. *American Women in Poverty.* Greenwood Press, 1989.

# *Writing Persuasive Essays*

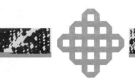
In this chapter, we will examine one piece of persuasive writing about elderly people and poverty to illustrate the parts of a persuasive essay. Read the persuasive essay below until you have a basic understanding of its main points. Then go on to work through the rest of this chapter.

### LEARNING STRATEGY

**Forming Concepts: Referring to an example as you learn new information can help you understand that information better.**

# Poverty and the elderly

We read newspaper articles about them, how they used to live in terrible poverty but now live in luxurious retirement homes, going on fabulous vacations, driving expensive cars, drinking the best wines. We hear stories of previously low Social Security[1] and pension[2] payments that now let them live in affluence while the rest of us work hard just to stay at the same standard of living. We even hear stories of them voting against school taxes or the construction of parks for children because their interests in children ended decades ago when their own children left home to strike out on their own. We are speaking of the elderly, of course, those sixty-five years and older, and while part of us is relieved that these people who have worked hard all their lives can rest in the comfort they have earned rather than face the pover-

ty conditions of decades past, another part resents the taxes all of us must pay to keep these "greedy" people so comfortable. However, while it is widely believed nowadays that the elderly are living the good life, we must not be fooled into believing that the old problem has been replaced by a new one. Instead we must recognize that there are many more elderly who are living a desperate life, unable to live in even the barest comfort. (1)

To some extent, the widely held belief nowadays that the elderly are living the good life is based on facts. Only one in six elderly persons is unable physically to take care of himself. Most elders can expect to live to age 82. Financially, their incomes have increased more than 98 percent since 1950, resulting in great improvements in the number of elderly who are in poverty. About 12 percent of the elderly were in poverty in the mid-1980s compared to 60 percent in 1950. (2)

Nevertheless, this is not the whole story. First, elderly families still have a far lower income than younger families. In 1988, families headed by elders earned only $21,705 while families headed by younger people earned $34,728. One explanation people often use to explain this gap is that the elderly choose to earn less because they want to retire. But the fact is that re-

tirees often are not given a choice about retirement, and even if they are, why must we assume that retirement wages should inevitably be less than working wages? A second argument often given to explain the gap in earnings is that the elderly have fewer needs and receive many government benefits which make up for the loss in wages when they retire. Admittedly, government benefits may do much to improve the opportunities for good

---

[1]Payments made by the government to retired workers or their spouses or children based on the previous earnings of the worker while he was employed. Each worker pays a social security tax on all earned wages during his working life.

[2]Payments made by a company to its retired workers based on the previous earnings of the worker. Not all companies give pensions.

medical care for the elderly, but they do nothing to pay the rent and utilities or put food on the table (unless the elder accepts public assistance[3] which has its own drawbacks). In any case, must one reduce his appetite and his need for clothes or entertainment simply because he is elderly? (3)

The assumption that the elderly somehow need less is part of the reason why statistics tend to show an improving standard of living for the elderly. It is not common knowledge that the U.S. Census Bureau actually defines poverty differently for the aged than for the non-aged. In 1988, it set the poverty level at $5,674 for aged individuals, while the level for others was $6,155. If the poverty rate for the aged were calculated in the same way as it is for others, it would be several points higher than the 12 percent rate found in 1988. In addition, the rate would rise still more if certain items that are excluded were included, such as health care, which accounts for a large part of the money spent by the elderly. In fact, a report from the Villers Foundation said, "Millions of the elderly are poor. Millions more are, if not officially impoverished, so close to it that any kind of unanticipated economic blow can knock them off the economic tightrope on which they struggle to walk." (4)

How do we reconcile the two worlds, the world of those who live in lush homes and take grand trips and the world of those who live from hand to mouth?[4] In fact, there are two different worlds for the aged. There are the privileged elderly who have private pensions, large savings accounts in their banks and investments; and there are more than 10 million elderly persons who depend on social security from month to month just to survive. While we may feel relieved or even resentful about the first group, it is the second group which needs more of our attention. We must not assume that all elderly are living the good life, for if we do, who will strive to improve their circumstances? (5)

Mattera, 1990, p.152–165.

[3]Payments made by the government to people in poverty for rent and food. People receiving public assistance may be embarrassed.

[4]Having barely enough money to pay for immediate necessities such as housing and food.

**EXERCISE:** Check your understanding of the article by summarizing aloud the two opposing opinions expressed in it. What does the author believe about the elderly and poverty? What do other people like former President Reagan commonly believe?

# PART II: DEFINING PERSUASION

One of the most common reasons for writing is for the writer to persuade an audience to agree with, or at least respect, a certain opinion. When writing persuasively, the writer has reason to believe that the audience has a different opinion than his or her own. The writer's goal, then, is to cause the reader to have a new opinion—the writer's opinion. In order to accomplish this, the writer must make this opinion clear, in the thesis statement, and support this opinion with strong evidence.

If you recall Chapter 2, you will remember that the English writing style tends to be very direct. This is especially true in persuasive writing, and it is a pitfall to be wary of in your persuasive writing if you come from a culture that tends to be less direct. Your English-speaking audience will be confused if your essays look like persuasion in some parts but look like reports of two or more opinions in other parts. (We call this second type of paper a "pro/con" essay; it is not the same as a persuasive essay, which does not present two or more sides evenly.)

Successfully writing a persuasive essay involves, most importantly, knowing the audience and predicting what the audience might be thinking while reading the essay. The most persuasive essay is the one that answers the audience's arguments as they arise. Therefore, the writer must know all sides of the issue, even though he or she supports only one side.

# PART III: WRITING PERSUASIVE THESIS STATEMENTS

The most important characteristic of the persuasive thesis statement is that it states an opinion about which others could disagree. In other words, it is argumentative. Read the following theses. Does each state an opinion that could cause disagreement?

1. Poverty is a problem that the poor make for themselves, so they should solve it for themselves.
2. A school's main function should be to socialize children.
3. It can be hard to cope with personal problems.
4. A father's place is at work, not at home.
5. Both fathers and mothers have important roles in their children's lives.

Statements 1, 2, and 4 seem to be the most argumentative. There are many people who believe that the problems of poverty are caused by an unfair social system. These people would strongly disagree with statement 1. The second statement expresses a sentiment held by many people, but it is by no means universal. There are many people who believe that schools should help students develop their individual talents as well as make them into useful citizens. Finally, statement 4 is argumentative because it implies that a father's only function is to earn money, not to be a valuable part of the home life and a child's emotional development. Many people would disagree with this.

Statements 3 and 5 are not argumentative. Everybody knows that it is hard to cope with personal problems—that's what makes them problems! Likewise, everyone believes that fathers and mothers play important roles in their children's development, even if they may disagree about what those roles are exactly.

Notice that our knowledge of whether or not a topic is argumentative depends on our knowledge of our audience. We have to imagine what our audience might answer after hearing our thesis. In particular you must be careful about forming arguments for people from other cultures since not all cultures share the same biases or assumptions. Statement 4 is quite argumentative in the United States; it may simply be a statement of fact in your native country.

**EXERCISE:** Practice writing *persuasive* (or *argumentative*) thesis statements with one or more of your classmates for the following topics. Indicate which audiences would probably find your thesis statements to be argumentative. Be sure that there can be disagreement about your theses.

1. (the father's role in the family)

   _____

2. (mothers and jobs outside the home )

   _____

3. (equality among the races)

   _____

4. (the purpose of an education)

   _____

5. (women being elected to political offices)

   _____

6. (teaching young people to oppose government authorities when necessary)

   _____

Paragraph 1 of the article at the opening of this chapter, "Poverty and the elderly," contains the thesis statement. What is it? Examine it in its context. How does it show that the article is persuasive?

# PART IV: SUMMARIZING THE OPPOSING OPINION

It may surprise you to know that when you are persuading your readers to agree with your opinion, you must also summarize for them the opinions that oppose yours. Some of your readers will already have formed opinions on the topic. If you ignore their opinions or the facts which support their opinions, you run the risk of alienating or angering your audience, making it difficult for them to pay attention to what you are saying about your own opinion. In addition, it will be easier for your audience to respect your opinion if they see that you are very well aware of the issue on all sides yet *still* hold the opinion that you do.

However, this is not to say that you have to devote as much time to the other opinions as you do your own. Instead, you may briefly summarize the opposing view, mentioning the most important points. Then you may go on to say why these points are not valid, or acceptable.

While you are summarizing the opposing opinion, it is important to make it clear to your reader that this is not *your* opinion. You can do this by using certain phrases such as those below:

- Some people say/think . . .
- We are told . . .
- It is sometimes believed . . .
- It is commonly thought . . .
- . . . is/are said to be . . .

When you are showing why the opposing opinion is not valid (called *rebutting the opposing opinion*) you may have to admit that certain facts of that opinion are true. You do this by using the following language (X = statement of opposing opinion; Y = statement of writer's opinion):

• Admittedly, X. However, Y.

(Admittedly, many senior citizens live quite comfortably. However, a large number also live in terrible poverty.)

• Granted, X, but Y.

(Granted, the statistics indicate that poverty has decreased among the elderly, but these statistics have changed in part because the methods for calculating them have changed.)

• While X, Y.

(While many senior citizens are living a well-earned life of leisure, there are still far too many who are suffering from poverty.)

• It is true that X, yet Y.

(It is true that the percentage of elders who are in poverty seems to have decreased, yet the statistics belie the actual situation.)

Paragraph 2 and part of 3 in the article above express the claims of the opposing point of view. Part of paragraph 3 and paragraph 4 answer these claims. Examine these two paragraphs. Does the author successfully neutralize the opposing arguments? How?

**EXERCISE:** Practice predicting opposing opinions for the topics below with some of your classmates. For each, list what that opinion is and at least three reasons why some members of your audience might have that opinion. The first is done for you.

| AUTHOR'S OPINION | OPPOSING OPINION | REASONS |
|---|---|---|
| **1.** The father's main role in the family is to be the breadwinner (wage earner). | Fathers should have an equal role to the mothers' in taking care of the child's daily needs. | Children need male role models more than money.<br><br>Children with absent fathers are more often involved in crime.<br><br>Women are now in the workplace because of economics; it is unfair to have them earn money and take care of the home too. |

| AUTHOR'S OPINION | OPPOSING OPINION | REASONS |
|---|---|---|
| **2.** Mothers should not have jobs outside the home until their children are in school. | | |
| **3.** Free education for all children should exist for the sole purpose of creating good citizens in society. | | |

## SHORT WRITING (100–125 WORDS)

Practice writing opposing opinions with one of the three topics in the exercise above. Use appropriate transition words from the list given above.

# PART V: SUPPORTING YOUR OPINION

The writer's opinion in the article at the beginning of this chapter is expressed both in the parts where he shows why the opposing opinion is wrong and in new information contained in these paragraphs. How successful is the author in supporting his opinion? What effect do the statistics have on your own opinion? Which of his points do you find most persuasive?

## Evidence

When you are writing your own persuasive essays, you will use a variety of evidence, not only statistics, depending on the topic. The topic in the article above is particularly well-served by *statistics.* But sometimes, topics require *logical explanation* much like "If A = B and B = C, then A = C." At other times, the evidence you have might be *quotations from experts* or accounts of *your personal experience.*

You should be aware that some types of evidence are more persuasive than others. Of the four types mentioned above (in italics), how would you rank them for persuasive value?

**EXERCISE:** Using the same topics from a previous exercise, determine which types of evidence might be most useful to support the opinions: statistics, logical explanation, quotations from experts, personal experience.

- The father's main role in the family is to be the breadwinner (wage earner).
- Mothers should not work outside the home until their children are in school.
- Free education for all children should exist for the sole purpose of creating good citizens in society.

There is one other type of evidence that can be useful when no other type is available. This is the *hypothetical* example. In this type of evidence you *imagine* someone in a certain situation and describe the situation in such a way as to create a feeling or image in your reader's mind. Hypothetical examples can be very effective with some readers, particularly when they are based on emotion, but they are less effective than the types of evidence named above. After all, they are not real.

*PITFALL!* Avoid basing an argument completely on *emotion* or *religion*. Especially in the United States and many other western countries, there are numerous religions. A religious argument may be effective only to those who practice that religion. Arguments based on emotions tend to be ineffective because emotions differ so widely from person to person. You may feel strongly about a topic, but that doesn't mean your reader does.

What types of evidence does the article at the beginning of this chapter employ? Is the evidence successful? Would other types also have been successful? Does the article base any of its arguments on emotion?

## PART VI: CONCLUDING

The conclusion in a piece of persuasive writing offers one more chance to make your main point about your topic. As such, it tends to restate the thesis or summarize the main pieces of evidence presented in the essay. But the pitfalls mentioned in Chapter 2 still apply: Don't simply *repeat* your thesis word for word, and don't summarize all of your main points if your essay is short.

The conclusion in the article above finds a way to reconcile or combine two apparently opposing opinions about whether the elderly are impoverished. Is it successful?

### SHORT ESSAY (250–300 WORDS)

Write a short essay on one of the topics described in this chapter in which you persuade your reader to agree with your opinion. Be sure to consider opposing opinions and to provide evidence to support your own opinion.

### Thesis Statements

*DO*       State an opinion about which others could disagree. Follow all the charac-
           teristics of thesis statements discussed in Chapter 2.

*DON'T*    *Mention both the opposing point of view and your own equally—em-
           phasize your own view more.*

### The Opposing Opinion

*DO*       Mention briefly the main points of those who oppose your opinion. Use
           appropriate transition words to indicate that this is the opposing opin-
           ion and not your own. Rebut the opposing opinion carefully; show why
           it is wrong point by point.

*DON'T*    *Explain the opposing opinion too much—it will sound like your own
           opinion and confuse your reader.*

### Evidence

*DO*       Use expert quotations, statistics, logical explanations and personal experi-
           ence to support your opinions. Give the sources of your evidence.
           Always consider your audience.

*DON'T*    *Base your arguments on emotion or religious beliefs if you can avoid it.
           Base your arguments on hypothetical examples unless you can think
           of no other evidence.*

## Bibliography

Mattera, Philip. "Tarnishing the Golden Years." In *Prosperity Lost.* Reading, Mass.: Addison-Wesley, 1990.

# Education and
# Empowerment

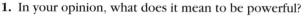

1. In your opinion, what does it mean to be powerful?
2. In what ways can you be a powerful person in your own life?
3. Has your education until now taught you how to be powerful in these ways?

## Topic Orientation

### Threads

The English word "power" derives from the Latin *posse*—to be able.

In order to begin understanding the topic for this chapter, discuss the following questions with two or three of your classmates.

1. What is your most important goal for the future?
2. How successfully has your education until now prepared you for this goal?
3. What role might further education play in helping you to achieve this goal?

## *LEARNING STRATEGY*

**Managing Your Learning: Choose a topic that you will probably be able to handle but one that is also a little more difficult than you are used to.**

# PART II: WRITING THE FIRST DRAFT

## Major Essay Assignments

Write the first draft of a major essay of approximately 750 words on one of the following topics (or a topic of your choice which you have discussed with your instructor). Choose the type of essay that you feel competent to write but that will also provide a bit of a challenge for you. Use the questions in the assignments to help you begin the assignment, not to limit your ideas.

   **1. Descriptive Essay.** Describe the *one* most significant aspect of your education so far. You will need to consider first what "significant" means to you. It may, for example, mean memorable, useful, empowering, or confidence-building. Before choosing your final topic, brainstorm about the teachers who have had an impact on you, any particular courses that have intrigued you, or extracurricular activities (such as athletics, music, or clubs) that have been important to you. Choose *one* particular aspect of your education, then make your reader understand why it has been important to you.

**2. Narrative Essay.** In the second reading, Mark describes his first day at school in such a way that we learn how empowering education can be for people in his situation. Describe your first day at a particular school. In what ways did you feel powerless in this new situation? In what ways did you feel powerful? What did you do to get some control or power for yourself in this new situation? How did the school match or not match your expectations? By the end of that day, how did you feel about your new school and yourself?

**3. Analytic Essay.** It is likely that you will be continuing your education in the future, in one way or another, perhaps in a school or institute or perhaps in your profession. Explain the steps you can take to achieve an education that empowers you. What can you do to get an education that will help you to develop to your fullest potential? You will need to explain to your reader exactly what an empowering education is, in your opinion. You will probably also need to give your reader some background about the educational systems in your country if your education will continue there, since your readers' systems may be different.

**4. Persuasive Essay.** Argue whether public education should take as its main goal to prepare socially useful citizens or whether it should enable individuals to develop to their fullest potentials (or both). Keep in mind as you are writing that your reader may not have experience with the same type of educational system as you have. Your reader will also need to know exactly what *you* mean by an "empowering" education.

## LEARNING STRATEGY

**Understanding and Using Emotions: Don't expect perfection on your first draft because your ideas and language abilities will continue to develop as you write each draft of this essay.**

## INTRODUCTORY READING

### Vocabulary Enrichment

Look at the underlined words, as well as the meanings of the sentences around them, in the Toffler passage that follows and find:

**1.** a noun that means "the higher part of the organization" _____

**2.** two verbs that mean "change" _____

and _____

**3.** an adverb that means "very much" _____

**4.** an adjective that means "obvious" _____

**5.** an adjective that means "mindless" or "repetitious" _____

*VOCABULARY LEARNING STRATEGY:* Choose one or more of the words from this vocabulary exercise which you feel will be useful in your writing. Enter them into the Vocabulary Checklist at the end of this chapter.

We are accustomed to thinking of education as a tool by which people prepare for their futures. In this passage, Alvin Toffler points out that public, mass education was not established for individual achievement but rather for the needs of industrial society, which he refers to as Second Wave society. What needs does industrial society have?

# The covert curriculum

As work shifted out of the fields and the home, children had to be prepared for factory life. The early mine, mill, and factory owners of industrializing England discovered, as Andrew Ure wrote in 1835, that it was "nearly impossible to convert persons past the age of puberty, whether drawn from rural or from handicraft occupations, into useful factory hands." If young people could be prefitted to the industrial system, it would vastly ease the problems of industrial discipline later on. The result was another central structure of all Second Wave societies: mass education. (1)

Built on the factory model, mass education taught basic reading, writing, and arithmetic, a bit of history and other subjects. This was the "overt curriculum." But beneath it lay an invisible or "covert curriculum" that was far more basic. It consisted—and still does in most industrial nations—of three courses: one in punctuality, one in obedience, and one in rote, repetitive work. Factory labor demanded workers who showed up on time, especially assembly-line hands. It demanded workers who would take orders from a management hierarchy without questioning. And it demanded men and women prepared to slave away at machines or in offices, performing brutally repetitive operations. (2)

Toffler, 1980, p. 29.

## ELABORATING ON THE READING

1. What social purpose does Toffler assign to mass education?
2. Which behaviors in classrooms are usually rewarded, and which are punished?
3. Which types of students tend to be rewarded most often, and which tend to be punished?
4. How do these rewards and punishments reinforce the social behaviors described by Toffler?

## Preparing for Short Writing: Writing Skills

### BRAINSTORMING

The act of searching your mind for any ideas related to the topic you plan to write about is called brainstorming. Some people sit with a piece of paper or a notebook and write everything they, alone or with others, can think about the topic. They may, at the same time, try to organize the information into groups or lists, but the important thing is that they do not reject *any* piece of information immediately. Brainstorming is not about making decisions; it is about creating possibilities. Others prefer not to write the information at all. They go about their regular activities with the topic in the backs of their minds and occasionally think about it consciously, sometimes over several days. When they become more comfortable with the topic and begin to see the ideas they can write about, they begin writing a draft.

**BRAINSTORMING EXERCISE:**   With a classmate, brainstorm as many ways as you can think of for a school to socialize its students. Two items are included for you as examples.

### Ways that Schools Socialize Students

• requiring them to be quiet in the classroom

• requiring them to have "hall passes" in order to leave the classroom

•

•

•

•

## SHORT WRITING (150–200 WORDS)

Describe one way in which your own previous education socialized you, that is, served your society's needs more than your own. You may use a topic from the previous brainstorming exercise.

### *LEARNING STRATEGY*

**Forming Concepts: Increase your learning potential by sharing your work with some of your classmates and taking notes on their ideas; "two heads are better than one!"**

Share your short writing with several members of your class. Take notes on any ideas you believe may be useful for you later in this chapter or when you write your essay.

*NOTE:*   Be careful not to use your classmates' work as if it were your own. This is called *cheating* and is a punishable behavior.

### IN-DEPTH READING

**Vocabulary Enrichment**
Examine the contexts in which the following words or phrases appear in the story which follows. Then determine their parts of speech (noun, verb, adjective, or adverb) and likely meanings. Use a dictionary or grammar reference if you are unsure of the part of speech.

| | PART OF SPEECH | MEANING | | |
|---|---|---|---|---|
| 1. revered | _____ | disliked | admired | forgot |
| 2. captivated | _____ | attacked | confused | interested |
| 3. lacking | _____ | absent | good | pleasant |
| 4. priority | _____ | goal | choice | chance |
| 5. contemplated | _____ | hated | considered | fought |
| 6. tyrannous | _____ | kind | unhappy | cruelly powerful |
| 7. ample credence | _____ | a silly idea | easy work | enough |
| and | | | | |
| | _____ | | | evidence |
| 8. allegiance | _____ | loyalty | anger | interest |
| 9. scarcely | _____ | easily | clearly | hardly |
| 10. reluctant | _____ | ready | disappointed | hesitant |
| 11. pretext | _____ | false reason | plan | preparation |
| 12. neglecting | _____ | caring for | ignoring | remembering |
| 13. magnitude | _____ | strength | importance | length |
| 14. destiny | _____ | fear | luck | certain future |
| 15. altered | _____ | changed | completed | hidden |

## Threads

Empowerment involves individuals gaining control of their lives and fulfilling their needs, in part, as a result of developing the competencies, skills, and abilities necessary to effectively participate in the social and political worlds.

Seth Kreisberg, *Transforming Power: Domination, Empowerment, and Education*, State University of New York, 1992

**Remember Your Vocabulary Checklist!**

## LEARNING STRATEGY

**Personalizing: Improve your understanding and memory of the story by imagining yourself as one of the characters.**

As you read the following story, imagine yourself in the little boy's situation. How would you feel about these events?

The author of the book from which the following passage is taken, Mark Mathabane, writes of his enrollment more than two decades ago in a black school in the country of South Africa, where education for blacks was limited by whites, who controlled the country. Why would the whites in South Africa want to limit the education of blacks?

# Chapter 21: "Education will open doors where none seem to exist."

**W**hen my mother began dropping hints that I would soon be going to school, I vowed never to go because school was a waste of time. She laughed and said, "We'll see. You don't know what you're talking about." My philosophy on school was that of a gang of ten-, eleven- and twelve-year-olds whom I so <u>revered</u> that their every word seemed that of an oracle. (1)

These boys had long left their homes and were now living in various neighborhood junkyards, making it on their own. They slept in abandoned cars, smoked glue and benzene, ate pilchards[1] and brown bread, sneaked into the white world to caddy and, if unsuccessful, came back to the township to steal beer and soda bottles from shebeens[2], or goods from the Indian traders on First Avenue. Their life-style was exciting, adventurous and full of surprises; and I was attracted to it. My mother told me that they were no-gooders, that they would amount to nothing, that I should not associate with them, but I paid no heed. What does she know? I used to tell myself. One thing she did not know was that the gang's way of life had <u>captivated</u> me wholly, particularly their philosophy on school: they hated it and considered an education a waste of time. (2)

They, like myself, had grown up in an environment where the value of an education was never emphasized, where the first thing a child learned was not how to read and write and spell, but how to fight and steal and rebel; where the money to send children to school was grossly <u>lacking,</u> for survival was first <u>priority.</u> I kept my membership in the gang, knowing that

---

[1]pilchards: a type of South African fish, similar to the herring or sardine

[2]shebeens: taverns or bars

for as a long as I was under its influence, I would never go to school. (3)

. . .

The sun was beginning to rise from beyond the veld when Granny and my mother dragged me to school. The streets were beginning to fill with their everyday traffic: old men and women, wizened, bent and ragged, were beginning their rambling; workless men and women were beginning to assemble in their usual coteries and head for shebeens in the backyards where they discussed how they escaped the morning pass raids and <u>contemplated</u> the conditions of life amidst intense beer drinking and vacant, uneasy laughter; young boys and girls, some as young as myself, were beginning their aimless wanderings along the narrow, dusty streets in search of food, carrying bawling infants piggyback[3]. (4)

As we went along some of the streets, boys and girls who shared the same fears about school as I were making their feelings known in a variety of ways. They were howling their protests and trying to escape. A few managed to

---

[3]piggyback: on one's back

break loose and make a mad dash for freedom, only to be recaptured in no time, admonished or whipped, or both, and ordered to march again. (5)

As we made a turn into Sixteenth Avenue, the street leading to the tribal school I was being taken to, a short, chubby black woman came along from the opposite direction. She had a scuttle overflowing with coal on her *doek*-covered [cloth-covered] head. An infant, bawling deafeningly, was loosely swathed with a piece of sheepskin onto her back. Following closely behind the woman, and picking up pieces of coal as they fell from the scuttle and placing them in a small plastic bag, was a half-naked, potbellied and thumb-sucking boy of about four. The women stopped abreast. For some reason we stopped too. (6)

"I wish I had done the same to my oldest son," the strange woman said in a regretful voice, gazing at me. I was confounded by her stopping and offering her unsolicited opinion. (7)

"I wish I had done that to my oldest son," she repeated, and suddenly burst into tears; amidst sobs, she continued, "before . . . the street claimed him . . . and . . . turned him into a *tsotsi*." (8)

Granny and my mother offered consolatory remarks to the strange woman. (9)

"But it's too late now," the strange woman continued, tears now streaming freely down her puffy cheeks. She made no attempt to dry them. "It's too late now," she said for the second time, "he's beyond any help. I can't help him even if I wanted to. *Uswile* [He is dead]." (10)

"How did he die?" my mother asked in a sympathetic voice. (11)

"He shunned school and, instead, grew up to live by the knife. And the same knife he lived by ended his life. That's why whenever I see a boy-child refuse to go to school, I stop and tell the story of my dear little *mbitsini* [heartbreak]." (12)

Having said that, the strange woman left as mysteriously as she had arrived. (13)

"Did you hear what that woman said!" my mother screamed into my ears. "Do you want the same to happen to you?" (14)

I dropped my eyes. I was confused. (15)

"Poor woman," Granny said ruefully. "She must have truly loved her son." (16)

. . .

I didn't want to go to school for three reasons: I was reluctant to surrender my freedom and independence over to what I heard every school-going child call "tyrannous discipline." I had heard many bad things about life in tribal school—from daily beatings by teachers and mistresses who worked you like a mule to long school hours—and the sight of those canes[4] in the principal's office gave ample credence to rumors that school was nothing but a torture chamber. And there was my allegiance to the gang. (17)

But the thought of the strange woman's lamentations over her dead son presented a somewhat strong case for going to school: I didn't want to end up dead in the streets. A more compelling argument for going to

_____

[4]canes: sticks used to hit students for punishment

school, however, was the vivid recollection of all that humiliation and pain my mother had gone through to get me the papers and the birth certificate so I could enroll in school. What should I do? I was torn between two worlds. (18)

But later that evening something happened to force me to go to school. (19)

I was returning home from playing soccer when a neighbor accosted me by the gate and told me that there had been a bloody fight at my home. (20)

"Your mother and father have been at it again," the neighbor, a woman, said. (21)

"And your mother left." (22)
I was stunned. (23)
"Was she hurt badly?" (24)

"A little bit," the woman said. "But she'll be all right. We took her to your grandma's place." (25)

. . .

I ran, without stopping, all the way to the other end of the township where Granny lived. There I found my mother, her face swollen and bruised and her eyes puffed up to the point where she could scarcely see. (26)

"What happened, Mama?" I asked, fighting to hold back the tears at the sight of her disfigured face. (27)

"Nothing, child, nothing," she mumbled, almost apologetically, between swollen lips. "Your papa simply lost his temper, that's all." (28)

"But why did he beat you up like this, Mama?" Tears came down my face. "He's never beaten you like this before." (29)

My mother appeared reluctant to answer me. She looked searchingly at Granny, who was pounding millet with pestle and mortar and mixing it with sorghum and nuts for an African delicacy. Granny said, "Tell him, child, tell him. He's got a right to know. Anyway, he's the cause of it all." (30)

"Your father and I fought because I took you to school this morning," my mother began. "He had told me not to, and when I told him that I had, he became very upset. He was drunk. We started arguing, and one thing led to another." (31)

"Why doesn't he want me to go to school?" (32)

"He says he doesn't have money to waste paying for you to get what he calls a useless white man's education," my mother replied. "But I told him that if he won't pay for your schooling, I would try and look for a job and pay, but he didn't want to hear that, also." (33)

. . .

"Why do you want me to go to school, Mama?" I asked, hoping that she might, somehow, clear up some of the confusion that was building in my mind. (34)

"I want you to have a future, child," my mother said. "And, contrary to what your father says, school is the only means to a future. I don't want you growing up to be like your father." (35)

The latter statement hit me like a bolt of lightening. It just about shattered every defense mechanism and every pretext I had against going to school. (36)

"Your father didn't go to school," she continued, dabbing her puffed eyes to reduce the swelling with a piece of cloth dipped in warm water, "That's why he's doing some of the bad things he's doing. Things like drinking, gambling and neglecting his family. He didn't learn how to read and write; therefore, he can't find a decent job. Lack of any education has narrowly focused his life. He sees nothing beyond himself. He still thinks in the old, tribal way, and still believes that things should be as they were back in the old days when he was growing up as a tribal boy in Louis Trichardt. Though he's my husband, and your father, he doesn't see any of that." (37)

"He refused to go to school because his father led him to believe that an education was a tool through which white people were going to take things away from him, like they did black people in the old days. And that a white man's education was worthless insofar as black people were concerned because it prepared them for jobs they can't have. But I know it isn't totally so, child, because times have changed somewhat. Though our lot isn't any better today, an education will get you a decent job. If you can read or write you'll be better off than those of us who can't. . . . Education will open doors where none seem to exist. It'll make people talk to you, listen to you and help you; people who otherwise wouldn't bother. It will make you soar, like a bird lifting up into the endless blue sky, and leave poverty, hunger and suffering behind. It'll teach you to learn to embrace what's good and shun what's bad and evil. Above all, it'll make you a somebody in this world. It'll make you grow up to be a good and proud person. . . ." (38)

With tears streaming down my cheeks and falling upon my mother's bosom, I promised her that I would go to school "forever." . . . Scarcely aware of the <u>magnitude</u> of the decision I was making or, rather, the decision which was being emotionally thrusted upon me, I chose to fight on my mother's side, and thus my <u>destiny</u> was forever <u>altered</u>. (39)

Mathabane, 1987, pp. 123-134.

## ELABORATING ON THE READING

1. Why did Mark's mother want him to have an education?
2. Why did Mark's father disapprove of Mark's going to school?
3. Whose opinion, Mark's father's or his mother's, better reflects the main idea of the *Third Wave* passage earlier in this chapter? How?
4. Describe Mark's future if he didn't go to school. How would his life be different if he did go to school?
5. Which would give Mark more power over his life: going to school or not going?

## Preparing for Short Writing: Writing Skills

### CHRONOLOGICAL AND SEQUENTIAL DESCRIPTION

When writers describe sequences or processes, there are several things they keep in mind. First, they must determine which steps are the most important ones to include in their explanation. Then, they generally try to explain the steps in the order in which the steps occur. (Creative writing, including novels and short stories, is an exception to this rule.) If you compare this information to the explanation of physical description above, you will see that these characteristics are similar: It is easier for readers to organize and remember information which follows a "map." In this case, the map is from past to present or first to last.

It is also important for writers who are giving chronological or sequential information to be sure to include all the necessary steps. Sometimes a writer who understands a process or sequence very well tends to forget that his or her readers may not be very familiar with it. In fact, writers should assume that their audience is relatively naive about the process being described; otherwise, they wouldn't need to read the description of it.

Finally, it is often important to give background about some or all of the steps involved. Reasons why the steps are necessary or background on how they developed can help readers understand the steps more completely and, thus, remember them more easily.

**EXERCISE—Listing Steps:** Prepare a list of the steps involved in Mark's father's actions leading up to and including Mark's first day of school. Be sure to put the list in chronological order.

## SHORT WRITING (150–200 WORDS)

We can often get insights from readings by imagining the story from another person's mind. In this reading, we read the story from Mark's point of view, and we also learned a great deal about his mother's viewpoint. However, we learned very little about his father's viewpoint.

Write approximately 150 words *in which you retell the story as Mark's father saw it, using his voice.* Why was he so angry about Mark's beginning school? What did he think about Mark's future and about his wife's taking Mark to school? What did Mark's father know from his own experience? Be sure to tell the story in chronological order.

## Drafting Your Essay

Have you ever discussed a problem with a friend? Can you remember talking about the problem, *not* getting any advice from your friend, but arriving at a solution yourself, just because you had put the problem into words? This same process applies to writing.

One of the most important ways writers develop their ideas is simply by sitting down and writing. Typically, even professional writers begin and begin again until they manage to strike up an attitude or idea that pleases them. As they write, new ideas enter their minds, and already existing ideas develop more concretely. This is the reason why drafting and revision are so important to writers. There is no good writer who can write something worth reading without going in false directions a few times or without having to go back over a draft and adding, deleting, or reorganizing information. Notice that this method of generating ideas differs from freewriting in the sense that freewriting is uncontrolled, without decision making. Drafting is very much dependent on making decisions.

This text is organized in such a way that you will (depending on your teacher's schedule) write three drafts of each major essay. Despite the fact that you will receive feedback from your classmates and teacher, you will also have an opportunity to provide feedback to yourself through the use of "reflections," included in each chapter of this text. You will discover, as you reflect on your writing, that the only sure end to the drafting process is your teacher's deadline— there's always another idea to add or change that will improve your writing. Therefore, use all the instruction on writing and language skills in the chapter to improve your writing, draft by draft.

## Making Your Draft Clearer: Writing Skills

### SIMPLE TRANSITIONS

One way to keep your readers aware of the topic you are discussing and the direction in which you plan to lead them is to use simple transitions. (On page 133 you will find a discussion of phrasal and sentence transitions.)

Simple transitions such as *however, on the other hand, in addition,* and *therefore* act as signals in writing. Imagine that you were going to travel across a country like the United States. You would have a map, but how would you identify the roads you needed to travel on? By road signs, of course. And how many signs would you like to have? One every 100 miles? One every 10 feet? Of course not. Too few signs can lead to confusion, but so can too many.

Too often, students learn about simple transitions and apply the rule "if one is good, a hundred must be great." It is not helpful to your reader to begin every sentence in your writing with a transition. Instead, try to use them as aids to your readers' comprehension. In addition, be sure that your transitions name the relationship between ideas, but do not create the relationship. Simply adding *as a result* does not guarantee that the next sentence is truly a result of the previous one. Which transitions do you notice in this paragraph?

Simple transitions are often used to relate information in a subsequent paragraph to that in a previous one. However, they can also do the same between sentences within one paragraph. Some common ways to use transitions are given below. (More specific ways are given in Chapter 6.) Notice that simple transitions are always followed by commas.

- to show similarity or continuity in types of information: *in addition, in fact, moreover, also,*
- to show contrasts or differences in information: *however, nevertheless,*
- to show sequence: *first, second, next, finally,*
- to link examples with their generalizations: *for example, for instance,*
- to introduce summary information: *in short, in summary, to summarize, in conclusion,*
- to show results: *therefore, as a result, thus, consequently, hence,* (very formal)

**EXERCISE 1—Simple Transitions:** Read the following paragraphs until you understand them well. Then identify the simple transitions, and discuss the following with one or more classmates:

- the relative number of transitions compared to the length of the essay;
- the meanings of each transition and why these meanings are appropriate; and
- the clarity of the passage if the transitions were absent.

### ARE JAPANESE SCHOOLS ALWAYS BETTER?

There have been many comparisons recently between U.S. educational methods and Japanese methods. *As a matter of fact,* the implication has always been that U.S. educators have a lot to learn from their Japanese counterparts, since Japan has become such a highly industrialized, economically successful country in such a relatively short amount of time. It is likely that there are several areas that U.S. educators may choose to copy. *However,* not all Japanese educational methods are easily applied in the U.S.

*First,* we tend to admire the Japanese character for its emphasis on effort. It is this very effort that apparently explains the rapid economic rise of the country. *For example,* in some Japanese kindergartens, students go shirtless all year long to build endurance and some schools require boys to wear short pants during the winter. The Japanese six-day school week, which appears to us to be academically motivated, is, *in fact,* really a part of this emphasis on effort.

**Threads**

"Banking education" treats students as "receptacles" into which teachers "deposit" information; it "oppresses creative power." In "problem posing education, people develop their power to perceive critically the way they exist in the world, . . . to overcome authoritarianism. . . ."

Paulo Freire, "The 'Banking' Concept of Education," *Pedagogy of the Oppressed,* 1970

*Second,* emphasis on group responsibility is a characteristic of Japanese education. This tends to reinforce conformity, which Japanese society values highly. *For example,* techniques such as assigning a single grade to a whole class rather than to each individual and discussing issues in terms of group welfare reinforce this value. We should remember, though, that Japan has a great amount of racial unity. *As a result,* group responsibility may be easier to promote in Japan than in the U.S.

It may not be so easy to adapt Japanese methods to U.S. schools because of the differences in the two cultures. *Nevertheless,* this does not mean that there are no lessons to be learned from the Japanese, only that we must be careful in choosing what we wish to copy from Japan. (Fallows, 1991, pp. 55–59)

**EXERCISE 2—Simple Transitions:**   Take out your first draft, and examine your use of transitions. Are there enough to guide your reader? Are there so many that your reader is overloaded? Have you used transitions with the right meanings?

## Making Your Draft Clearer: Language Skills

### VERB TENSES WITH GENERALIZATIONS AND EXPERIENTIAL EXAMPLES

As you write many essays, you will generally find yourself moving between two time frames: the past and the present/future. The *past time frame* includes simple past, past perfect, past *-ing* forms, and verbs with *would, could,* and sometimes *should* and *might.* The *present/future time frame* includes simple present, present perfect, present *-ing* forms and future forms with *can, will,* and sometimes *should* and *may.*

We often use the *past time frame* when we are telling a story which proves the point we are trying to make. We generally use the *present/future time frame* when we are generalizing about our thoughts, beliefs, or opinions. Consider the following example. Where does the tense change from present to past? Why?

It can be very easy for an adult to forget how frightening school is for a young child. For the first time, the child spends a significant portion of his or her time outside of the home, without parents, familiar objects, siblings, or any of the things that he or she has come to rely on day in and day out. Thus, the child feels especially powerless, particularly if he or she is a shy child.

While I don't remember my first day of school, I do remember one day early in my school career very well, when I was six years old. My classmates and I had been taught to remove our coats and hats quietly by our desks at the beginning of each day and to wait until the teacher, who had often scared me because she was a nun,[1] gave us permission to go to the coat room to hang them up. One morning, my mother walked into my classroom. I was shocked and intently focused my eyes upon her trying to discern why she was there. Had I done something wrong? Was something bad about to happen? I was sure my teacher, who was actually a kind person, didn't like

---

[1]nun: religious woman who devotes her life to service to God

me very much and that I would be made to look very foolish in front of my young classmates.

As a matter of fact, I did look very foolish. For not only did I remove my coat and hat, but, engrossed in my thoughts about my mother's visit, I also removed my blouse and was working on my undershirt!

There is a very strong tendency in English to *maintain* a time frame unless there is a good reason to change it. Writers tend to see their papers in *functional parts*. Thus, if one functional part gives opinions or states facts, it will be in present tense. If another functional part is telling a story, it will be in the past. Because of this tendency, writers write sentences when storytelling such as "His name *was* Hiro," (even though his name still *is* Hiro) or "She *was* from Egypt," (even though she still *is* from Egypt).

In the story above, find examples of this.

Within one paragraph, you may find both the past and present time frames. This generally happens when one or more statements gives an opinion or fact (the generalization) and the next statements provide story-telling evidence (examples from personal life or history). Consider the following example continuing the story above.

Why did I react that way? Surely many six-year-olds in my class would not have reacted as I had. I think partly it was that I was very insecure about my relationship with my teacher and partly that I hadn't yet learned to feel comfortable at my school. There are many children who can handle a situation like mine with great strength of character. (They don't strip!) They are not shy children and they don't depend on familiar surroundings in order to feel secure. Their security is inside themselves, in their own self-esteem. Mine was somewhere outside myself, in my home, my family, my neighborhood friends. To me, then, school became an alien place in which I had to learn to believe in a new "me."

Where do the verb tenses change from past to present or present to past? Can you explain why these changes occur?

**EXERCISE—Verb Tenses in Generalizations and Examples:** Determine whether the verbs in parentheses in the paragraphs below should be in the present or past time frame. Then put them into the appropriate form.

Most teachers (*understand*) quite well what (*constitutes*) good teaching in an ideal world. In courses for "gifted" children, methods such as individualized study, hands-on experience, cooperative learning among classmates, and peer instruction *(are be)* all employed to develop young, intelligent minds. Yet, teachers in the classrooms of poor neighborhoods often *(fall)* into the trap we *(call)* the "pedagogy of poverty," which *(has have)* far different goals from those of the gifted classroom.

In the pedagogy of poverty, the teacher and the textbooks *(are be)* regarded as the sole sources of information from which students are to learn the proper facts. Rayburn High School, located near a public housing[1] complex, used

---

[1] housing for the poor, subsidized by government funds

to be just a such a school. At Rayburn, teachers *(exist)* to dispense information. They *(will)* ask questions, give directions, monitor student performance, and reward and punish students. In short, the teacher *(be)* in charge and the only experience students gained *(be)* in obeying authority.

In most pedagogy of poverty classrooms, teachers *(can)* become virtual police who *(monitor)* student behavior in order to maintain control in the classroom. Keeping records on absences, grades, disciplinary actions, and analyses by specialists is done very precisely by the teacher to protect the school from legal action by students or parents. Teachers *(watch)* students carefully during class, lunchtime, free play periods, and even between classes to prevent behaviors which poor children *(be)* "known" to indulge in, such as fighting, smoking, and criminal acts. A good poverty teacher's daily goal *(be)* to control noise and *(prevent)* loss of control by the teacher, not *(encourage)* good studying.

Students at Rayburn *(be)* lucky because they *(have)* concerned parents, some of whom *(can)* recognize that their children *(be)* not receiving the kind of education that they *(will)* need in a competitive world. They *(take)* their concerns to the school board and *(ask)* for specific changes. Today, while nobody *(consider)* Rayburn a school for gifted children, it *(be)* much more than a house of discipline.

Children of all socioeconomic groups *(need)* equally good educations. We must abandon the pedagogy of poverty and teach in ways that empower all students, not only the gifted. (Haberman, 1991, pp. 290–294)

Now, go back to your draft of the major essay, and check your verb tenses. Have you maintained the appropriate time frames?

## LEARNING STRATEGY

**Understanding and Using Emotions: Encourage yourself by emphasizing the positive and congratulating yourself for your successes.**

## Reflecting on Draft One

After you complete your first draft to your satisfaction, consider the following.

1. Describe one thing you intended to do in your essay that you think you succeeded in doing. How do you know?

   _____

2. If you haven't already given your essay a title, give it one which could be given only to your essay and no other. Why did you choose this title?

   _____

3. Identify the audience you had in mind when you were writing your essay.

   _____

4. Describe one thing you wanted your reader to receive from your essay.

   _____

5. Describe one change you would like to make in the next draft. Why?

   _____

# PART III: WRITING THE SECOND DRAFT

In Part III, you will work on revising the first draft of your major essay. In particular, you will gain valuable ideas by reading more on the topic, learn how to add examples, put these examples into an effective order, and increase the sophistication of your language with new vocabulary and sentence structure choices.

## FURTHER READING

**Vocabulary Enrichment**

Using an English-English dictionary, write *brief definitions and the parts of speech* for the following words from the article which follows.

1. eclectic _____

2. rigor _____

3. well-rounded _____

4. innovations _____

5. nurture _____

6. exceed _____

**Remember Your
Vocabulary Checklist!**

*LEARNING STRATEGY*

**Managing Your Learning:** *Gradually* **make your writing sound
more academic by adding *a few* vocabulary items from this
chapter to your essay in appropriate places.**

The following article describes a private school in California, U.S.A. Private schools offer what is sometimes perceived to be a stronger education than public schools can offer, in part because the students must pay tuition. (Public education is free to students, paid for by government tax dollars.) How does the Polytechnic School compare with your own high school?

*LEARNING STRATEGY*

**Remembering New Material: When you read useful or interesting
ideas, underline, highlight, or take notes in the margins to help
you remember the information and to make it accessible for
later use.**

# Private education with a conscience

From its <u>eclectic</u>, slightly timeworn campus off California Boulevard, Polytechnic School in Pasadena has for decades practiced a style of private education that mixes academic <u>rigor</u> with a strong social conscience, prizes the arts as much as athletics and makes room for the poor alongside the rich. "The youngsters here have an ability to care for and respect one another, to care about society and, for the most part, to really care about their studies," said David Murphy, a Poly parent for 14 years and president of the 21-member board of trustees that governs the independent, college preparatory school. (1)

One of the Los Angeles area's most highly regarded private schools, Polytechnic turns out <u>well-rounded</u> scholars, requires its students to participate in community service projects and shares its resources and <u>innovations</u> with surrounding public schools. . . . (2)

Like most of the area's top private schools, Poly is expensive and tough to get into. Tuitions range from $6,055 [per year] for pre-kindergarten and kindergarten to $8,730 for grades nine through 12, plus other costs such as books, uniforms, lab fees and field trips. . . . From the day it opened in 1907, the school has offered scholarships to children whose families could not afford the tuition. . . . almost 9% of this year's operating budget . . . goes for financial aid. . . . The 820-student school has space for about 100 new students each year but usually draws more than 1,000 applicants. (3)

"About 70% of those who apply would have a successful experience at the school," Murphy said. "That means we have to turn away a lot of really good kids, and that is very painful for us. Those who survive the anxiety-ridden rounds of interviews and entrance tests are admitted to a world of small classes (student to faculty ratio is 10.5 to 1), inspired teachers and an enriched curriculum that has all third-

graders studying the violin and sixth-graders conjugating verbs in French, Latin or Spanish. (4)

Lower School students—pre-kindergarten through fifth grade—are introduced to science, mathematical concepts and reading by cooperative learning techniques that foster attitudes of helping one another. In the Middle School, sixth- through eighth-graders begin the transition from self-contained classrooms to the departmentalized courses of high school. Each student is assigned a faculty member who monitors his academic progress. Upper School students often spend as much time each day on homework as they do in class. They study one foreign language for at least three years, and some take on more. In keeping with the school's goal of turning out well-rounded individuals, everyone who goes out for an athletic team is accepted. (5)

To add to classroom instruction and foster the atmosphere of "caring and camaraderie," the school tries hard to <u>nurture</u>. Middle School and Upper School students go off together with staff for several days to such places as Catalina Island, the Green River in Utah or a ranch near San Luis Obispo. . . .

The 15-acre site near the California Institute of Technology . . . contains two libraries, a computer room, media center, fully equipped science laboratories, gymnasium and a theater and fine arts center. The Upper School's main building is a graceful mansion, set among fine old trees, which was built in the 1920s for a prominent Pasadena family and later donated to the school. . . . (6)

Academically, Poly students are standouts. On the Scholastic Aptitude Test, a widely used college entrance examination, the class of 1991 scored an average of 615 out of a possible 800 in the verbal part of the test and 675 in math. The national averages for public high school students were 419 and 473 respectively, according to the college Board, which sponsors the exam. . . . Last year, 38 students, or 51% of the class of 1991, were National Merit or National Achievement honorees. (7)

But it is the school's strong tradition of community service that makes Headmaster Alexander B. (Mike) Babcock proudest. The community outreach program begins with class projects in pre-kindergarten and by middle school, students are encouraged to tutor at public schools, make decorations for the Pasadena Senior Citizen Center, collect food and clothing for the needy, make sandwiches for the homeless or volunteer at an orphanage in Mexico. For several years, Upper School students have been required to do volunteer work in order to graduate, and Babcock said many <u>exceed</u> the requirement. "I think kids who graduate from here have a social consciousness, feel a need to give back to the community . . .," he said. (8)

Like many parents, Hannah and Mark Farbstein of San Marino were attracted to Poly by its small classes and enriched curriculum but quickly came to appreciate the "good values they are teaching" as well. "Our kids have had some really good opportunities to be friends with kids of different races, religions, backgrounds," said Hannah Farbstein, head of one of the parents' groups that work closely with the school. (9)

Merl, 1992, Sec. A, pp. 1, 30–31.

## ELABORATING ON THE READING

With one or two of your classmates, analyze "Private Education with a Conscience," looking in particular for two kinds of information: examples of how Poly reinforces society's values and examples of how Poly helps individuals develop to their full potentials. List these examples below so that you will have ideas for your major essay later.

| POLY REINFORCES SOCIETY'S VALUES | POLY FACILITATES INDIVIDUAL DEVELOPMENT |
| --- | --- |
| | |
| | |
| | |
| | |
| | |
| | |
| | |
| | |
| | |

**Threads**

High schools around the U.S. are starting to base instruction on cooperative learning, where students study in groups and teachers act as guides rather than lecturers. The old "teacher-centered" way was thought to turn kids into passive sponges of knowledge.

"The Group Classroom," *Newsweek*, May 10, 1993

## TAKING THE IDEA FARTHER

Discuss with some of your classmates which of the following principles of "good teaching" are empowering and which are socializing. Place an *E* next to those that are empowering and an *S* next to those that are socializing. (Note: You may have disagreements.)

1. _____ Students leave the classroom for field trips, visits that give them real-life experience on some topic they have been studying.

2. _____ Students are required to be respectful of authority figures.

3. _____ Students memorize large amounts of factual information.

4. _____ Students help the school make decisions involving such rules as safety regulations, dress codes, and school newspaper censorship.

5. _____ Students are encouraged to form their own opinions rather than adopt their teachers' opinions.

6. _____ Students help to plan their class schedules and curricula.

7. _____ Students are taught to meet deadlines by handing in assignments on time.

8. _____ Students are taught to question "common sense" opinions.

9. _____ Students are taught to connect what they learn in class with how they live.

10. _____ Students are taught to be competitive with their classmates when their teachers give grades and reward those with appropriate behavior.

11. _____ Students are taught to be cooperative when they work in teams on assignments.

12. _____ Students are taught to depend on authority when they listen to lectures and take notes.

13. _____ Students must stand when the teacher enters the room and when they answer his or her questions.

14. _____ Students must recite the "Pledge of Allegiance" (a loyalty oath to the United States) at the beginning of each day.

15. _____ Students must carry a "hall pass" whenever they are outside of the classroom during class time to show that they have permission from the teacher.

Could any of these ideas be useful in your major essay? If so, develop those you like for your essay, explained in your own words.

### LEARNING STRATEGY

**Managing Your Learning: Increasing your contact with native speakers increases your ability to speak and listen effectively in a second language.**

## Gathering Data—A Poll

A poll involves asking a number of people to answer the same questions so that the researcher can find out opinions about a topic. It is very common in the United States for people to be stopped on the street or in a shopping area and asked for their opinions.

In small groups of three or four students, prepare a very short poll on the topic of "The Most Important Qualities in a Good Education." Then go out into the community around your school or neighborhood and ask people to answer your questions, being careful to keep a record of their answers. Explain to the people that you are a student conducting a poll. Ask them if they would mind answering (three or four) questions. Prepare your results and explain them to your class.

*HINT:*  Be sure to limit the number of questions—no more than five. When people are on their way to a destination, they have little time to stop and talk. Also be sure that your questions can be answered with a short answer. Long answers will be hard for you to write down.

Compare your results when you return to class.

## Preparing for Short Writing: Writing Skills

### USING AND ORDERING EXAMPLES

Look at the article on Poly, which includes examples of reinforcing society's values and developing individual power. Consider its use of examples.

1. How important was its use of examples to your understanding the points raised in the article?
2. Which examples had the greatest effect on you? Which examples made you believe that Polytechnic is a good school? Which examples had little or no effect on your opinions?
3. Do you believe the article would have been as effective if it had had no examples?

Examples are the backbone of good writing. They bring pictures to readers' minds, persuade, and instruct. There are two ways that writers order their examples. The first is *least important to most important.* Writers save their best examples for last so that their readers can finish reading their essays and have the writers' strongest information most recently in their minds. The last impression is thus a good impression. Imagine, for example, that a writer is writing an essay about why children who live in poverty receive worse educations than children who do not. The writer has three reasons why he believes this is true: impoverished children are undernourished and thus are unable to learn as easily when they are hungry; teachers of impoverished children generally do not expect their students to do well, so the children do not; and impoverished children's schools generally lack quality facilities, equipment, and teachers. In the writer's mind, although all of the reasons are important, the second reason (teacher expectations) is the most important because it is most easily changed. The least important (to the writer, not to the children) is that they are hungry, because this is the most difficult to change. Therefore, he will discuss the examples in the following order: children's hunger, lack of facilities, teacher expectations. Notice that another writer might have a different opinion regarding which of the examples is most or least important and would order them differently. Check the Polytechnic article. Did it order its examples from least to most important, in your opinion?

Another principle writers keep in mind is to present *information that is more familiar to their readers first* and present less familiar information later in the essay. This helps writers orient their readers and makes them feel more comfortable and accepting of the writers' main points earlier in the writing. It is especially useful to present familiar information early in an essay when writers suspect that their readers will not accept the writers' points easily. Notice that this principle requires writers to have a fairly good idea of exactly who their readers are. Let's continue with the above example of why impoverished children receive a poorer quality education and see how the order might change when the audience changes. If the writer's audience is a group of people who are training to become teachers, the most familiar example will be the one about teacher expectations. However, if the audience is the government, the most familiar example will be the one about facilities and equipment, since these are paid for by the taxes generated and appropriated by government. Did the Polytechnic article order its examples from most to least familiar?

In some cases, the same example will have mixed priorities, least important and least familiar or most important and most familiar. In such cases, the writer must make an authorial decision about how best to use the information. When the audience is not well-known or when it is mixed, he or she will probably rely on the importance of the examples rather than their familiarity to the readers. Remember, however, that there are usually not "right" answers in writing; there are only decisions to be made by writers based on predictions they make about their audiences and the information available about their topics.

**EXERCISE—Importance and Familiarity:**   Brainstorm examples for each of the following assertions. Then practice ordering examples by putting them in order once according to importance and a second time according to familiarity. Which method do you believe would be more useful in each group for your readers? Why?

- ways teachers can help students develop self-confidence
- ways students can gain real-world experience
- school activities other than academic classes that help students mature

## SHORT WRITING (150–200 WORDS)

Imagine you are the director of a school which needs additional funds, and you are competing with two other schools for a $100,000 grant from an educational foundation. Write a letter to the foundation explaining what you would like to do with this money. Choose between order of importance and order of familiarity as you describe examples of how the money can be spent at your school.

## Making Your Draft Clearer: Language Skills

### A. THE "PERFECT" VERBS

There are three grammatical groups of verbs in English: the *simple verbs,* the *progressive verbs,* and the *perfect verbs.* The most problematic of the three are the perfect verbs, particularly in comparison with the simple verbs.

In your writing, you will most often use the simple verbs. These include simple present (*I go, you go, he goes,* and so on) and simple past (*I went, you went, he went,* and so on). This is because simple verbs are used to express facts, give opinions, make assertions and generalizations (present), and tell about events that have already happened (past). Most writing consists of these functions.

You have already learned in Part II of this chapter that there is a strong tendency in English writing to maintain a verb tense within one functional part. Occasionally, however, it is necessary in writing to show differences in time *while maintaining the overall time frame.* This is the main use for the perfect verbs, which act as bridges between two times in English.

**1. Present perfect verbs** (such as *has seen, have gone, have looked*) are present-tense verbs. They are often used to maintain a present time frame while referring to past events. Consider the following example. Notice in particular where the verb forms change from simple present to present perfect. While the time frame is present throughout, the functions of the verb forms change. Why does the author change the verbs from simple present to present perfect?

In our lives, we often discover the value of precious things when we don't have them. One knows the importance of food better when he is hungry than when he has a full stomach, and he knows the value and power of money better when he is in need of money than when he has plenty. Likewise, a person learns much about what a proper education should provide him when his education fails to provide it. In that sense, coming to America <u>has been</u> one of the most precious experiences of my life. As an explorer makes his way through an unknown area, I <u>have been</u> a traveler in the 'jungle' called America trying to figure out what it really looks like from outside. Knowing practically nothing about American people or their ways, I <u>have been</u> born again in America learning the new ways from school. In doing so, I <u>have come</u> to realize the difference in teaching styles between two nations, America and Korea, which, in turn, <u>has led</u> me to discover the empowering teaching aspect of American schools, which is what I <u>have been looking</u> for from my education. (Jay Lee, student)

**2. Past perfect verbs** are past time frame verbs. Thus, they are used in functional parts of writing which are already in the past tense. Similar to present perfect verbs, *past perfect* verbs are used to name actions which took place earlier than the past actions already named, that is, earlier in the past. For this reason, it may be helpful to remember this verb form as "double past" because it is actually two steps back in the past. Re-examine the following story, paying particular attention to the underlined "double past" verb forms. Why is this form used instead of simple past?

While I don't remember my first day of school, I do remember one day early in my school career very well, when I was six years old. My classmates and I <u>had been taught</u> to remove our coats and hats quietly by our desks at the beginning of each day and to wait until the teacher, who <u>had often scared</u> me because she was a nun, gave us permission to go to the coat room to hang them up. One morning, my mother walked into my classroom. I was shocked and intently focused my eyes upon her trying to discern why she was there. <u>Had I done</u> something wrong?

**Threads**

In 1989–90 the U.S. federal government contributed only 6.1% of the money spent on public kindergarten through high school education; the rest came from local and state governments.

*Newsweek,* April 19, 1993

Summary of Verb Forms That Usually Occur Together

| Group 1<br>PAST TIME FRAME | Group 2<br>PRESENT/FUTURE TIME FRAME |
|---|---|
| Simple Past (verb + -ed) | Simple Present (verb + -s/ø) |
| Past Modals | Present Modals |
| (would/could + verb | (can/will/should/might/must + verb) |
| should have + past participle | |
| had to + past participle, etc.) | |
| Past Progressive | Present Progressive |
| was/were + verb + -ing | (is/am/are + verb + -ing) |
| **Past Perfect** | **Present Perfect** |
| had + past participle | (has/have + past participle) |

NOTE: It is not possible to use past perfect verb forms with present/future time frames; nor is it possible to use present perfect verb forms with past time frames.

## B. SPECIAL CONDITIONS OF SUBJECT-VERB AGREEMENT

When the subject of a sentence or clause is *singular* (other than *I* and *you*), the verb has an *-s* ending in the present tense. However, there are some special conditions of subject-verb agreement that can cause problems for student writers.

1. Sometimes a subject and verb are separated by other words, especially prepositional phrases and adjective clauses. However, make sure the verb agrees with its true subject.

   a. **Students** in a gifted classroom **receive** special methods of instruction.
   b. The **instruction** that is given to these students **empowers** them.

2. Subjects joined by *and* usually take plural verbs.

   a. Cooperative learning **and** independent study **are** two important techniques in the gifted classroom.
   b. Memorization **and** discipline **do** not find an important place in gifted classrooms.

3. When parts of a subject are joined by *or* or *nor*, the verb agrees with the last part of the subject. If one part is singular and the other plural, we generally try to put the plural part second.

   a. Neither a test **nor** grades **encourage** students to take risks in their learning.
   b. Roleplay **or** acting **becomes** an empowering learning activity.

4. Use singular verbs with the following indefinite pronouns: *anybody, anyone, each, either, everybody, everyone, everything, nobody, no one, somebody,* or *something.*

   a. Almost **everybody believes** that education is important for a good future.
   b. **Nobody wants** children who are so empowered that they are misfits in society.

**EXERCISE—Subject-Verb Agreement: Special Conditions:**   Write the correct present tense verb form for each verb in parentheses below.

Probably the one group of students that *(achieve)* the most empowering education *(be)* the so-called "gifted" students. Gifted students generally have an I.Q. (intelligence measure) of at least 125 (with 100–110 the average). Because they seem to have more potential for learning, they are put in special courses which *(provide)* more challenging material to learn and methods which *(allow)* each student to develop his or her individual potential.

There are a number of techniques which characterize the gifted classroom. One of these *(be)* individualized learning. With this technique, students choose the areas they are most interested in learning about and *(proceed)*, at their own pace, with only a little direction from the teacher, to investigate that area, study it, and produce a project related to it such as a research paper, a poem or song, a painting, a videotape, or whatever the children's creativity *(lead)* them to.

The fact that the teacher provides only a few suggestions *(be)* central to the gifted class methodology. Teachers are not bosses or directors, but rather they are "facilitators"; that is, they make it easier for the children to indulge their exploratory instincts while learning. One way teachers take a back seat to class activities *(be)* by having students engage in "peer instruction." Everyone *(become)* a resource to his or her classmates. Learning from their friends, getting feedback from their classmates, and making judgments for themselves, the students become independent learners who *(go)* on to learn the rest of their lives, inside or outside classrooms. The old method of seeking an all-knowing authority, the teacher, to give them "the answer" is not an empowering method.

Nobody *(disagree)* that gifted students may need more challenging classwork. However, the average student or below-average student also *(benefit)* from studying challenging material in class.

## Making Your Draft Clearer: Language Skills

### REDUCING ADVERB CLAUSES

Adverb clauses are sentence-like structures that contain subjects and verbs, begin with a connecting word like *before, because,* or *even though,* and are attached to a complete sentence. In the following examples, the adverbial connector is underlined and the adverbial clause is **bold.**

1. <u>**When**</u> **schools experience reduced funding,** they inevitably make budget cuts in "soft" courses such as the arts or foreign languages.
2. Rayburn High School was forced to cut Russian from its curriculum <u>**despite the fact that**</u> **parents requested it be retained.**

In order to add more variety to your sentence structure, it is possible to reduce adverb clauses when the subject of the adverb clause is the same as the subject in the main clause. We generally do this by deleting the subject and any helping verbs from the adverb clause and changing the verb from a main verb to a verb-like form called a "participle." When the main verb is active (the subject does the action of the verb) we change it by adding *-ing.* When it is in passive form (the subject receives the action of the verb) we use the *-ed* or *-en* form. Consider the following examples:

1. a. Children maximize their opportunities, according to some, **when they are sent to private schools.** (full clause with a passive verb)
   b. Children maximize their opportunities, according to some, **when sent to private schools.** (reduced clause)

2. a. **Although society professes to need educated citizens,** it actually established mass education to prepare people for factory jobs. (full clauses with an active verb)
   b. **Although professing to need educated citizens,** society actually established mass education to prepare people for factory jobs. (reduced clause)

What differences can you see between the *a* and *b* versions?
What differences can you see between the number 1 sentences and the number 2 sentences?

However, note the following incorrect reduction, which we call a "dangling" clause [an asterisk (*) before a sentence indicates a badly formed sentence]:

3. a. **When the Department of Education's authority was limited,** parents' involvement increased.
   b. ***When limited,** the parents' involvement increased.

Because the subjects of the two clauses are different, it is not possible to delete one of the subjects in order to reduce the clause.

In some cases it is also possible to delete the connecting word (*while, when, after, before, until, although, though, even though*). Do this only when the meaning of the sentence will continue to be clear despite the deletion.

*NOTE:* *Because* and *since* (the two "cause" connectors) cannot be deleted; *from the moment that* can become *upon* or *on* in reduced classes; *despite the fact that, in spite of the fact that,* and *due to the fact that* become *despite, in spite of,* and *due to* in reduced clauses.

**EXERCISE—Reducing Adverbial Clauses:**   Reduce the clauses in **bold** print below whenever possible. Be careful! Some of the clauses will dangle if you reduce them.

**From the moment that I entered elementary school,** I was identified as a very good student **despite the fact that I scarcely studied.** My teachers never cared that I neglected my homework **because I knew how to play the game of "school."** I remember, for example, that I was quite reluctant to study mathematics. No matter how long I contemplated problems in class, their difficulty always exceeded my ability to do them. This was probably **due to the fact that I was neglecting my homework.** Mathematics was not one of my priorities. My teacher rarely questioned me about this; in fact, I always received high grades in math class. I suppose my teacher gave me these grades under the pretext that I wasn't giving him any trouble in class. He was extremely strict about obedience but not about learning. **Since mathematics had no part in my destiny,** it did not intrigue me. However, **although I was not captivated by mathematics,** I was not overt about my feelings.

**After I graduate high school this year,** I will be going to the university. Before then, I'll have some time to think, and I'll also have to earn some money to pay for my education. The truth is, **since I want more from my education than good grades now,** I've altered my way of thinking a bit. **Because the university is vastly more important to my life than high school was,** I will choose those courses that help me become a well-rounded person. In order to do this, I will have to apply more rigor to my studies. **Since university professors are much less tyrannous than my high school teachers were,** they won't be interested in disciplining me. I'll have to discipline myself.

**While I still don't exactly revere mathematics,** I'll have an ample number of courses, so I can afford to be eclectic. In the meantime, I have no allegiance to any particular topics. I just want to nurture my mind for a while. My high school teachers would be amazed to see how much my attitude has shifted.

Now go back to your second draft, and increase its level of sophistication by finding a few places where you could reduce some clauses like those in the previous exercise. Don't overdo it.

## Editing Strategy: One Line at a Time

When we read, our eyes move quickly over the words. When we read our own writing, our eyes tend to move even more quickly, because we already know (or think we know) the content of the writing. Because our eyes are moving so quickly, they miss details, including errors such as spelling, missing endings, and verb tense changes. One editing strategy is to take an index card or piece of paper and force your eye *not* to move too quickly by covering subsequent lines of writing with the card or paper and revealing only the current and previous lines. (You can also block previous lines if desired.) Try this on your second draft before you hand it in.

## Student Writing: Practice Peer Response

Read the following student essay, in which the author prescribes a more narrow use for education. After you finish reading the essay, fill out the peer response that follows to analyze it. Your instructor may ask you to do this with or without your classmates and may provide additional questions.

## THE GOOD THINGS ABOUT MY EDUCATION

*Ali Nemat*

The word empowering can have many different meanings. To me the word empowering means something that would put you above everyone else. With the education system we have we learn many facts and figures which are useless. To be a doctor one has to go to 12 years of elementary school and high school and another 8 to 10 years of university and medical school.

What is the point of education? Why do people spend most of their lives going to school? Education was totally different in the past. Schools were only for the rich people and the royalty. Careers were passed down through generations. In the old days a doctor knew only how to cure people. A mechanic knew only how to fix things. A farmer was able to farm only. Now that our attitude toward education has changed we want everyone to be well-rounded. We believe a doctor should not only be able to cure sick people, but he also should be capable of understanding politics, know how and in what way concepts of physics work and etc.

In the 22 years that a doctor goes to school he learns a lot of things. He will learn anything from ancient history to human physiology. Some of this knowledge will make him a better well-rounded person and others will make him a better doctor. For him to be able to emphasize on the thing that would make him a better doctor will empower him to be a better doctor.

For me the first 10 years of my education were useless. I learned many things that were useless. The only thing that I believe was important was learning how to read and write but that will not empower me because everyone else can read and write also. Maybe the reason that those years were not empowering me was because I did not value education that much. I did not care about what I was studying. The only reason I was going to school was because all of my friends were going to school.

During my junior year in high school I realized I had to have an education if I wanted to do anything in my life. I also realized that not any education would be helpful. I had to have one that would be empowering me to be above the rest of my peers. I started to emphasize science classes. I knew classes like art, drama, music and etc. would not empower me to be a good doctor although they could help me be a more well-rounded person. I started to take chemistry, biology, and physics. I was lucky enough to have teachers who took their job seriously. I did not have teachers that would ask me to read a chapter and test me on it. They got involved in the class. They forced students to think for themselves.

As I have said before a good education should put you above everyone else. Having good teachers, a good school, and a healthy environment are all part of an empowering education. The absence of one of these factors will result in very little empowering education. My teachers in high school were very helpful. They took time out of their schedule to help me with any problems I had in my classes. My chemistry and calculus teachers encouraged me to study more than they taught. They made me realize that what they taught me in class was basic things, things which were useless. They taught me how to think logically. The ability to think logically and to be able to reason out any problem is the one thing that separates intelligent people from the average person. A good education is the line which separates the empowered people from the powerless. We have to realize that power is not handed to us, but we have to go after it. To do so we have to first choose what we want in life and then go after it.

Now, exchange your paper with one of your classmate's papers and complete the same peer response after reading it.

> ## Threads
>
> **Knowledge emerges only through invention and reinvention, through the restless, impatient, continuing, hopeful inquiry people pursue in the world, with the world, and with each other.**
>
> Paulo Freire, "The 'Banking' Concept of Education"

## Peer Response to Draft Two

**Personalizing: Put yourself in your classmate's position and respond to his or her paper as you would like him or her to respond to yours.**

1. Congratulate the author on something you particularly enjoyed or found interesting in this essay. Try to explain to the author why it had this effect on you.

   _____

   _____

2. Tell the author about any parts of his or her essay that were confusing to you. Try to explain why they confused you.

   _____

   _____

3. Were there any places in the author's essay where you wanted more information or a different kind of information? Explain these to the author.

   _____

   _____

4. Were there any places in the author's essay where there was unnecessary information that you weren't interested in reading? Point these out.

   _____

   _____

5. Explain to the author the overall effect his or her essay had on you. Which parts are you likely to remember from it several days from now?

   _____

   _____

# PART IV: WRITING THE THIRD DRAFT AND ASSESSING YOUR LEARNING

In Part IV, you will once again revise your major essay, this time taking into consideration comments from your readers: yourself, your peer reviewer, your instructor, and any other readers who may have read your essay in or out of class. As a result

of reader comments, you are likely to find yourself revising content and organization in one of three ways.

**Adding Information:** Your reader(s) may have needed more examples, more background explanations, other evidence to prove your point (such as statistics or quotations from experts or the articles in this chapter). If you agree with your readers, try to add the information they needed.

**Deleting Information:** Your readers may have found the amount of information you gave in your second draft unnecessary or overwhelming. They may have thought some of your information was off topic. If you agree with your readers, try to remove the information they didn't need.

**Reorganizing Information:** Your readers may have needed some information earlier than you gave it, for example, background information. They may have thought that the more interesting information should have been placed in a different place or they may have disagreed with you about which information was important or more familiar. If you decide they are correct, make the necessary changes.

In addition to revising content and organization, you must once again proofread and edit your essay. Make corrections (especially verb agreement and verb tense corrections) and other changes which will increase the clarity and improve the academic tone of your paper. Continue trying to use some of the vocabulary from this chapter as well as reduced adverbial clauses where appropriate.

## Punctuation Note: Punctuating with Simple Transitions

Simple transitions can be used in two locations: at the beginning of a complete sentence or between two main parts of a sentence. The punctuation that must be used depends on the location of the transition.

1. At the beginning of a sentence: Use a comma (,) after the transition. You may also combine two sentences with simple transitions with a semi-colon (;) at the end of the previous sentence and a comma after the transition.

   a. Knowledge is power. **Therefore,** the more schooling one has, the more power one can have.
   b. Knowledge is power; **therefore,** the more knowledge one has, the more power one can have.

2. Between two main parts of a sentence, such as the subject and verb or the verb and object: Use a comma both before and after the transition.

   a. Knowledge, **consequently,** is power.
   b. The more knowledge one has, **however,** the more power one can have.

Go back to your third draft. Check your use of simple transitions, and in particular, check your use of commas and semicolons. Make any necessary changes.

## STUDENT WRITINGS FOR FURTHER DISCUSSION

The following student-written essay presents views that contradict those of the student essay you read earlier in this chapter. With which opinion do you agree? Which essay is better in your opinion? How would you improve the essay below if you were to revise it?

### THE VALUE OF EDUCATION

*Stephanie Lo*

Getting power is one of the important things in life. Education provides people with an unlimited amount of power. The more education people get, the more it empowers them. It gives people the ability to do many things in this society such as a better career, higher social status and personal satisfaction.

One way people become empowered is by raising their social status with education. People tend to look up to people that have a good education. The reason is that people with a good education show how ambitious and diligent they are. They also show that they are the type to strive towards a goal instead of laying back and waiting for something like a welfare check. By being educated, a person's opinion is honored more by other people because they have been exposed to many types of knowledge and refinement. Also, when someone is educated, it means a better job and higher class. For example, a person that wants to be a doctor has to go through many years of school. Because of so much training, he will get a better job because he is qualified to be a doctor whereas a person that is a high school dropout will only get a minimum wage job. When a person has a better job, it makes him a higher class because he has the ability to make more money, own more material things and possess more refinement and culture. All of these result from a good education. A good education opens up people's eyes and makes them strive for higher goals. On the other hand, the people with no education will be the opposites. An uneducated person has no culture and social upbringing. Even if the person gets rich overnight, from a lottery, put him in a room with lawyers, doctors and engineers, he will feel out of place and inferior, as a result of his lack of education. The only way that a person can climb up from "the bottom of the ladder" is to educate himself and to get himself out of his ignorance. As for the social upbringing part, put him in with "high class people," he will learn

**Threads**

The illiteracy rate in the United States is approximately 3%.

*Rand McNally Almanac of World Facts*

because he is, in a sense, at their level. Therefore, he is at a higher social status than before.

Another way of being empowered is personal satisfaction. For me, to have knowledge gives me a certain satisfaction. Whenever I play Trivial Pursuit, when I get the answer right, I feel a lot of pride. To possess this knowledge and actually to use it makes the learning part better. Learning things such as physics, history, and art don't affect life that much. Great, I know about Kepler's laws, how Canada became a nation and that Leonardo da Vinci painted the "Last Supper," but what good does it do? I really don't need that knowledge for everyday life, but why do I still want to learn it? The reason is because it gives me personal satisfaction. To possess knowledge about my country, the United States, makes me feel patriotic and at the same time gives me personal satisfaction. To know what other people are talking about makes me feel "smart" and it also gives me personal satisfaction. To feel the pride of possessing knowledge that can be used builds more confidence in me. When my friends are arguing against me about a controversial subject, and when I know about the subject very well, it gives me confidence to defend my opinions.

From these two examples, it shows how education is good for the society and personal interest. To possess knowledge from being educated makes a person feel very good inside because education is an accomplishment. The rewards from being educated are definitely worth the years of suffering, pain, and stress in school. Even if there is suffering for a while, it's better than the whole lifetime because of the limited amount of money due to lack of education.

## DISCUSSION

1. Which essay do you find yourself agreeing with more?
2. Which aspects of each essay do you find most persuasive?
3. Which aspects do you find least persuasive?
4. If you were to offer one or both of the writers suggestions for revision, what would those suggestions be?

## Reflecting on Draft Three

1. Describe one change you made in your second draft and tell why you made it.

   _____

   _____

2. Evaluate how successful this change was.

   _____

   _____

3. Look over the three drafts of this essay. Then write a few sentences evaluating how much you think you improved your essay from the first to the third draft and why you think it is better. Consider content, organization, and language.

   _____

   _____

4. Scan this draft (the third draft) of your essay, and find a couple of word choices or phrases of which you are particularly proud. Copy them, and explain why you are proud of them.

_____

_____

5. Describe one thing you learned from writing the three drafts of this essay that you can apply to the writing of your next major essay.

_____

_____

## LEARNING STRATEGY

**Managing Your Learning: Learn from your experience by purposefully reconsidering your successes, failures, and feelings about the process.**

## Writer's Notebook

Consider the following questions in your writer's notebook after you write the drafts of this chapter's major essay.

1. How difficult was it for you to start writing the essay? Did you start over many times? Did you think the difficulty was influenced by your inexperience as a writer, your unfamiliarity with the topic, or your language abilities?

2. Did you use any of the strategies for generating ideas discussed in this chapter? Which one(s) worked best for you? Why?

3. Would you generally describe yourself as a confident or unconfident writer? Do you think confidence is an important part of writing? Do you imagine that professional writers have more confidence?
   Can you detect a difference in your confidence level when you write in your native language as opposed to English? What do you think you (and perhaps your teacher or classmates) can do to increase your confidence?

4. Did you find it necessary to write an outline or a list of topics to discuss before you began writing your essay or at any point while you were writing? Did you find it to be true that the writing process itself (drafting) led to your thinking of more ideas? If you did not, why do you suppose you didn't (even when most professional writers claim they do)?

5. Did you make it a point to use some of the vocabulary words from this chapter in your essay? Why might it be a good idea to learn some of these words,

even if you already know simpler words to convey the same meanings? Why do you think it is probably not a good idea to use as many difficult vocabulary words as possible in your essays?

## Vocabulary Checklist

Add vocabulary words from this chapter that you believe will be useful for your essay or your life in general. Several additional useful words have been added for you.

| WORD | PART OF SPEECH | MEANING | PREPO-SITIONS | SAMPLE SENTENCE |
|---|---|---|---|---|
| 1. promote | (verb) | encourage | ø | Schools typically promote values such as obedience by rewarding obedient students and punishing rebellious ones. |
| 2. reinforce | (verb) | make stronger | ø | One way schools reinforce obedient behavior is by giving some advantages to obedient students. |
| 3. potential | (noun, adj) | possibility for developing | of | A school should try to develop the potential of each student. |
| 4. | | | | |
| 5. | | | | |
| 6. | | | | |

| WORD | PART OF SPEECH | MEANING | PREPO-SITIONS | SAMPLE SENTENCE |
|------|----------------|---------|---------------|-----------------|
| 7. | | | | |
| 8. | | | | |
| 9. | | | | |
| 10. | | | | |

## Bibliography

Fallows, James. "Strengths, Weaknesses, and Lessons of Japanese Education." *The Education Digest,* Oct. 1991, pp. 55-59.

Haberman, Martin. "The Pedagogy of Poverty Versus Good Teaching." *Phi Delta Kappan,* Dec. 1991.

Mathabane, Mark. *Kaffir Boy: The True Story of a Black Youth's Coming of Age in Apartheid South Africa.* New York: Macmillan Publishing Company, 1986.

Merl, Jean. "Are Private Schools Any Better?" *Los Angeles Times,* March 29, 1992, Sec. A, pp. 1, 30, 31.

Rebeck, George. "Is Voc Ed a Dead End?" *Utne Reader,* Sept./Oct. 1992, pp. 34-35.

Toffler, Alvin. *The Third Wave.* New York: Bantam Books, 1980.

# Fathers: Are They Central or Peripheral?

# PART I: INTRODUCTION

Think about the following questions as you work on this chapter.

1. What was your relationship with your father or the most significant man in your life like?
2. What is a father's most important role in the family?
3. Men, what kind of father would you like to be? Women, what kind of father would you like for your children?

### *LEARNING STRATEGY*

**Forming Concepts: In the following section, check your under-standing of your culture's customs regarding fatherhood by comparing them with those of one or more classmates from your culture and/or contrasting them with those of one or more classmates from other cultures.**

## Topic Orientation

In order to begin understanding the topic for this chapter, discuss the following questions with two or three of your classmates.

1. What constitutes masculine behavior in your culture?
2. What kind of daily contact does a father in your culture typically have with his children when they are babies? When they are older?
3. Is the contact a father has with his children different from the contact a mother has?
4. In the case of divorce or death, could the father take care of his children as well as the mother?
5. The stereotype of fathers (at least in the United States) is that they are better at disciplining children than mothers are. Do you agree? What else might a father add to the child's life that the mother alone may not add?

# PART II: WRITING THE FIRST DRAFT

### MAJOR ESSAY ASSIGNMENTS

Write a first draft of your major essay for this chapter of approximately 750 words. Try to challenge yourself with the essay topic you choose. You may create your own topic related to fathers in cooperation with your instructor. The questions for each topic are designed to help you generate ideas, not to limit you. Use the freewriting technique you are about to learn to help you generate ideas if you wish, and keep in mind the principles of organizing comparisons explained later in this chapter if you choose to compare in your essay.

### LEARNING STRATEGY

**Personalizing: Choose an assignment in which you have a strong interest. Remember, you'll be working on it for quite a while.**

1. **Narrative/Descriptive Essay.** Describe your relationship with your father or with someone to whom you are as close as a father. Would you characterize your relationship with him as more like the one expressed in the first reading, "My Father Worked Late," or the one in the second reading, "Helen, Mr. Mellow, and the Briefcase"? In what ways do you depend on him? Are you able to tell stories about one or more instances when he nurtured you? Have there been times when you felt distanced from him?

2. **Analytical Essay.** Compare the roles of fathers and mothers in your nation. Do fathers function primarily as economic providers (or "breadwinners") for the family, or do they also take part in the primary care of the child (feeding, dressing, cleaning, teaching, showing affection)? Do mothers function solely as caregivers or do they also function as economic providers?

Are the roles of mothers and fathers changing in your nation? How are people reacting to these changes? Do businesses support maternity and paternity leaves for their employees, for example? Is child care easily available to working parents? Do people easily accept fathers, instead of mothers, staying home to care for their children? Are fathers often awarded custody of children in divorce cases?

3. **Persuasive Essay.** Argue whether, in the case of divorce, it is appropriate to grant custody of the children automatically to the mother, unless she is found to be incompetent. Is it reasonable to assume, for example, that mothers *instinctively* care better for children than fathers? Should the law consider fathers to be equally capable of caring for children?

As you write this essay, keep in mind that your readers may strongly disagree with your perspective. You must, therefore, carefully predict your readers' reactions and arguments; then you can include appropriate counterarguments in your essay. Also remember as you prepare your arguments that your reader may not hold the same cultural values as you do.

## INTRODUCTORY READING

**Vocabulary Enrichment**

Study the following definitions and sample sentences. Then complete the exercise that follows.

## Threads

**Fathers should be neither seen nor heard. This is the only proper basis for family life.**

Oscar Wilde

1. **bounce:** (v.) move quickly up and down, as with a ball

   My sister and I bounced on the furniture in excitement when we saw our father's car coming up the driveway.

   We bounced on his stomach, laughing and shouting in our excitement.

2. **pitch:** (n. [countable*], v.) throws; uncontrolled movements forward or down (a wild pitch, in baseball, is an out-of-control throw at the batter)

   We pitched some old clothes into a truck gathering clothing for poor children.

   The woman pitched the burned dinner into the sink with an angry exclamation.

3. **grab:** (v.) reach for suddenly, roughly

   We grabbed his beard and pulled hard, laughing to hear him shriek.

   My father grabbed my brother and threw him high in the air, never dropping him.

4. **wrestle:** (v.) sport fighting by holding the other's body

   My brother wrestled in high school and won several competitions.

   When I was young, my father, sister and I would wrestle on the livingroom floor, laughing and enjoying the closeness we felt with each other.

5. **to "have" someone:** (v.) to succeed in capturing someone

   My dad chased the puppy, and we thought he had it, but it disappeared again.

   I sat on Dad's chest, and Billy was on his legs. We finally had him!

6. **cradle:** (n. [countable], v.) hold tenderly in the arms (a cradle is a small bed for a baby)

   I had never seen my father cry until the day I saw him cradle my newborn sister.

   I cradled my little brother in my arms, singing nonsense songs to calm him.

7. **headlock:** (n. [countable]) holding an opponent's head so that it cannot move

   My dad got me in a headlock and started tickling me. (tickle = touch someone to cause uncontrollable laughing)

   I loved my dad's headlocks because they felt like embraces to me.

8. **embrace:** (v., n. [countable]) wrapping one's arms around another in a show of affection (also called "hug")

   As long as I can remember, my father never embraced my brother; they shook hands a lot.

   My mother and I embraced often, even when saying hello or good-bye.

9. **communion:** (n. [uncountable†]) Christian ceremony involving the eating of bread and drinking of wine; sharing of intimate feelings

   The high point of the mass was the distribution of communion to the participants.

   The distance we sometimes felt from our parents left our communion incomplete.

---

*NOTE: Countable nouns may be used in the plural form and may have *a* or *an* before them. They also may use *many* and *(a) few* as determiners.

†NOTE: Uncountable nouns may not be used in the plural form and may not have *a* or *an* before them. They can use much and (a) little as determiners before them.

10. **intimate:** (adj. [n.: intimacy]) close sharing of feelings, very personal

   Mark loved his father, but their relationship couldn't be described as intimate.

   As far as he knew, his father wasn't intimate with anyone, including his wife.

11. **affection:** (n. [adj.: affectionate]) gentle liking or love

   We always knew our father loved us, but he rarely showed his affection overtly.

   People show affection by touching, hugging, kissing, saying gentle words. Dad was unable to do this.

12. **to give:** (v.) from "give up," meaning admit defeat

   He tickled us until tears rolled down our cheeks, and we shouted, "I give, I give."

***VOCABULARY LEARNING STRATEGY:*** Choose one or more of the words from this vocabulary exercise that you feel will be useful in your writing. Enter them into the Vocabulary Checklist at the end of this chapter.

**EXERCISE 1:** Divide the 12 words above into two categories: those expressing roughness and those expressing gentleness. Which word can have both characteristics?

| ROUGHNESS | GENTLENESS |
| --- | --- |
| _____ | _____ |
| _____ | _____ |
| _____ | _____ |
| _____ | _____ |
| _____ | _____ |
| _____ | _____ |

## INTRODUCTORY READING

In the United States, as in many other cultures, the father's role in the family has been thought to be primarily economic. The following poem by Jim Daniels expresses a son's distress about the "economic father."

### *LEARNING STRATEGY*

**Personalizing: Understand by comparing the experience of the sons in this poem with your own childhood experiences with your father or another significant male.**

## My Father Worked Late

**Threads**

In a 1990 poll by the *Los Angeles Times,* 39% of fathers said they would quit their jobs to have more time with their children.

1
Some nights we were still awake
my brother and I, our faces smearing[1] the window
watching the headlights <u>bounce</u> up the driveway
the wild <u>pitches</u> of light
5
thrown by a tired moon.
We breathed in the huge silence after the engine died
then ran to the door, <u>grabbing</u> his legs
as if we could hold him there
10
through night, morning, forever.

Some nights when he wasn't too tired
he took off his shirt
and sat in the middle of the floor.
We <u>wrestled,</u> trying to pin
15
back his arms, sitting on his chest
digging our heads into the yellow stains
under the arms of his T-shirt.
Each time we thought we <u>had</u> him
*Do you give, huh, do you give?*
20
he sat up, <u>cradling</u> us both in <u>headlocks</u>
in the closest thing to an <u>embrace</u>
that I remember, and carried us to bed.

Other nights he looked right through us
mechanically eating his late dinner
25
yelling at anything that moved.
Some mornings we woke to find him
asleep on the couch, his foreman's[2] tie twisted
into words we couldn't spell.
We ate our cereal as carefully as <u>communion</u>

---

[1]smearing: creating unclear images through movement across a surface
[2]foreman: factory supervisor

until our mother shook him ready for another day.
My father carries no wallet full of lost years
carries no stubs[3], no guarantees, no promises.
We could drive toward each other all night
and never cross the distance of those missing years.

Today, home for a visit,
I pull in front of the house.
My father walks down the steps
limping from his stroke[4]
he is coming toward me
both of us pinned to the wind
he is looking at me as if to say
*give, give, I give,*
as if either of us
had anything left to give.

Daniels, 1985, pp. 5–6.

**Threads**

**72% of men say they experience stress while trying to balance home and work.**

James Levine, Fatherhood Project, Families & Work Institute, New York City

## ELABORATING ON THE READING

**EXERCISE 1:** Some of the imagery in this poem depends on double meanings for single phrases or words. Explain the double meanings in the following.

1. (line 19) "Do you give?"

_______________

2. (line 18) "each time we thought we had him"

_______________

3. (line 20) ". . . cradling us both in headlocks"

_______________

4. (line 29) "communion"

_______________

5. (line 31) "wallet full of lost years"

_______________

6. (line 42) "give, give, I give"

_______________

[3]stub: ticket receipt

[4]stroke: broken blood vessel in the brain which may lead to loss of bodily function

**EXERCISE 2:**   Study the poem and discuss the following questions with two or three of your classmates to figure out the author's intention in this poem. You may have disagreements.

1. What is the father's primary activity in the poem? How do you know?
2. What do the sons want from their father? How do you know?
3. Why is it difficult for the sons to get what they want from their father?
4. Why is there distance between the father and the son? Do you believe they feel the same distance with their mother?
5. What message do you think the author of this poem is trying to communicate to his reader?
6. Do you think the father in the poem is a bad father?

## Preparing for Short Writing: Writing Skills

### FREEWRITING

Freewriting is a technique for generating ideas for written communication. Like brainstorming, freewriting aids writers in discovering *possibilities* rather than making decisions about their writing. Freewriting involves putting pen to paper and attempting to write anything that enters the writer's head regarding the topic *without stopping the writing until the freewriting session ends.* Inevitably, the freewriter is self-conscious at first, but a few moments into the process, a topic begins to take hold in the writer's mind. Freewriting does not result in unified paragraphs with topic sentences and proper coherence techniques. Instead, it can result in ideas to which the writer was unable to gain access consciously. Freewriting attempts to gain access to these ideas subconsciously. Most beginning writers find freewriting tiring to sustain for longer than ten minutes. You may want to begin with five-minute sessions if you choose to use this technique.

Following is a sample of freewriting related to the topic of this chapter:

> Freewriting is strange. My teacher wants me to do it. What do I say? I should talk about fathers. Fathers, fathers, my father is a busy man. He works hard. He spends a lot of hours at work, but he never complains. I am grateful that he has a good job and can earn a lot of money for our family. His company is famous in my country. We are proud of his work. He is proud too. Sometimes he tells us about his job, but I have never seen his company. I don't see him very much either—maybe an hour or two in the evenings. When he's tired, I leave him alone. When I was little, he scared me so much that I cried when he came home. I hardly recognized him. Did that hurt his feelings?

As a result of this freewriting session, the writer generated several new ideas, among them that he is grateful for his father's work but that his father may have been hurt by the writer's early interactions with him. Without the freewriting session, these new ideas may not have surfaced.

**EXERCISE:**   Freewrite for approximately five minutes on *one* of the following topics:

- the kind of father you want to be
- the ideal father
- a time when you felt especially close to or distant from your father (or other significant male in your life)

What new detail(s) did you discover as a result of this freewriting exercise? How did you feel doing it?

**Understanding and Using Emotions:** If you do not enjoy freewriting after giving it a good try, focus your efforts on some of the other idea-generating techniques mentioned in this text.

## SHORT WRITING (150–200 WORDS)

The poem "My Father Worked Late" was written from a young son's point of view. Imagine that you are the father. Write several paragraphs (or a poem, if you like) *as if you were the father.* How did you feel about your work, your sons, and your relationship with them over the years?

## IN-DEPTH READING

### Vocabulary Enrichment

**EXERCISE 1:** Examine the words on the left, below, in their contexts in the passage above. (They are listed in order from the passage.) Then choose the meaning on the right that best defines each word.

| | | |
|---|---|---|
| 1. _____ prior to | **a.** extremely clear | |
| 2. _____ contemplate | **b.** without energy | |
| 3. _____ resist | **c.** strong | |
| 4. _____ initially | **d.** very quiet | |
| 5. _____ vivid | **e.** longer than necessary | |
| 6. _____ belittle | **f.** avoid, fight against | |
| 7. _____ prolonged | **g.** unusually early in development | |
| 8. _____ stunned | **h.** at first | |
| 9. _____ perpetually | **i.** insult, cause to feel unimportant | |
| 10. _____ vitally | **j.** shocked, surprised | |
| 11. _____ vigorous | **k.** before | |
| 12. _____ precocious | **l.** very necessary, important | |
| 13. _____ vulnerable | **m.** always, forever | |
| 14. _____ coming around | **n.** starting to understand | |
| 15. _____ elated | **o.** very happy | |
| 16. _____ listless | **p.** easily hurt, weak | |
| 17. _____ somber | **q.** become less developed, go backwards | |
| 18. _____ regress | **r.** think carefully about | |
| 19. _____ thrive | **s.** growing easily and quickly | |
| 20. _____ nurturing | **t.** loving and caring | |

**EXERCISE 2:** Write ten sentences explaining what you think parents' and children's roles should or should not be. Use at least ten of the vocabulary words from the previous exercise.

1. _____

_____

2. _____

_____

3. _____

_____

4. _____

_____

5. _____

_____

6. _____

_____

7. _____

_____

8. _____

_____

9. _____

_____

10. _____

_____

## Threads

The father—any father
—should be sharing
with the mother the
day-to-day care of
their child from birth
onward. . . . This is the
natural way for the
father to start the
relationship, just as it is
for the mother.

Dr. Benjamin Spock, 1974

**Remember Your
Vocabulary Checklist!**

The following passage is from a book by Kyle D. Pruett, a researcher at Yale University. The book explains the results of research he conducted for more than five years on 17 families in which the *father* was the primary caregiver for their children, from their birth. In most cases, it was not planned for the father to take this role; instead it happened because of the father's and mother's job situations.

This story is about Ben, his daughter Helen, and her mother Ann. Before Helen was born, Ann received a promotion in her job while Ben's job was not going very well. Together, the new parents decided that Ben would stay home with Helen while Ann went to work and became the sole breadwinner for the family.

What advantages did both the child and the father gain from this arrangement?

### LEARNING STRATEGY

**Personalizing: Understand the following story better by imagining yourself in the little girl's or the father's position.**

# Helen, Mr. Mellow, and the briefcase

In describing these early days with Helen after Ann returned to work, Ben said, "Suddenly, I began to figure her out. My wife, though she really loved our little girl, never seemed quite able to understand her, maybe because they're so much alike. I don't know. I was reluctant to admit that *I* had figured her out at first. I kept it to myself. But Helen became crystal clear to me. You know, like whether she was either tired, or wanted to eat, or play—that stuff. She responded instantly when I guessed right. That made me feel confident about what I was doing. Really, it was kind of like all of a sudden the feelings of being an outsider left, and I began to feel overwhelmed with the wish to raise her, to develop her the way *I* wanted her developed. It may sound crazy, but I started to almost look forward to her waking up at night just to be with her." (1)

During the first week after his wife had returned to work, he was often anxious: "What was going to happen to *me,* though? I didn't want to watch the soaps and go 'stupid,' so I comforted myself in the afternoon by turning off the TV, and going out to buy a copy of the *Wall Street Journal.* I didn't have the chance to read much of it, but, amazingly, it helped just having it." (2)

Since the beginning, Mr. Mellow had continued to "read" his daughter well. He said, "I eventually developed my own style." He fed her in a fashion different from that of his wife; for example, he allowed Helen more finger play with her food than Anne did. (3)

I had initially speculated that when these new fathers got into everyday difficulties, they would call up images of what their wives would do, but within weeks if not days after the mothers were gone, most of the fathers, like Mr. Mellow, were using their own intuitions about what was useful in particular situations for their babies. They were, with the help of their babies, raising the children in their own unique styles. . . . (4)

When Anne returned to work some-

what before the end of her allotted eight-week maternity leave, she worried only about her husband "being a softy. In fact, he still is." As evidence, she reported that she had been the one to help her daughter end a sleep disturbance at nine months by insisting that Helen "cry it out in bed. I had to make him leave her alone. He was always going in to comfort her, he said, but I think they were just playing around." (5)

. . .

Just <u>prior to</u> the conception of Helen, Anne had gone to work for a subsidiary firm as an accountant. Ben was contemplating a job change amid rumors that his office was soon to be "absorbed," and in the interim, to his wife's surprise and delight, had made his decision to raise Helen. (6)

. . .

One of the things that most bothered him in his role as "housefather" was his being the only father he knew who was raising an infant. Early in his days as the "main man," he was invited by several women in the neighborhood to join them on their morning "baby stroll" around their pleasant suburban neighborhood. He <u>resisted initially,</u> re-

porting a <u>vivid</u> memory of the times his sisters had tried to urge him in taunting, <u>belittling</u> fashion to "play dolls" and push their "babies" around in carriages with them." (7)

. . .

While we had been talking, Helen had returned to the kitchen and crawled up into Ben's lap and buried her head in his chest. He paused and looked lovingly into the eyes of his daughter, who was just beginning to stir in his arms and said, "But I'm not sure she's ever going to get rid of me." (8)

This theme of resisting separations from the important objects in his life had already affected his feelings about Helen. In order to keep his "finger in the job pie" he had had to leave for ten days on what he called a "job safari" the month before, which had marked the first <u>prolonged</u> separation between him, his wife, and their daughter. He was <u>stunned</u> to find out from his wife during his absence that Helen's appetite had decreased, her mood and temperament had disintegrated, she'd become clingy and was almost <u>perpetually</u> tearful. He reported that he had felt so awful upon hearing this that he had lost *his* appetite. "I'm sure I blew an interview, maybe even on purpose. I took the red-eye[1] flight to get home early." (9)

. . .

A <u>vitally</u> important part of the study was the careful examination of the children's development, the so-called "proof of the pudding."[2] Helen was the first child to be evaluated . . . using first the Yale Developmental Schedules and then a diagnostic play interview. The developmental testing was constructed to examine carefully the overall developmental competence of the children intellectually, physically, emotionally, and socially. (10)

When her father brought her to the child study center, Helen, now eleven months, was a <u>vigorous</u>, bright-eyed, smiling, well-scrubbed little girl who leaned forward immediately from her father's arms to examine my mustache, which bore some likeness to her father's. She looked back and forth between the two faces for a moment, looked at the door of the examining room, and peremptorily ordered, "Go!" (11)

. . .

Although 44 weeks at the time of the testing, she exhibited a 52- to 56-week profile in her personal, social, and language function. The quality of her performance was also interesting. Helen would clap her hands in an excited fashion, breaking into a broad smile whenever she successfully assembled a particular puzzle or achieved the desired block design sequence. (12)

Helen's problem-solving skills were equally advanced. But it was her play that was most <u>precocious</u>. She exhibited a broad range of skills with the unfamiliar toys presented to her in the testing situation, often organizing surprisingly complex play involving both her father and me. I felt as though I were in the presence of a budding stage director! (13)

As the obvious competence of his daughter emerged, I invited Helen's father to tell me some of his experience with children prior to his becoming a father to one. His response was typical of much of the fathering population in the study. I was continually surprised to find so little experience with young children in the study fathers. Twelve of the seventeen fathers had few, if any, extensive prefathering experiences with children. (14)

At our next interview, I turned my focus to Anne [Helen's mother] in order to complete the family portrait. (15)

. . .

Anne had "always planned to have children" and had fully intended to raise them. She was at a <u>vulnerable</u> stage in her career, having just been promoted when she got pregnant with Helen. "There were three of us competing for one job, these two guys and myself. I knew that the particular job was perfect for me. But I wanted this baby so badly. . . . I was so torn up about it, I just couldn't think about what to do. Ben's decision to stay home with her was just the perfect thing . . . just perfect, though he and I were the only ones who thought so at the time! My parents did a 'slow roll.'[3] They couldn't begin to understand it. They're <u>coming around</u>, now, but I've really missed their support—especially my father's. (16)

. . .

Two and a half years after this initial contact with Helen's family, a younger brother, Bruce was born. . . . Ben [who had returned to work a year before] had planned to renew his "half-time paternity leave"[4] from his firm and to stay in touch with his business through his computer terminal, but his request was denied. His boss informed him that his company only allowed "one paternity leave per family." As a result, when I interviewed the family at the time that Bruce was four months old, Anne was now the stay-at-home parent, having recently acquired an extended leave of absence (without pay) from her own firm. Helen, now three and one-half, was at nursery school four mornings a week. She had been attending day care[5] three afternoons a week until her brother was born. Now she attended nursery school only. (17)

Ben was not doing so well. Anne had been the first to notice that he'd become less involved at the end of her pregnancy, almost immediately after being informed that he would have to return to his job actively or lose it altogether. Unlike the first pregnancy, he could remember no dreams, and he experienced a weight *loss* instead of gain. [He had gained weight during her first pregnancy.] At the time of the delivery, and this one he did attend, he had felt <u>elated</u> as he had on first becoming a father but found himself repeatedly handing his son back to his wife after picking him up. (18)

Once Bruce was home from the hospital, Ben did not hear his son's cries at night (again unlike Helen), and his wife had to awaken him to "take his turn" at the night-time feedings. Helen had begun to complain that "Daddy wasn't funny anymore." He reported he was "driving home after work at 50 miles an hour, instead of 60 like before." (19)

Mr. Mellow spontaneously reported during the interview that he was very troubled by the distance he felt between himself and his son. "I don't think it's just the boy-girl stuff. I just don't feel as important in his life. I miss that a lot—more than a lot!" . . . (20)

During the period after Bruce's birth, Helen's nursery school teacher reported that she looked <u>listless</u> and <u>somber</u> much of the time. She spoke animatedly and with pride, even exhibitionistically, about her brother but had also <u>regressed</u> to protesting her father's departures in the morning when he dropped her off at nursery school on his way to work. It was hard to tell whether this was due to Helen's feeling displaced by her brother's arrival or whether she might have been following her father into some depression. (21)

Though Helen continued to <u>thrive</u>

---

[1]the red-eye: very late night/early morning transportation (causes the eyes to be red from lack of sleep)

[2]proof of the pudding: evidence that something works

[3]slow roll: becoming angrier and angrier

[4]paternity leave: time away from work for new fathers; this is becoming more common in the United States.

[5]day care: care facility for children who are not in school and whose parents are at work during the day

in general, this family was involved in a difficult transition, not wholly of its own choosing. Though the mother was doing well, the father had regressed, referring to himself several times as "the odd man out." The denial of the opportunity to father the second child in the manner he wished depressed him significantly, and Helen seemed to be partially following suit. By the time of the reevaluation's completion, however, Mr. Mellow was feeling somewhat healed after he had decided, with his father's advice, to seek legal counsel to challenge his company's paternity leave policies. (22)

His decision, though an intensely personal and risky one for him, serves as witness to what may be required to solve the father problem and free men to develop fully their <u>nurturing</u> capacities. (23)

Pruett, 1987, pp. 88-97.

## *LEARNING STRATEGY*

**Forming Concepts: Try to add the information you learned about the father in the previous reading to your knowledge of fathers in general.**

## ELABORATING ON THE READING

**EXERCISE 1—Discussion:**  Discuss the following questions with some of your classmates and your teacher.

1. How did the Mellow's family choose to structure the parental roles? Why?
2. How did their family, neighbors, and employers react to their choice?
3. Were there positive effects on Helen's development? Were there negative ones?
4. What effects did this arrangement have on the father? The mother?
5. Do you think it is normally possible for a father to care for his child as well as the mother can? Does he do it in the same ways?
6. How does a mother usually learn how to be a good mother?
7. How does a father usually learn how to be a good father? How did Ben Mellows learn?
8. Do you think Helen's mother was a bad mother? Do you think Ben Mellows parented Helen as well as her mother would have?

**Threads**

A 1989 survey of medium and large private employers found that only 1% of employees had the option of paid paternity leave.

Nancy R. Gibbs, "Bringing up Father," *Time,* June 28, 1993, p. 55

**EXERCISE 2:**  With two or three of your classmates generate a list of typical descriptions of mothers. Then go on to list typical descriptions of fathers. An example is given of each.

| | MOTHERS' BEHAVIOR | FATHERS' BEHAVIOR |
|---|---|---|
| 1. | *patient* | *strict* |
| 2. | | |
| 3. | | |
| 4. | | |
| 5. | | |
| 6. | | |

Do you think these typical descriptions are the truth or stereotypes?

**EXERCISE 3:**    Consider the poem and passage you've read so far in this chapter. Then, with two or three of your classmates, generate a list of characteristics that many societies *expect* of fathers and those that societies *resist.* The list is begun for you.

| SOCIETY *EXPECTS* THESE CHARACTERISTICS | SOCIETY *RESISTS* THESE CHARACTERISTICS |
|---|---|
| 1. *Fathers play roughly with their children.* | 1. *Fathers cry over their children.* |
| 2. _____ | 2. _____ |
| 3. _____ | 3. _____ |
| 4. _____ | 4. _____ |
| 5. _____ | 5. _____ |

## Preparing for Short Writing: Writing Skills

## WRITING COMPARISONS

When comparing two things, writers must find a clear way to organize the many details involved in the comparison. This can be difficult because not only are there likely to be many descriptive characteristics to be included, but the number increases by virtue of the fact that the writing compares two or more items. The most effective way of presenting these characteristics is to determine a plan of action, make this plan clear to the reader early on, and follow it throughout the comparison, not deviating toward another plan midway.

There are three basic techniques for organizing comparison information. Each is illustrated below.

### TECHNIQUE 1: ALL OF ONE / ALL OF THE OTHER

When writers choose this technique, they describe the two items to be compared separately. First one item is described fully, without connection with the second item. Then the second item is described, often referring back to the first item with transitions such as *similar to, like, unlike, different from, whereas,* and *however.* Often, if there is enough information, the two items are described in separate paragraphs as well. The following passage illustrates Technique 1 by comparing two fathers' reasons for neglecting child support payments.

Many noncustodial parents, primarily fathers, refuse to pay child support when ordered to do so by the courts. They have varying reasons for doing so. Ted says he never chose to be a parent, and in fact, he does not believe that he is the father of his daughter, though paternity tests indicate there is a 99.91 percent chance that he is the father. He prefers to forget that he has a child and says, "Family life scared me. I don't want the responsibility." In addition, Ted feels that the payments would create a financial hardship for him.

While Adam is also upset about his child support situation, unlike Ted, Adam is more angry about losing control over the situation rather than questioning his child's paternity. Now that he is divorced and his ex-wife has custody, Adam feels he has no input into the way his child is raised or how the money he sends is spent. "Can't they make her [his ex-wife] show receipts?" he asks. (Waldman, 1992, pp. 46–49)

Notice how the technique that is used in this paragraph is made clear within the first two sentences. In particular, the sentence, "They have varying reasons for doing so," shows that *different* reasons will be shown. As soon as the reader sees "Ted" in the next sentence, he or she knows that this text will show differences between someone named Ted and one or more other fathers. Nevertheless, these other fathers are not mentioned again until Ted's story is completed and Adam's is introduced.

Second, notice how Ted's opinions and Adam's are expressed separately, in this case in different paragraphs. While Ted's story in the first paragraph is not influenced by Adam's, there are several references to Ted in Adam's story. Sentences and phrases like "While Adam is also upset by his child support situation," "unlike Ted," and "rather than questioning his child's paternity" are all overt comparison's to Ted's situation.

Writers prefer to use Technique 1 when the items being compared have entirely different qualities. For example, Ted's reasons involve paternity and finances. Adam's reasons involve control over the situation. If they both had opinions on paternity, control, and finances, Technique 2 would be more effective.

## TECHNIQUE 2: MIXED TOGETHER

When the two items are to be compared using the same types of details, writers mix the items together, detail by detail. Below is a paragraph comparing two television fathers popular in the United States. Dr. Cliff Huxtable, played by a famous actor/comedian named Bill Cosby, is generally understood to be a near-perfect father. Homer Simpson is a cartoon character father on the Simpsons. He is generally understood to be a poor example of a father.

Perhaps some of society's expectations of fathers come from the ways they are portrayed on television. In recent times, there have been two types of fathers on television, which we can refer to as the "Cliff Huxtables," from the *Cosby Show,* and the "Homer Simpsons," from the *Simpsons.* In both shows, the fathers' professions are clear, and we often see the fathers at work. Whereas Cliff is a professional man, a physician, Homer is a blue-collar worker in a nuclear power plant. Cliff has an office in his home, which allows him to see more of his children than the typical father. Homer, of course, works outside of his home and arrives home each evening tired and ready to "vegetate" in front of the television. Both fathers spend a good deal of time with their children, although Homer, perhaps, is less nurturing toward his children than Cliff. Yet when all is said and done, both fathers show tenderness toward their children in their own fashions.

Examine the paragraph above. Which sentence gives the reader the first clue that this is a comparison? Which words specifically refer to the comparison? Finally, which information about the two men is *similar,* and which is *different?*

## TECHNIQUE 3: SIMILARITIES AND DIFFERENCES

A third technique for organizing comparison information is to separate the similarities and the differences. This technique is especially effective in making text clear when there is an equal or almost equal number of similarities and differences or when the similarities and differences are complicated and need additional explanation.

> There are "deadbeat"[1] moms too. Similar to deadbeat dads, mothers who do not pay child support when ordered to generally may neglect to do so out of the anguish over losing custody in the first place. They may also perceive child support payments as, in a way, paying the ex-husband rather than the children. And finally, they may also feel, like fathers, that the payments place an undue hardship on them.
>
> However, unlike fathers, mothers who lose custody of their children suffer especially acute embarrassment since society and the courts still generally consider the mother to be the preferred custodial parent. In addition, whereas men are commonly required to make child support payments, it is less common for ex-wives to make such payments. It may, then, feel especially "unfeminine" for a woman to make financial payments to a man who has custody of the children she feels are her right to keep. The woman avoids the anguish of the situation by ignoring the situation entirely. (Waldman, 1992, pp. 46–49)

Which sentences provides the clue to the comparison that follows? Which language makes that comparison obvious? Could either of the other organizational techniques have been used instead?

### LEARNING STRATEGY

**Overcoming Limitations: Choose a type of comparison organization which you can manage well, and limit the number of points you will raise in the next short writing to a manageable number.**

## SHORT WRITING (150–200 WORDS)

Compare fathers in your society to Mr. Mellow or the father in the poem. In your society, is it easy or hard for men to nurture their children? Is working more important to the men in your society than spending time with children? Are fathers' roles changing?

Share your short write with several members of your class. Take notes on any ideas you believe may be useful for you later in this chapter or when you write your essay.

---

[1]deadbeat: someone who refuses to pay his or her bills

## IN-DEPTH READING

**Vocabulary Enrichment**

Match the following words with their *opposites*. Check their contexts in the reading below before completing each item.

1. _____ benevolent          **a.** enabling

2. _____ detachment          **b.** admirably

3. _____ void                **c.** involvement

4. _____ pathetically        **d.** cruel

5. _____ disabling           **e.** fullness

The following article, written anonymously, was printed in *The New York Times* for Father's Day, a holiday celebrated in the United States on the third Sunday in June each year. In it, the father shows the differences in his attitudes toward fatherhood when he became the father of a son twenty-five years ago and when he again became a father to twin daughters recently.

# Fatherhood: The second round

His first round of fatherhood, a quarter-century ago, was done the old-fashioned way—as a benevolent by-stander. He and his new bride were children. In their 20's. With not the slightest idea of how to nurture a child or share a household. (1)

A father, as they understood it, put bread on the table, played with his child after work and went along on family outings, leaving the hard and dirty chores to mother. The day his baby was due, he dropped his wife at the hospital and was shooed[1] off to work by the doctor. Later, he got a call. It was a boy, healthy, 7 pounds 5 ounces. (2)

Neither he nor his wife found anything odd in his detachment. Family lore[2] held that he had changed only a single diaper. Whenever asked to pitch in,[3] he loved to reply, "Bring the man-child to me when he is 21." (3)

Looking back, his years of fatherhood seemed largely a void, broken by a few sporadic memories. Belly-tickling. Hide-and-seek[4] in the apartment. A temper tantrum at the shoe store. Embarrassed retreats from restaurants. (4)

Father's Day, in his experience, was the very opposite of Mother's Day—less homage for a job well done than mandatory annual torture. Like that hectic outing at the zoo, where his son squirmed into the bear enclosure, or the sweltering picnic at the lake, engulfed by mobs and rotting fish. (5)

Just a few weeks ago, while on vacation together, he asked his son, now 27, what he recalled of his Daddy. It was pathetically little. The father felt he had known his son least as a child—and loved him most as a young man. (6)

His second stab[5] at fathering is being done the new-fashioned way—tuning in, not out. His second wife, with a career of her own, was not about to let him sit on the sidelines. Not with twin daughters. (7)

They arrived 10 weeks early, so tiny only a doll's clothes would fit them. And as they struggled for breath and life in the intensive-care nursery, he came every day to root them on,[6] cradle them in the crook of an arm, or deliver a vial of breast milk. Daily, their bonds grew stronger. (8)

Later, when they came home, he fell easily into the role of chief attendant. Older, wiser and looser now, he became a champion diaper changer. In the mornings, he ruled over breakfast, pleased that his toaster waffles and instant hot cereal became the standard of excellence. (9)

He is still no Mr. Mom. Too much childish prattle bores him, and a full day of girl-tending can be disabling. But he is involved, and having fun. As his daughters approach their fourth birthday, he is enraptured by their beauty, their brilliance, their individuality. (10)

Though twins, they are not identical. One is gregarious, empathetic, cautious. The other a loner, moody, reckless. He basks unashamedly in their adoration.

---

[1]shooed: kindly told to leave
[2]lore: legend
[3]pitch in: help complete a task

[4]hide-and-seek: a children's game
[5]stab: attempt

[6]root them on: encourage them

In the evenings, tired from work and commute, he will often ignore his keys and reach for the doorbell, setting off squeals of delight and a pell-mell rush to admit him. (11)

For weeks now the girls have been preparing his Father's Day[7] cards, and picking shirts of his favorite color. But there will be no special trip to the zoo or the lake; it's not necessary. For in this new and better age, Father's Day is not an annual event. It occurs daily. (12)

----

[7]Father's Day: a U.S. holiday honoring fathers every June

*The New York Times,* 1991, Sec. 4 p. 16.

## ELABORATING ON THE READING

1. What similarities do you notice between the father in this reading and the father in the poem? What similarities do you notice between this father and Mr. Mellow?
2. Why did the father in this reading get a second chance? What were some of the differences the second time around?
3. Does this father take care of his baby daughters as completely as Mr. Mellow took care of Helen?
4. How does Father's Day with his daughters compare to Father's Day with his son two decades ago?
5. Which of the methods of organization for comparisons mentioned above does this reading use? Why do you think the author chose this method?

## SHORT WRITING (150–200 WORDS)

Describe the similarities between the father in the reading above *with his son* and the father in the poem. Then go on to describe the differences between the father in the reading above *with his daughters* and the father in the poem.

## Making Your Draft Clearer: Language Skills

### PRONOUN REFERENCE

**A. They, he, she, it**

A pronoun is a word which takes the place of and means the same thing as a noun which occurs near it. Examples of pronouns include *she, her, he, his, him, they, their, them, it,* and *its.* These pronouns can be particularly problematic for writers when one paragraph contains more than one possible referent for a pronoun. Consider the following single-sentence examples:

Fathers and sons may have particular problems developing relationships because *they* have not been taught how to interact lovingly.

What is the referent (the meaning) of *they?* Is it *fathers?* Is it *sons?* Is it both? Because the referent is ambiguous, the sentence is unclear for the reader. Now consider the following edited versions:

Fathers and sons may have particular problems developing relationships because *the fathers* have not been taught how to interact lovingly.

or:

Fathers and sons may have particular problems developing relationships because *neither* has been taught how to interact lovingly.

By removing the pronoun and substituting a full noun phrase, the writer is able to achieve more clarity in the sentence.

**EXERCISE 1:** Paragraph 1 contains many uses of the pronoun *they* and *their.* Circle each instance of this pronoun. Then determine whether its referent is clear. If not, edit to clarify.

> 1.  "A staggering number of American men have difficult or unsatisfying relationships with their fathers. As boys, they learned little from them; they were at best a benign influence. As adults, they have fashioned an uneasy co-existence, a relationship shaped by silence and unspoken distance." (Clancy, 1992, p. 18)

Now do the same with paragraph 2, this time focusing on *he* and *him.*

> 2.  [The West African] Lele honored fatherhood. A boy was taught, "Your father is like God. But for his begetting, where would you be? Therefore honor your father." He was taught that the debt which he owed him for his care of him in infancy was unrepayable, immeasurable. It was very shameful for a him show disrespect to him. A father was expected to avoid his grown son, so that he should not feel bowed down with the burden of respect. (Adapted from Douglas, 1963, p. 114)

### B.  This *vs* it

It is common for writers to refer back to information contained in a previous sentence using either *this* or *it.* When the information writers are referring to is a complex concept, they use *this.* When the information is a simple word or phrase, they use *it.* Examine the following sentences.

> The notion of fatherhood in the U.S. has varied depending on the moment in history. This has resulted in varying opinions on the purposes of father-hood in present day society. (*This* refers to the complex concept "the no-tion of fatherhood has varied depending on history.")

> In the earliest phase, the father's role was quite well-defined. It was "moral teacher." (*It* refers to "the father's role" only.)

**EXERCISE 1:** In the following paragraphs, circle either *this* or *it* according to the needs of the sentences.

> **A.** At about the time when America was industrializing, a change oc-curred in the father's role. (*It/This*) became "breadwinner" rather than moral teacher. While fathers still retained some responsibility for teaching their children good values, the role of breadwinning became the most important characteristic of a good father by the mid-nineteenth century. (*It/This*) con-tinued through the Great Depression in 1929 and the early 1930s.
>
> By the end of the mid-1940s, although remaining central as breadwinners and moral teachers, fathers' primary role developed into "sex-role model."

(*It/This*) is thought to have happened as a result of the disorder caused by World War II. In fact, many professionals wrote articles claiming that fathers were not providing strong images for their sons to imitate. (*It/This*) was often portrayed humorously in television shows.

By the mid-1970s, the new "nurturant" father became the ideal. Fathers were supposed to be active caretakers of their children. This new definition of fatherhood was very popular in the media. (*It/This*) appeared in several popular movies and television shows and in fact is still the dominant definition. (Lamb, 1987, pp. 5-6)

**B.**  In Japan, a strong emphasis on educational achievements, referred to as "schoolism," shapes social status. (*It/This*) has profoundly influenced parenting, child development, and family dynamics. The mother, known as the "education mom," takes most of the responsibility for her children's schooling. (*It/This*) leads to her dominance in the educational domain. The father, on the other hand, works long hours, and (*it/this*) causes him to spend little time with his family. Although the man enjoys much higher social status than the woman outside of the home, schoolism contributes to the maternal power and paternal weakness inside the home. (*It/This*) also makes the father the model of economic success. (Shwalb, Imaizumi, and Nakazawa, 1987, pp. 251-252)

**C.**  In most small Italian towns, the family is nurtured and molded by community norms. (*It/This*) is shown, for example, by the fact that young people are not considered as adults until they have children, even though they might be married. The word *sposi* is used to refer to married people who have not had children, no matter how long they have been married. Reinforcement of family values is also accomplished in other ways. (*It/This*) exists in sayings like: "A family without children is like a garden without flowers."

Not only does the Italian society aid in forming family units, but it also aids in strengthening them. (*It/This*) does this by promoting "family time." The most important part of each day is *pranzo,* the midday meal, when family members return home. For most people, the family relationship is important. (*It/This*) provides social and cultural support. (New and Benigni, 1987, pp. 149-50)

Now check your draft for pronoun problems. Make changes where necessary.

## Reflecting on Draft One

After you complete your first draft to your satisfaction, consider the following.

**1.**  In only one sentence, tell what your paper is about.

_____

**2.**  Describe one thing you did very well in this draft. What makes it so good, in your opinion?

_____

**Threads**

In 1992, Japan enacted a new law giving both fathers and mothers the right to take child-care leave from their jobs.

*Los Angeles Times,* July 6, 1993

3. Identify one place in your paper where you are worried your audience might not understand what you are trying to express.

_____

4. Identify a part of your paper which you are not happy with but which you cannot figure out how to improve.

_____

5. Identify one improvement which you are already planning for Draft 2 but which you could not accomplish in this draft because you ran out of time.

_____

# PART III: WRITING THE SECOND DRAFT

Write a second draft of your essay for this chapter. As you work on this draft, you will learn how to use expert quotations in your writing. Find places in your essay where adding quotations from outside sources (either the articles in this chapter or other articles which you can find in the library) could strengthen your paper. You might, for example, use a quotation to heighten reader interest at the beginning or end of your paper, to provide evidence of your opinions, or to convince your reader of the seriousness of your topic. You will also learn ways to make your use of language clearer and more sophisticated.

## FURTHER READING

**Vocabulary Enrichment**

**EXERCISE 1:** Examine the following words in their contexts in the passage below. Then determine which is the closest meaning for each word.

| | | | |
|---|---|---|---|
| **1.** meticulously | stupidly | carefully | happily |
| **2.** to the exclusion | misunderstanding | helping | ignoring |
| **3.** contend | lie | state strongly | dislike |
| **4.** deprive | give freely | help | take away |
| **5.** stable | unchanging | expensive | clear |
| **6.** rite of passage | trip | sign of maturity | law |
| **7.** on a massive scale | very much | sometimes | rarely |
| **8.** plateau | end of growth | reward | rate |
| **9.** out of wedlock | uneducated | unhealthy | unmarried |
| **10.** startling | comforting | surprising | expected |

## Threads

Kids learn from their moms how to be aware of their emotional side. From Dad, they learn how to live in society.

Jerome Lee Shapiro, psychologist, author of *A Measure of the Man* and two other books on fatherhood

| | | | |
|---|---|---|---|
| 11. complacent | friendly | self-satisfied | afraid |
| 12. pressing | heavy | very important | written |
| 13. sporadic | irregular | physical | planned |
| 14. well-adjusted | healthy | wealthy | happy |
| 15. better off | happier | healthier | wealthier |
| 16. be prone to | accustomed to | surprised about | likely to suffer |
| 17. rage | strong anger | fear | hunger |
| 18. vulnerability | weakness | truth | doubt |
| 19. self-esteem | self-doubt | self-respect | self-defense |
| 20. fragile | strong | easily hurt | surprising |
| 21. at ease | obvious | healthy | comfortable |
| 22. potential | possible | expensive | unimportant |

**EXERCISE 2:**   Use ten of the vocabulary words from Exercise 1, and write sentences explaining the problems a child might experience when his or her parents divorce and the mother receives sole custody of the child.

1. _____

_____

2. _____

_____

3. _____

_____

4. _____

_____

5. _____

_____

6. _____

_____

7. _____

_____

8. _____

_____

9. _____

_____

10. _____

_____

**Remember Your
Vocabulary Checklist!**

In the United States, fathers may play small roles in their children's lives for several reasons: loss of child custody after divorce, fatherhood without marriage, or traditional division of sex roles ("stay-at-home" mother and "working" father). Their absence from their children's lives has profound effects on society as a whole. The following passage from the article discusses some of the consequences of absentee fathers.

# Life without father

We meticulously talk in gender-neutral terms about "single-parent households" and "parenthood." But discussion about the particular importance of fathers is rare. In this feminist age, [David] Blankenhorn [president of the Institute for American Values, a New York think tank that studies family issues] contends, there's an assumption that women can do just fine by themselves, thank you. They survive as independent women, as single mothers, . . . and even as welfare[1] recipients (such social critics as Barbara Ehrenreich have argued that it's perfectly rational for poor women to find welfare checks more reliable and less troublesome than men). Even the nation's social-services system focuses its financial and counseling assistance on mothers—often to the exclusion of fathers, critics contend. (1)

But many researchers now single out fathers as providing a form of child-rearing distinct from that of mothers—and just as essential to a child's development. Whether they are roughhousing with a 5-year-old or scaring the bejesus[2]

out of a delinquent teen, fathers bring a different style to parenting, says Kyle Pruett, psychiatry professor at the Yale Child Study Center and author of *The Nurturing Father.* (2)

Social thinkers across the political spectrum are beginning to emphasize the role of fathers in building safe communities. Conservative sociologist James Q. Wilson contends that while "neighborhood standards [are] set by mothers, they are enforced by fathers. . . . The absence of fathers deprives the community of those little platoons that effectively control boys on the street." Likewise, New Jersey legislator Wayne R. Bryant, a liberal African-American, describes the difference between the boy who throws a bottle on the ground in a stable suburb and one who does the same in an almost-fatherless housing project. The first boy picks it up when challenged by the man next door; the second responds to a female neighbor's request with a menacing "Don't you tell me what to do." Without men around as role models, adolescent boys create their own rites of passage: perhaps getting a girl pregnant or dealing drugs or murdering a rival. (3)

---

[1]welfare: a system of financial assistance provided to poor people by the government; comfort, health, and happiness

[2]bejesus: slang, used with "frighten" and "scare" to mean "completely"

Throughout history, men have been torn from their families by war, disease and death. But in "'90s America," men are choosing to disconnect from family life on a massive scale, and at far higher rates than other industrialized countries. "Men are drifting away from family life," says Blankenhorn. "We are in danger of becoming a fatherless society." (4)

That is especially true in minority communities, where poverty rates are the highest. In nearly two-thirds of black households and in one-third of Latino households, only one parent—usually the mother—is present. Divorce rates, though still high, have reached a plateau. The most important factor behind the increase in fatherless households is the seemingly unstoppable rise in out-of-wedlock births. In 1989, a startling 66% of black children and 36% of Latino children were born to unwed parents. (5)

But fathers are harder to find in white suburbia as well. Nearly a quarter of white homes are headed by one parent, and the percentage of white children born to unwed parents has nearly doubled over the last decade, to almost 20%—a much faster growth rate than that found in black communities. Lest[3] white Americans become too complacent: Blankenhorn has crunched Census Bureau figures to show that white families now experience break-

---

[3] lest: old-fashioned way to say "in case"

ups at the same pace as black families did in 1965, when President Johnson called "the breakdown of the Negro family structure" one of the most pressing issues of the era. (6)

All across America tonight, one-third of the nation's children will go to bed without their biological fathers in the next room. And most of them won't see their fathers the next day, either. According to studies by Frank F. Furstenberg Jr., a University of Pennsylvania sociologist, about 40% of the children who live in fatherless households haven't seen their fathers in at least a year; for many others, contact is sporadic. In any month, only one in five of these children sleeps even one night in his father's home. "It's a minority of [absent] fathers that has at least once-a-week contact," says Furstenberg. (7)

Researchers are quick to note that plenty of single mothers raise well-adjusted children, and that children are better off not living with emotionally or physically abusive fathers. But, they add, the odds are stacked against fatherless children—particularly those who live in poverty. Children with fathers tend to do better in school, are less prone to depression and are more successful in relationships. "It shows up on cognitive achievement, on social achievement, every-where," says San Diego psychiatrist Martin Greenberg, author of *The Birth of a Father.* Greenberg describes the fatherless young criminals he counsels as brimming with rage

over being "abandoned." And fatherless girls, Greenberg and other researchers note, often experience low self-esteem and rocky romantic relationships as they search for the ideal father substitute. Most of the time, stepfathers can't begin to fill the void. (8)

That vulnerability is evident in the comments of Lori Thompson and mothers like her, who worry about the periods of depression they see in their children. Ask the normally buoyant Jason about his father, and his mood darkens. Little-boy fingers drop to his lap and tug at each other fitfully. A tiny tear surfaces, and he swats away the unwelcome drop. "He's OK," Jason says. Then comes the halting, deep breath. "I don't know when he's telling the truth or when he's actually going to show up." (9)

Another mother . . . says that no matter how much she tries to bolster her 9-year-old son, his self-esteem remains fragile. Outwardly, he appears to be a cheerful, well-adjusted child thoroughly at ease in the company of adults. But his mother confesses that he has frightened her with talk about wanting to kill himself. "Issues of potential loss affect him deeply," she says. "I've been dating a guy for one week, and he already wants me to marry him and make him his daddy." (10)

---

Easton, 1992, pp. 15–16.

## ELABORATING ON THE READING

### Threads

In 1990, 25% of children were living only with their mothers.

*Time,* June 28, 1993

**EXERCISE 1:**   Study the passage above and discuss the following issues with two or three of your classmates.

1. Scan the article to find reasons why men are "choosing to disconnect from family life." Brainstorm other possible reasons as well.
2. List some benefits of fathers' involvement in families.
3. List some negative consequences of fathers' absence from families.
4. Which details in this passage impressed you the most? Why?

Forming Concepts: After you figure out what impresses you as a reader, apply that knowledge to your own writing so that you can impress your readers as well.

## SHORT WRITING (150–200 WORDS)

Compare the qualities that a father brings to a child's life with the qualities a mother brings.

## TAKING THE IDEA FARTHER: SIMULATION ACTIVITY

**A.** In this exercise, you will act out a court proceeding to determine which parent will receive custody of two children. In order to do this, you must determine what the most important issues are in caring for children. With your classmates, list these below.

| IMPORTANT ISSUES IN CARING FOR CHILDREN |
| --- |
| |
| |
| |
| |
| |
| |

**Threads**

Children from broken families are almost twice as likely to drop out of high school as children with two-parent families.

*Time,* June 28, 1993

**B.** Now consider the details of the case.

**Situation:** Two of your classmates have been married for nine years and are about to divorce. They have two children, one three-year-old boy and one seven-year-old girl. The girl is in her second year of elementary school; the boy is too young for school.

**The Decision:** Should one parent receive custody of the children, or should the parents share joint custody, meaning that the children spend equal time in each parent's home? Note that noncustodial parents are usually required to help support the children financially regardless of custody arrangements. If only one parent receives custody, how often should the children visit the noncustodial parent?

## Threads

More than 40% of all children born between 1970 and 1984 are likely to spend much of their childhoods in single-parent homes.

*Time,* June 28, 1993

**The Players**

*The plaintiff* (the one seeking custody) [*plain* is the root, from *complain*]
   *attorney for the plaintiff, witness for the plaintiff*

*The defendant* (the one defending himself or herself against the plaintiff's request)
   *attorney for the defendant, witness for the defendant*

*The minor children* (children under the age of 18)

*The judge* (Referred to as "your honor," the judge may make the final decision on how to assign custody of the children, or your teacher may ask the class to vote on the decision. The judge also supervises the proceedings and decides which of the lawyers' questions are appropriate and which are not.

*The attorneys* (Each parent has an attorney who organizes the flow of information to the judge in such a way that the parent can win custody. The attorney first does this by preparing a list of questions to ask the witnesses for his or her own client so that all the supporting information will be available to the judge. Second, the attorney prepares questions to ask the other side's witnesses so that their testimony will not hurt his or her client's case or will hurt themselves.)

*The bailiff* (maintains order in the court, gives the oath to witnesses to "swear to tell the truth, the whole truth, and nothing but the truth.")

*The witnesses* (In the United States, civil cases, as opposed to criminal, often rely on character witnesses, people who testify to the good character and behavior of one of the people in question, as well as other types of witnesses.)

**C.**   In two groups, plan the most important points the following witnesses should mention as they give testimony. Add more witnesses if you wish. Then plan questions for the attorneys to ask during the proceeding.

| *ON THE MOTHER'S SIDE* | *ON THE FATHER'S SIDE* |
|---|---|
| the mother | the father |
| the mother's parents | the father's parents |
| a child psychologist | a child psychologist |
| a friend | a friend |

**D.**   Prepare questionnaires for the two parents and all the witnesses to fill out. This will ensure that information (such as age, job, address, and religion) is available to everybody before the trial begins. It will also help ensure that nobody changes his story while he is giving testimony. What information would you like to include in the questionnaires?

   Also prepare and give to the judge before the trial all physical evidence (called exhibits) such as photographs and papers that will be used to support one side during the trial. No physical evidence may be added during the trial.

**E.**   You are now ready to assign the parts above to some of your classmates, study the procedures and special vocabulary below, and roleplay the proceeding.

**F.   Procedures and vocabulary associated with custody trials in the United States.**

THE PROCEDURE

   The bailiff calls *"Order in the Court. All stand, the honorable [judge's name] presiding. . . . Be seated"* (after the judge arrives)

The judge tells the attorney for the plaintiff to begin.

The attorney for the plaintiff makes a brief opening statement summarizing what he or she plans to prove when calling witnesses later.

The attorney for the defendant does the same.

The attorney for the plaintiff calls one witness at a time.

The attorney for the defendant may also question each witness when the plaintiff's attorney finishes.

The attorney for the defendant calls the witnesses one at a time; they are also each questioned by the attorney for the plaintiff.

Each attorney makes a brief closing statement summarizing what has been proved.

The judge (or the class) makes a decision on how custody will be arranged.

SPECIAL VOCABULARY

*The attorneys:*

*"The [defendant/plaintiff] calls [witness] to the stand."*

*"Objection, your honor! / I object!"* (The attorney disapproves of the other attorney's or witness's behavior.)

Reasons to object: *"That question is irrelevant. / The attorney is badgering [attacking] the witness."*

*"I refer to Exhibit [letter], entered into evidence."*

*"Your honor, I request permission to treat this witness as a hostile witness."* (The attorney expects the witness to lie or evade.)

*The judge:*

*"The witness will please answer the question."* ("Stop avoiding the question!")

*"Overruled."* (The judge disagrees with an attorney's objection. This comment must be followed by a new command from the judge such as, "The witness will answer the question.")

*"Sustained."* (The judge agrees with an attorney's objection. This comment must be followed by a new command from the judge such as, "The witness will ignore that question.")

*"This court finds in favor of (the defendant / the plaintiff)."* (Who wins?)

*"Custody is granted to (the mother / the father) with visitation rights to (the mother / the father)."*

## LEARNING STRATEGY

**Personalizing: Identify what you learned during this simulation activity about fathers' roles in their children's lives, and use this information to improve the content of your essay.**

## SHORT WRITING (150–200 WORDS)

Explain to your instructor how you felt about the custody trial. Was it decided fairly? What did you learn about U.S. courts in general and custody battles in particular?

**Managing Your Learning: Increasing your contact with native speakers increases your ability to speak and listen effectively in a second language.**

## Gathering Data: A Poll

A poll involves asking a number of people to answer the same questions so that the researcher can find out opinions about a topic. It is very common in the United States for people to be stopped on the street or in a shopping area and asked for their opinions.

In small groups of three or four students, prepare a very short poll on the topic of "A Father's Role in the Family." Then go out into the community around your school or neighborhood and ask people to answer your questions, being careful to keep a record of their answers. Explain to the people that you are a student conducting a poll. Ask them if they would mind answering (three or four) questions. Prepare your results and explain them to your class.

*HINT:*   Be sure to limit the number of questions—no more than five. When people are on their way to a destination, they have little time to stop and talk. Also be sure that your questions can be answered in a short answer. Long answers will be hard for you to write down.

Compare your results when you return to class.

## Making Your Draft Clearer: Language Skills

### GENERALIZING WITH SINGULAR AND PLURAL NOUNS AND *THE*

When writing about topics such as fathers, mothers, sons, and daughters it is very important for the writer to make one particular decision right from the beginning: Will he or she write about "father*s*" and "mother*s*," "the father" and "the mother," or "a father" and "a mother"? All are possible and correct, but what is *not* correct is to mix both singular and plural forms in the same essay.

Once the writer decides to write using the plural "fathers," he or she must make all other details related to these fathers plural as well. Consider the following phrases and sentences, which are absolutely impossible. Why?

1. Fathers are traditionally more interested in their job.
2. Mothers are stereotyped as the perfect housewife.
3. It is perfectly normal for men to win custody of their child.
4. Mothers typically stay in their home while men concentrate on their career.

There are essentially three forms writers can choose from when they are generalizing about whole groups of people.

1. They can write in the plural, making sure to match all nouns and pronouns to the plural form of the topic. In this case the preceding sentences are corrected to:
   a. *Fathers* are traditionally more interested in *their jobs.*
   b. *Mothers* are stereotyped as perfect *housewives.*
   c. It is perfectly normal for *men* to win custody of *their children.*
   d. *Mothers* typically stay in their *homes* while *men* concentrate on *their careers.*

2. They can write in the singular using the general article *a.* In this case the sentences are changed to:
   a. *A father* is traditionally more interested in *his job.*
   b. *A mother* is stereotyped as *a perfect housewife.*
   c. It is perfectly normal for *a father* to win custody of *his* children.
   d. *A mother* typically stays in *her home* while *a father* concentrates on *his career.*

3. Contrary to the normal use of *the,* we can also use *the* plus the singular noun to refer to every member of that class identified by the noun. Therefore, *the father,* when used to make a generalization, refers to "every man in that group called *father.*" In fact, this form is often preferred over the form discussed in (2) above because it sounds more intellectual. As a result, the above sentences become:
   a. *The father* is traditionally more interested in *his job.*
   b. *The mother* is stereotyped as *the perfect housewife.*
   c. It is perfectly normal for *the father* to win custody of *his children.*
   d. *The mother* typically stays in *her home* while *the father* concentrates on *his career.*

**EXERCISE—Editing Singular/Plural Errors:** Find the errors in singular/plural nouns and related language in the paragraphs below and make corrections by choosing one of the two *singular* methods discussed above and using it consistently throughout.

   A.   Fathers in this society are depicted as being someone who never shows his soft side; someone who looks out for the well-being of his family. His job is to provide food and protection for his family. But in reality, fathers are expected to be a lot more than the typical family leader. He needs to show love and affection toward his children. Most of these fathers fail to realize that their children are suffering. The children need their father to be around them. Children who are neglected by their father do not have the same happy life that children with caring fathers do. (adapted from Trung Xa, student)

Now make changes in the following paragraph so that all nouns and pro-nouns are *plural* and match each other.

**B.** Growing up with a single parent isn't always so easy, and it is especially tough for single parents to raise the child alone. In most cases of divorce, mothers usually get custody of the child unless evidence shows that she is incompetent. There are such myths that women show more affection towards the child, that mothers are more caring, and that they are very cautious of the child's daily routine and attitudes. Such myths are not always true, and they exist because society tends to stereotype a mother as being the perfect housewife—staying at home cooking, cleaning, and taking care of the kids. Well, this is the 90s, and things do change. Now it is perfectly normal for men to win custody of their child, and they do a great job of raising their kids too. (adapted from Xuan Vo, student)

Now check your own essay for this chapter. Have you made any singular/plural errors such as those discussed above?

## Making Your Draft Clearer: Writing Skills

### APPEALING TO EXPERTS BY QUOTING AND PARAPHRASING

Examine the reading, "Life without Father," which begins on page 97. As you scan this reading, highlight or underline all quotations used by the author. Then discuss the questions below with your classmates and instructor to gain an understanding of how quotations are best used.

1. In paragraph 1, is the material in quotation marks quoted from expert sources, or is it in quotations for another reason?
2. In paragraph 2, information is attributed to Kyle D. Pruett, an expert at Yale University. In paragraph 3, information is attributed to James Q. Wilson. Wilson's information is in quotation marks, yet Pruett's is not. Can you explain why?
3. Can you explain why the author of "Life without Father" may have felt that it was necessary to quote Wilson's words exactly but not to quote Pruett's?
4. When examining the quotation from Blankenhorn in paragraph 4, which general rules can you formulate regarding the following conventions?
   a. the placement of the comma (,) in relation to the quotation marks (")
   b. the use of the verb "says" and its subject
   c. the name of the person who spoke or wrote the quotation
   d. the use (and nonuse) of capital letters within the quotation

5. At the end of paragraph seven, why do you think the word "absent" is placed within brackets [ ]?

6. List the experts who are quoted in this article. List also their professional titles or affiliations.

| EXPERT | AFFILIATION |
|---|---|
| James Q. Wilson | conservative sociologist |
| | |
| | |
| | |
| | |
| | |

Why is it important for the reader also to know their titles or affiliations? Which titles or affiliations are most impressive to you? Does this influence your acceptance of the information given by the experts?

7. Analyze the following quotation from paragraph 6. What is the *subject* of this sentence segment? What is its *verb?* What is its *object?* Does the portion in quotation marks follow the grammar rules of the whole sentence, or is it entirely separate from the grammar of the rest of the sentence?

> . . . when President Johnson called "the breakdown of the Negro family structure" one of the most pressing issues of the era.

8. How many quotations appear in the article in total? What percentage of the entire article is quoted? Is there other information from experts that is not directly quoted? Why do you think the author sometimes quotes and sometimes paraphrases (uses his own words to express the experts' opinions)?

9. If you were an expert who had published on a certain topic, and somebody used your information without using quotation marks or even telling his or her readers that you were the original source, how would you feel? What might you do about it?

*NOTE:* Using another writer's material, either (1) by directly quoting or (2) by indirectly paraphrasing, *without giving credit to the original source* is called *plagiarism.* It is a form of stealing. Students who plagiarize can receive a failing grade for their projects or their entire classes, or they can be suspended or expelled from school. Professionals who plagiarize can lose their jobs or be taken to court for action against them.

## Making Your Draft Clearer: Language Skills

### EXPRESSING IMAGINARY MEANINGS

English, like some other languages, distinguishes between two types of information: that which is *likely* to be true and that which is *unlikely* to be true, just a fantasy or imaginary. We generally use verbs such as *could, would,* and *should* to describe unlikely situations along with *if* or *wish* to indicate a situation we believe is unreal or imaginary.

All statements about *imaginary* events use *past* verb forms. Examine the following examples:

> The son *wished* his father *would spend* more time with his sons. (The son is fantasizing; it's impossible.)
>
> *If* we *had asked,* my father *could have taken* time off work to be with us. (He didn't because we didn't ask.)

Note that *hope* represents a likely event: "I *hope* my parents *will* get married again" (possible). *Wish* represents an unlikely event: "I *wish* they *would* get married again" (impossible).

**EXERCISE 1—Recognizing Likely and Unlikely Events:**   Determine whether each of the following events expressed in the following statements is *likely* (L) or *unlikely* (U). Some sentences have more than one event. Remember to look not only for words like *if* and *wish* but also for the verb tenses.

1. _____ If I have children, I want to spend a lot of time with them.

2. _____ The fathers who didn't pay child support could have sent part of their payments if they had been having financial problems.

3. _____ If Ben had known for sure that he was little Kenny's father, he would have been willing to pay child support on time.

4. _____ New fathers are able to become vital members of their families from the beginning if they are routinely given paternity leave at every company.

5. _____ Twenty years ago, few fathers hoped to stay home from work on paternity leave.

6. _____ All across America tonight, hundreds of children will wish that their fathers were with them to say goodnight.

## Past vs. Present Unlikely Events with *If*

*If* statements may express unlikely (or imaginary) events in the past or present. However, in order show the reader that the event is imaginary, only past verb forms are used. A general rule of thumb is that the simpler past verb forms express present unlikely events. More complex past verb forms express past unlikely events. Compare the verb forms in the following two sentences. The result of the condition is expressed with a modal verb: *would, could,* or *might,* also in either a simpler form (*would go* = present) or a more complex form (*would have gone* = past).

> If I *were* a father, I *would spend* a lot of time with my children. (present meaning)
>
> However, if I *had been* a father twenty years ago, I *might have been* like the father in the poem. (past meaning)

Summary: Unlikely Verb Forms with *If* and *Wish*

| | PRESENT MEANING | PAST MEANING |
|---|---|---|
| **CONDITION** | | |
| *if* or *wish* | "simple past" (*-ed*) | "double past" (*had* + PP) |
| **RESULT** | | |
| | *would* *could* *might* + verb | *would* *could* *might* + *have* + PP |

| | **Condition** | **Result** |
|---|---|---|
| **Examples:** | If the children *saw* the new movie, | they *would be* frightened. |
| | If my friend *were*[1] home right now, | I *could invite* her over to dinner. |
| | If I *had been* in New York last week, | I *would have seen* the big blizzard. |
| | I wish I *had known* my father better when I was a child. | |
| | He probably wishes we *could spend* more time together now. | |

[1]When expressing unlikely conditions, we always use *were* instead of *was,* even when the subject of the sentence is singular.

**EXERCISE 2—Unlikely Statements with *If*:**   Determine whether the following unlikely events are expressed in past time or present. You might begin by identifying the verbs.

1. If my son were more like me, we could probably do some activities together.
2. I could have spent a lot more time with my son if my job hadn't required so much of my time.
3. If I had spent more time with him, I would have developed a closer relationship with him through joint activities.
4. Because my company has a paternity leave policy, I would be able to spend time with my children if I had more children.
5. But I know my sons' feelings for me couldn't have been any stronger even if we had had more time together.
6. Mr. Mellow wishes his company had had paternity leave at the birth of his second child.
7. Many fathers wish they were with their children more often.
8. If fathers were the same as mothers, children wouldn't need both.

**EXERCISE 3—*If* and Imaginary Meanings:**   You and your spouse (wife or husband) have just had a child. The husband's company does not have a paternity leave policy but you are planning to write a letter to his supervisor to get paternity leave this time. There is a small chance that you will be successful. This is the husband's second marriage; he did not receive paternity leave when he had children during his first marriage. Brainstorm information about the first and present situations to use as evidence in your letter. You might consider the following questions to start.

If the husband had had paternity leave before:

- how would his feelings for his first children have been different?
- how would their feelings for him have been different?
- how would the leave have affected his work (positively or negatively)?
- what effects would the leave have had on his marriage?

If the husband received paternity leave this time:

- what impact would this have on his family life?
- what impact would this have on his working ability when he returned?
- what advantages would his company receive in return for granting leave?

## Making Your Draft Clearer: Language Skills

### PACKING INFORMATION INTO NOUN CLAUSES

Examine the following sentences. Each illustrates one of the three roles that nouns can play in sentences.

1. Four factors are important to understanding *the amount* of paternal involvement in families. (*amount* is the object of *understanding*)
2. *The data* suggest that more than half of all U.S. fathers do not want to spend more time with their children. (*data* is the subject of *suggest*)
3. There is no unanimity about the *desirability* of more paternal involvement in families. (*desirability* is the object of the preposition *about*)

In English, it is also possible to use whole clauses in the same way that we use simple nouns. These are called *noun clauses.* You will recall that a clause is a subject + verb. Writers use the particular type of clause called noun clause to include more information in their sentences or to vary the pattern of their sentences from the basic subject + verb + object pattern. Examine the following sentences and notice the function of each italicized noun clause in its sentence.

1. *What children care most about* is not so much who is at home but how that person feels about spending time at home. (subject noun clause)
2. Some fathers are unable to see *that they should be more involved in their children's day-to-day lives.* (object noun clause)
3. Researchers are not unanimous about *whether the father's involvement in his children's lives is as important as the mother's.* (noun clause as an object of a preposition)

Notice again that we have examples of a *subject noun clause,* an *object noun clause,* and a *noun clause as the object of a preposition.*
Circle the subject and verb in each clause above.
Write the word that appears before each noun clause:

_____

_____

_____

These are *noun clause connecting words.* They introduce noun clauses and connect them to the main sentence (or main clause).

### Noun Clause Connectors

the "wh-" question words: *who, what, where, when, why, how*
> (Notice when these noun clauses are used as subjects, the verb is in *-s* form in the present tense.)

> *How fathers treat their children* often depends on how their fathers treated them.

> My father never told me *where he was* during all those years of absence.

> I've always been curious about *why men's and women's roles seem so different in the family.*

> *What families need* is more opportunities to be together.

the *-ever* words (meaning "any person, any place, any time"): *who(m)ever, whatever, wherever*

> *Whoever said that parenting is easy* was obviously never a parent.

> Many men want to be able to do *whatever they please.*

> Children will become close to *whomever spends the most time with them.*

*that* (Notice that we often use *that* clauses with *it* + (*be*) + adjective.)

> *That society expects so little from fathers other than breadwinning* is amazing.

> It is amazing *that society expects so little from fathers.* (This form places more emphasis on "amazing" and less emphasis on "society expects so little from fathers," compared to the previous example.)

> Societies often believe *that the mother should be the primary caregiver of children.*

*Whether* and *if:* Use these connectors when you wish to express doubt or a question that can be answered yes or no about the topic you are writing about. (*If* is slightly less formal.)

> *Whether the man has skill in dealing with children* can be a very important factor in his level of involvement with his children.

> Paternal involvement in families also depends on *whether the mother wants her husband to be more involved.*

In the first sentence, the noun clause could be expressed as a yes/no question: Does the man have skill in dealing with children? The same is true for the second sentence: Does the mother want her husband to be more involved?

*NOTE:*  Although we use question words as noun clause connectors, notice that we are not writing questions, so *we do not use the question word order.* We use the clause word order: subject + verb.

**EXERCISE 1—Completing Sentences:** Complete the following sentences by writing noun clauses for the indicated places. Add any additional information that you desire.

1. ( . . . . . . ) is to develop some confidence in fathers so that they will not feel incompetent at taking care of their children..

   _____

2. Once fathers begin to realize ( . . . . . . ) they will find it easier to spend time with their children.

   _____

3. It is very important for new fathers to know ( . . . . . . ).

   _____

4. The most frequently discussed question about the father's role in the family is ( . . . . . . ).

   _____

5. In relation to the father's involvement, mothers are often most worried about ( . . . . . . ).

   _____

6. Some mothers worry about ( . . . ).

   _____

7. High parental involvement makes it possible for both parents to do ( . . . ).

   _____

8. Researchers in the area of fatherhood should find out ( . . . ).

   _____

9. ( . . . ) had a great influence on my development as a child.

   _____

10. A father's strictness with his children shows ( . . . ).

   _____

Now go back to your draft. Are there places where you can increase the amount of information in a sentence or its sophistication by expanding the subject, object, or object of a preposition into a clause? Are there places where you used noun clauses with the wrong word order? Make changes where necessary.

## Editing Strategy: Reading Aloud

One way to find out how your writing will "sound" to your reader is to read it aloud and listen to how it sounds to you. Reading aloud has several editing advantages: First, it allows you to imagine how an audience might react to what you are saying in your paper because your own ears can be your audience. Second, it slows down the rate at which you are reading (because it takes time to speak the words) and thus gives you a chance to catch any missing words or other errors. Finally, reading aloud may help you catch errors if you speak more correctly than you write. It is very important to read *exactly what you see on your paper* when you are reading aloud as an editing strategy. It is quite common for beginning writers to read, instead, what they *think* is on the paper.

*NOTE:* A similar read-aloud technique suitable for examination situations is to move your lips without using your voice.

**EXERCISE:** Read your second draft aloud as you keep a pen or pencil in your hand. Mark any changes you wish to make on your paper.

## STUDENT WRITING: PRACTICE PEER RESPONSE

Read the following student essay in which a writer from Vietnam discusses his complicated relationship with his father. After you finish reading the essay, fill out the peer response that follows to analyze it. Your instructor may ask you to do this with or without your classmates and may provide additional questions.

### MY FATHER AND I

*Trung Xa*

1   A father in American society is depicted as being someone who never shows his soft side, someone who never looks out for the well being of his family. His job is to provide food and protection for his family. But in reality, the father is expected to be a lot more than the typical family leader. He needs to show love and affection toward his children. Most fathers fail to realize that their children are suffering. The children need their fathers to be around them. Children who are neglected do not have the same happy lives that children with caring fathers do.

2   My father is different from the average fathers in America. Most fathers in this country do not devote enough time to their children because of their busy working schedules. My father, on the other hand, was a tailor in Vietnam. But in this country, because of his age, he cannot work. He spends a lot of his time with me at home.

3   My father and I have a relationship that is very similar to the father-son relationship in the poem "My Father Worked Late." We love each other very much, but we have trouble expressing our feelings toward each other. Unlike the child in the poem, I get to spend more time with my father because he did not have to work. Looking at my childhood, I think I was very lucky. My father and I did a lot of things together. For example, during our early days in America, I was fortunate enough to have my father hold my hand and take me to places that I had never been to before. With the few English terms that my father had acquired from watching TV, we managed to explore places such as Disneyland and the mall. These are the special moments that I will cherish for the rest of my life.

4   My father's love for me was witnessed most when I had surgery on my knee. It was during this time that he made me believe that no person on the face of this earth could love me more than he. My father spent three long sleepless nights at the hospital. His weary face brought tears to my eyes when his frail body walked into my room.

5   As in most father-son relationships, our relationship drifted further apart as I grew older. It seemed like there was a force that existed in each man which prevented him from expressing his love toward the other. Although fights and

arguments occurred regularly, I knew that deep down inside he cared for me very much.

6    My father's pushing me to become a better person, at times, made me very angry. As a result, communication between the two of us often broke down. Most of our conversations always ended in arguments. Sometimes after these arguments, I sensed a feeling of sadness on my father's face, the kind of feeling a mother would feel if she lost her baby. It looked as though he wanted to come over and hug me but something held him back. I could not understand what it was.

Now, exchange your paper with one of your classmate's papers and complete the same peer response after reading it.

## Peer Response to Draft Two

**1.** Tell your author some of the main points you understand from his or her essay.

_____

**2.** Describe to your author an image that appeared in your mind while you were reading his or her essay, almost as if it were a movie.

_____

**3.** Briefly tell your author about a memory from your own experience that was triggered by reading his or her essay.

_____

**4.** Write down one or more of the author's words or phrases which you admired.

_____

**5.** Ask your author for any information that you felt was missing from the essay or any questions that came to your mind while you were reading.

_____

# PART IV: WRITING THE THIRD DRAFT AND ASSESSING YOUR LEARNING

In Part IV, you will once again revise your essay. As you are doing so, be sure to consider your peer reader's comments, your teacher's comments, any issues raised in the practice peer response, and any changes you have been planning. In addition, check the following things:

- Have you used quotations and paraphrases to your writing's advantage?
- Have you introduced them correctly, and have you identified your sources?

- Have you described hypothetical or imaginary events grammatically?
- Have you written any awkward sentences that would sound better with noun clauses?
- Can you find places to use some of this chapter's new vocabulary in place of less sophisticated words in your paper?

## Punctuation Note: Quotation Marks

We surround material which we have taken directly from another source (using the same words) with quotation marks (" "). When the material we take from these sources is in the form of a complete sentence, we must be careful about where we put the end punctuation of that sentence in relation to the quotation marks. Below are some examples.

"The father of us all is Roman law!" (Delaisi de Parseval and Hurstel, 1987, p. 61)

"Throughout Italy the family has traditionally dominated the individual's interest as well as loyalties." (New and Benigni, 1987, p. 145.)

"In brief, the paternal role was primarily that of an educator-disciplinarian, in addition to that of provider"; the mother was basically a nurturer in Chinese society. (Ho, 1987, p. 234.)

In Hong Kong, there is "considerable parent-child distance": as many as 56.1% of children keep their unhappy feelings secret from their parents. (Ho, 1987, p. 235)

You can see four different types of end punctuation at the ends of each quotation. What are they? Is each inside the quotation mark or outside?

In general, put commas (,) and periods (.) inside the quotation mark. Question marks (?) and exclamation points (!) also go inside if they are part of the material you are quoting. Otherwise, put them outside. Put semicolons (;) and colons (:) outside the quotation marks.

Check your draft, looking particularly at those places where you used quotations. Is your end punctuation in the correct location? Make any necessary changes.

### STUDENT WRITINGS FOR FURTHER DISCUSSION

The following essay was written in response to assignment three, Persuasive Essay, by a young woman from Thailand. In it, she makes a case for why fathers are *better* parents than mothers. Does she make a successful case?

### CUSTODY OF CHILDREN

*Pachuen Kongkitisupchai*

1    The majority of the population in America assumes that mothers are more capable of raising their children than fathers. In fact, most societies in general tend to believe that it is reasonable to assume that mothers "instinctively" care for their children better than fathers. Similarly, the court tends to follow the same assumption that mothers are better nurturers and guardians for most of

## Threads

**Seventy percent of children under 18 who have been in prison have spent at least part of their lives without fathers.**

*"Life Without Father,"*
*Los Angeles Times*

the vital years of the children's lives than the fathers. Thus, mothers generally are considered the preferred custodial parents and the court perpetually grants mothers custody of their children. However, is it appropriate to grant custody of children automatically to the mothers, unless they are found to be incompetent?

2      The answer to this question weighs heavily upon many factors, but the most vital element is the children themselves. The children should have the ability to determine who they prefer to live with because the outcome of the decision will directly affect them more than anyone else. Another important factor is the competency of the children's parents. Which of the two parties will be able to supplement the other party without a great amount of disturbance to the children's normal growth. Will the children be deprived of a normal and healthy environment for growth if they live with either party? If living with either parent and he or she retards the children's growth either mental or physically, then the children should not be placed in that party's custody. Thus, the main factor is the living environment of the children. After considering all the critical factors that determine the decision of who gets the custody of the children, I believe that the court can make a competent decision for the benefit of the children.

3      After carefully considering all the vital factors that help determine the decision of who gets custody of the children, I argue that mothers may not be the most beneficial choice for the children. Mothers may have the ability to "instinctively" care for their children, but that does not prove that the fathers can not produce an equally satisfactory result. Women are "instinctively" able to care for their children because they have seen how their mothers raised their younger brothers or sisters when they were little girls. Not only did they see that their mothers were raising their siblings, but they also saw that their fathers were providers of the family while the mothers did the housework. Whether they realize it or not the notion that "women nurture children while men are the providers for the family" is engraved into their unconscious minds. Therefore, the women's instincts are constantly being reinforced by the image of their mothers throughout their childhoods. By being constantly reinforced with how their mothers raised their siblings, women will tend to repeat the

same methods and routines to raise their own children. Thus, similar errors will perpetually occur. Women may acknowledge these faults and attempt to alter them, but these women have past exposure which may retard the progress of change. I believe that the best solution is to raise children with both the women's instinct and the men's naiveté. However, this possibility is an ideal solution and may not always be obtainable. In some cases, the fathers may be the better choice because they are not exposed to the images of their mothers raising their siblings. Thus, fathers will raise children by their own understanding and that may be best for the children.

4    Having a distinctive outlook upon life and lacking past exposure, men may be the preferred option for children. With the distinction between opinions and methods of how to solve general problems that men offer, a new method of raising children may come up and be beneficial to the society as a whole. Mill, a theorist, once said, ". . . on every subject on which difference of opinion is possible, the truth depends on a balance to be struck between the two sets of conflicting ideas. . . ." Men can provide this possible different view and the new option that may be the more preferred solution. In the beginning, the men may not understand the children like the women because they do not have the same continual practice since childhood. However, the men will eventually develop their own intuition and styles of how to raise their children. A great example is Mr. Mellow who became a homemaker while his wife went back to work. "During the first week after his wife had returned to work, he was often anxious," stated one of the analysts. He continued, "Since the beginning, Mr. Mellow had continued to 'read' his daughter well. Mr. Mellow said, 'I eventually developed my own style.' He fed her in a fashion different from that of his wife; for example, he allowed Helen more finger play with her food than Anne (the mother) did."

5    Eventually the fathers begin to understand the children more than the mothers if the fathers are raising the children. To continue with the example, Mr. Mellow stated, "Suddenly, I began to figure her out. My wife, though she really loved our little girl, never seemed quite able to understand her, maybe because they're so much alike. . . . I was reluctant to admit that I had figured her out at first. I kept it to myself. But Helen (the daughter) became crystal clear to me." Not only was Mr. Mellow able to figure out the child, but Helen even began to progress at a faster rate than the other children. "Although 44 weeks at the time of the testing, she exhibited a 52 to 56 week profile in her personal, social, and language function." This proves that the children can progress just as quickly if not faster with fathers as the caretakers and this is one of the vital factors of the children's development. Both Mr. Mellow and Helen gain a special bond that is very different from a mother and daughter bond. When Mr. Mellow realized that he had to go back to work and could no longer stay home with Helen, he went into a depression. Most importantly, Helen also went into a depression like her father ". . . protesting her father's departures in the morning when he dropped her off at nursery school on his way to work. . . . She might have been following her father into some depression."

6    From Mr. Mellow's story one can see that mothers are not always "better" caretakers for children than fathers. I believe that the society should stop stereotyping mothers as better caretakers than fathers and view each case individually. In a situation, mothers may fulfill the vital elements of the children's growth better than fathers. But in other cases, fathers may be the better caretakers because fathers may replace the mothers much more successfully. If society does not stereotype mothers as the better caretakers, then maybe the society can have a truly open mind. If a society can openly accept a view contrary to the majority opinion, then this notion of equality of all can benefit all the citizens in that society. . . .

## Threads

**The world's most prolific father was the Emperor Moulay Ismail of Morocco, (1672–1727), who is believed to have had 548 sons and 340 daughters.**

*Guinness Book of World Records*

## DISCUSSION

In your discussion of the following questions, point to specific paragraphs and specific information to support your answers.

1. What is Pachuen's main point?

   _____

2. Which details does she offer to show that she understands the opposing point of view too?

   _____

3. What are the basic premises upon which she bases her main argument? In other words, what does she assume to be true about boys, girls, men, and women? Do you agree with her basic premises?

   _____

4. What evidence does Pachuen offer that is particularly persuasive?

   _____

5. Overall, how do you evaluate the persuasiveness of Pachuen's essay? What advice would you offer her for revising?

   _____

## Reflecting on Draft Three

### LEARNING STRATEGY

**Managing Your Learning: Evaluate the feedback that your class-mates, your teacher, and you have been giving your essay and consider the role this feedback plays as you write or revise.**

1. Identify one part of your essay that you believe was done well. It may be as small as a sentence or as large as a whole page.

   _____

   Why do you believe it was done well?

   _____

2. With a highlighter or colored pen, highlight or underline words, phrases, even whole sentences that especially please you.

   _____

3. Explain what you think makes these phrases special.

   _____

4. Describe what you hope makes your paper special or different from those of your classmates.

_____

5. Identify the most important thing you learned about your *topic* (not about good writing) while you were working on this essay.

_____

## Writer's Notebook

Consider the following questions in your writer's notebook after you write the drafts of this chapter's major essays.

1. What kinds of reading do you generally like? What are the characteristics of this type of reading that appeal to you most? Do you believe some of these characteristics might be usable in your writing for this course? Which ones?

2. What types of characteristics do you generally find memorable, enjoyable, or useful in your classmates' essays?

3. When you are writing your essay drafts, who do you imagine your audience to be? Your teacher? Your classmates? Yourself? How can it change your writing to imagine an audience other than your teacher only?

4. In what specific ways can you say that your understanding of your audience influences the choices you make while writing your essays?

5. Does having a clear audience in your mind make it easier or harder for you to write your essays? Why?

## Vocabulary Checklist

Add vocabulary words from the chapter that you believe will be useful for your essay or your life in general. Several additional useful words have been added for you.

| WORD | PART OF SPEECH | MEANING | PREPO-SITIONS | SAMPLE SENTENCE |
|---|---|---|---|---|
| 1. nurture | verb | provide an environment which allows one to grow well | ø | He nurtured his baby as if it were a tender flower. |
| 2. paternity | noun | the quality of fatherhood | of | Some men deny paternity of a child to avoid responsibility. |

| WORD | PART OF SPEECH | MEANING | PREPO-SITIONS | SAMPLE SENTENCE |
|---|---|---|---|---|
| 3. | | | | |
| 4. | | | | |
| 5. | | | | |
| 6. | | | | |
| 7. | | | | |
| 8. | | | | |
| 9. | | | | |
| 10. | | | | |

## Bibliography

Clancy, Frank. "Breaking Away." *Los Angeles Times Magazine,* June 21, 1992, pp. 18-19.

Daniels, Jim. "My Father Worked Late." In *Places Everyone.* Madison: University of Wisconsin Press, 1985.

Delaisi de Parseval, Genevieve, and Françoise Hurstel. "Paternity 'á la Française.'" In *The Father's Role: Cross-Cultural Perspectives.* Ed. Michael E. Lamb. Hillsdale, N.J.: Lawrence Erlbaum Associates, 1987.

Douglas, Mary. *The Lele of the Kasai.* London: Oxford University Press, 1963.

Easton, Nina J. "Life Without Father." *Los Angeles Times Magazine,* June 14, 1992, p. 15-16.

"Fatherhood: The Second Round." *The New York Times,* June 16, 1991, Sec. 4, p. 16.

Ho, David Y. F. "Fatherhood in Chinese Culture." In *The Father's Role: Cross-Cultural Perspectives*. Ed. Michael E. Lamb. Hillsdale, N.J.: Lawrence Erlbaum Associates, 1987.

Lamb, Michael. "Introduction: The Emergent American Father." In *The Father's Role: Cross-Cultural Perspectives*. Ed. Michael E. Lamb. Hillsdale, N.J.: Lawrence Erlbaum Associates, 1987.

New, Rebecca S. and Laura Benigni. "Italian Fathers and Infants: Cultural Constraints on Paternal Behavior." In *The Father's Role: Cross-Cultural Perspectives*. Ed. Michael E. Lamb. Hillsdale, N.J.: Lawrence Erlbaum Associates, 1987.

Pruett, Kyle D. *The Nurturing Father*. New York: Warner Books, 1987.

Schwalb, David W., Nobuo Imaizumi, and Jun Nakazawa. "The Modern Japanese Father: Roles and Problems in a Changing Society." In *The Father's Role: Cross-Cultural Perspectives*. Ed. Michael E. Lamb. Hillsdale, N.J.: Lawrence Erlbaum Associates, 1987.

Waldman, Steven. "Deadbeat Dads." *Newsweek,* May 4, 1992, pp. 46–49.

# Poverty: Could You Be Its Victim?

# PART I: INTRODUCTION

Think about the following questions as you work on this chapter.

1. Whose fault is poverty?
2. Do you think you could ever find yourself impoverished? Why or why not?
3. Should those who are not impoverished care about poverty?

## Topic Orientation

In order to begin understanding the topic for this chapter, discuss the following questions with two or three of your classmates.

1. With your group members, make a list of reasons why people usually find themselves impoverished.
2. Make a list of ways that you believe people can pull themselves out of poverty.
3. Make a list of characteristics which you believe cause people rarely or never to find themselves in poverty.

# PART II: WRITING THE FIRST DRAFT

## MAJOR ESSAY ASSIGNMENTS

Write a first draft of your major essay for this chapter of approximately 750 words. Choose the type of essay that you feel competent to write but that will also provide a bit of a challenge for you. Use the questions in the assignments to help you begin the assignment, not to limit your ideas. If you think of a better topic to write about, discuss this with your instructor. As you write your essay, be sure to make effective use of statistics, the readings, and outside sources where appropriate.

### LEARNING STRATEGY

**Managing Your Learning: Remember to challenge yourself in choosing your topic.**

1. **Descriptive Essay.** Describe the daily life of a particular group of impoverished people in your nation. Where and how do they live? How do they get food? clothing? transportation? medical care? Are there any programs designed to help them such as shelters, public assistance, or medical clinics? Are people in your country interested in helping this group of poor people?

2. **Analytical Essay.** Analyze the economic, social, and personal reasons why someone in your culture might become impoverished. You might consider such aspects as education, the economic and job systems of your country, the class system of your country, minority status, family status/divorce, and personal health/habits. Are there any particular characteristics which you believe may protect someone from poverty? Could you or someone you know become impoverished?

3. **Persuasive Essay.** Argue to your reader that a certain course of action should be taken in order to alleviate or end poverty. Explain why this particular action is appropriate, who ought to take this action, what exactly should be done, and how it can be done.

Since the causes of poverty can be so varied, you may want to limit your paper to the poverty of a particular group of people such as the elderly, children, the hardworking poor, or minorities.

## INTRODUCTORY READING

### Vocabulary Enrichment

Find meanings for the underlined words in the passage, "The Hardworking Poor," from among the words below. Then write the synonyms above the appropriate words in the passage.

### WORDS

| | |
|---|---|
| family | gather |
| possibility | warning |
| break | contradiction |
| make up | motivation |

***VOCABULARY LEARNING STRATEGY:*** Choose one or more of the words from this vocabulary exercise which you feel will be useful in your writing. Enter them into the Vocabulary Checklist at the end of this chapter.

Many people are accustomed to thinking that people can find themselves in poverty through their own fault. Sociologists refer to this as "blaming the victim." While it may be true that some people are poor through their own fault, the following passage shows us a different side of poverty.

## Threads

What differentiates the incomes of two people is not the physical output that each produces, but rather the value that society attaches to their products.

Bradley R. Schiller, *The Economics of Poverty and Discrimination*, p. 71

# The hardworking poor

If we include the <u>dependents</u> of household heads when we calculate the number of people in poverty, we find that there are over 4 million persons in families headed by individuals who worked all year round at full-time jobs. Why, we may ask, are so many people poor if their families work so much? Doesn't the existence of this <u>paradox</u> <u>violate</u> the very same principles that <u>comprise</u> our capitalist ideology? If we cannot guarantee economic security to those individuals who contribute their maximum work effort, what sort of <u>admonitions</u> or <u>incentives</u> can be directed to those who work less? . . .

If there is any moral to be <u>gleaned</u>, perhaps it is this: A poor janitor who works hard stands a very good chance of becoming a hard-working poor jani-

tor. There seems to be little <u>prospect</u> of economic security for the poor as a result of their own efforts. Too many people earn too little money.

Schiller, 1989, p. 65–69.

## ELABORATING ON THE READING

1. What would you say is the author's main point in this passage?
2. Why do you think the author felt it necessary to write a chapter in his book entitled "The Hardworking Poor"?
3. What do you think the author's intention was in writing the following sentence: "A poor janitor who works hard stands a very good chance of becoming a hardworking poor janitor." What tone do you notice in this quote?
4. Why do you think it is common for people to "blame the victim"? What do people say about the poor when they blame the poor for their own poverty?

## Preparing for Short Writing: Writing Skills

### USING STATISTICS

Compare the following pairs of sentences. Which is more effective to you? Why?

1. **a.** Many children were living in poverty in 1990.
   **b.** In 1990, twenty percent of all American children lived in poverty.
2. **a.** A large number of children were living in near-poverty in 1990.
   **b.** Twenty-five percent of children in 1990 were living in near-poverty.
3. **a.** Poverty among children rose greatly between 1970 and 1989.
   **b.** Poverty among children rose from 15% in 1970 to 20.5% in 1989. (Jansson, 1993, p. 304–305)

Now examine the following paragraph, noticing in particular how the statistics are inserted and how their sources are given.

The term *feminization of poverty* was coined to describe the extent of poverty in female-headed households. If only 23 percent of all poor families were headed by women in 1959, this figure had risen to 52 percent by 1989. About 51 percent of children in families headed by a woman were poor in 1989 compared to only 10 percent in two-parent families. Such families had high rates of poverty because females tend to be in lower-paying work and single heads can draw on only a single source of wage income.[1] Ozawa asserts that more women had become single heads of household because of increasing rates of teenage pregnancy and increasing rates of divorce.[2] (Jansson, 1993, p. 305)

Only one of the information sources is mentioned directly in this passage. How is this done?

What information do you find in the footnotes? Why would the reader want this information? (Note: There are a number of methods for writing footnotes. Find out which method is preferred by your course instructors, publisher, or supervisor. You will find more samples at the end of this chapter.)

## SHORT WRITING (150–200 WORDS)

The following table, containing information from the U.S. Census Bureau, shows data on the number of poor people who had jobs and how often they worked during the year. Study the information in Table 1 very carefully. Then write a description of the surprising relationship between poverty and employment. What makes this information surprising? Be sure to refer to statistics from the table specifically in your writing.

TABLE 1: How Much the Poor Work

| WEEKS WORKED | FULL-TIME WORKERS | PART-TIME WORKERS | TOTAL |
|---|---|---|---|
| 50–52 | 1,024,000 | 309,000 | 1,333,000 |
| 40–49 | 254,000 | 110,000 | 364,000 |
| 27–39 | 263,000 | 128,000 | 391,000 |
| 14–26 | 361,000 | 212,000 | 573,000 |
| 1–13 | 371,000 | 278,000 | 649,000 |
| Total employed: | 2,273,000 | 1,037,000 | 3,310,000 |
| Total unemployed: | | | 2,961,000 |

[a]Source: U.S. Bureau of the Census, 1987.

[1]Children's Defense Fund, *State of America's Children* (Washington, D.C., 1991), pp. 24–25.
[2]Martha Ozawa, "Introduction: An Overview." In Martha Ozawa, ed., *Women's Life Cycle and Economic Security* (New York: Greenwood Press, 1989), pp. 2–8.

## IN-DEPTH READING

**Vocabulary Enrichment**

**1. Prefixes, Stems, and Suffixes.** You may already be aware that many English words are related to Latin and Greek and are composed of parts: prefixes (the front parts), stems (the middle parts) and suffixes (the end parts). Prefixes and stems typically provide meaning, while suffixes provide both parts of speech and meaning. Examine the following prefixes, stems and suffixes:

| PREFIXES | | STEMS | | SUFFIXES | |
|---|---|---|---|---|---|
| dis- | "not" | -graph- | "writing" | -able | "able to" (adj.) |
| mal- | "bad" | -demo- | "people" | -ly | "the way" (adv.) |
| over- | "too much" | -domin- | "lord, rule" | | |
| pre- | "before in place, time, or importance" | | | | |

Can you list some words that contain one or more of these word parts?

_____

_____

_____

Using the information about prefixes, stems, and suffixes above, find underlined words in the following passage "Who Are the Poor?" that mean the following:

**1.** statistics about people _____

**2.** able to be hurt _____

**3.** poor diet _____

**4.** lack of specific physical or mental abilities_____

**5.** cause not to be believed _____

**6.** not the expected size _____

**7.** greater than others _____

### LEARNING STRATEGY

**Remembering New Material: Try to remember the stems and affixes you have just learned about by visualizing their meanings. For example, to remember the prefix "dis-" you might imagine a thumb pointing downward, indicating "no" (a typical North American gesture) or you might imagine a crowd for "-demo-." What other images can you visualize?**

**2. Definitions.** As you did earlier in this chapter, examine the underlined words in the passage above that you have not already defined. Choose the most likely definitions from the following list based on the context around the words.

continue without change      shocking
by chance      a very poor quality house
uncertain

**RememberYour
Vocabulary Checklist!**

The following passage describes, group by group, exactly who is afflicted by poverty in the United States. It may surprise you that almost no group is immune from poverty. As you read the passage, ask yourself: Could you fall into any of these categories? Could you find yourself living below the poverty line at some time in your life?

*LEARNING STRATEGY*

**Managing Your Learning: When you are reading material that is dense with details, remember your purpose in reading, and focus on those details of the reading which support your purpose, for example, your essay topic.**

As you read this passage, underline or highlight each mention of <u>common stereotypes</u> often believed about the poor.

# Who are the poor?

**I** t's Not in the Stars

Does poverty <u>randomly</u> afflict just anyone? The answer is an unequivocal no. Some citizens have a much greater probability of falling victim to poverty than others. Undoubtedly, the social class into which an individual is born serves as a fairly accurate predictor of whether or not that person will succumb to a lifetime of economic insecurity. The <u>demographics</u> of the nation's poverty population identify those who are most <u>vulnerable</u> to poverty. Contrary to the prevailing stereotypes regarding the poor, more than 80 percent of the poverty population consists of children (40 percent), the elderly (11 percent), and women (30 percent); and most (77 percent) of the poor live in families. Although a <u>disproportionate</u> number of poor Americans are nonwhite, the majority (69 percent) are white. One-sixth of this nation's poor children have at least one parent who works full-time, year-round. Society cannot hold these children responsible for the problems of their parents. Furthermore, those adults who are most vulnerable to economic insecurity—women and the elderly— are entitled to society's assistance when the "safety net" fails. (1)

## The Children

Most tragic of all are the children who live in poverty. Billy's story illustrates the <u>appalling</u> influence poverty can have on a child. (2)

When all of Billy's worldly possessions were gathered together, they did not even fill a plastic garbage bag. His father deserted the family when Billy was six years old. Although he had to give up the pet cat he loved so much in order to move into a Seattle emergency shelter,[1] Billy Todd Jr., 15 years old, was dismayed that he and his mother and brother were leaving the shelter. Billy had made friends at the shelter. Mack Litton, an out-of-work welder with a wife and kids of his own, taught Billy how to play ball and became a kind of substitute father to him. Mack described Billy as "a nice, quiet kid . . . a boy who worried whether other people would laugh at him. He didn't have nice clothes, and he had never had a father to teach him how to do things. He didn't know how to throw a baseball or a football right, for example. No one had ever shown him how." The housing Billy's mother found was "nothing more than a <u>shack</u>." Billy called it a "raggedy house." On the Sunday before they were to leave the shelter and move into the "raggedy house," Billy hanged himself in a closet (Greene, 1989). (3)

In 1990, one out of every five American children lived in poverty. If current trends continue, it is predicted that by the year 2000, one out of every three children will live in poverty. Many other children (15.6 million) live in conditions (25 percent above the poverty line[2]) which are virtually similar to the living conditions of the official poor, but they are not technically considered <u>to be living</u> below the

official poverty line. A 1990 study, conducted by the National Center for Children in Poverty at Columbia University, examined families with children that were living in near-poverty conditions. The study found that "many of these families have as much difficulty as officially poor families. When we look closely at children living in near-poverty, we find they are often indistinguishable from children living in poverty" (UPI, 1990, April 16). (4)

For minority-group children the situation is even more drastic. An astonishing 43 percent of black and 37 percent of Hispanic children live below the poverty threshold. Eighteen and a half million children live in the central cities; 29 percent of them live in poverty. The majority (71 percent) of poor children live in families with two parents present, and with one or both parents working. (5)

A recent 300-page report by the House Select Committee on Children, Youth, and Families (Report: Children locked in poverty, 1989, October 3) found that children comprise the largest segment of the U.S. poverty population. Among children, the poverty rate has risen from 15 percent in 1970 to 20.5 percent in 1989. (6)

Current estimates of the number of homeless[3] children in America range from 50,000 to 3 million. Whatever the exact number, documentation now exists which indicates high rates of disease and <u>malnutrition</u> plague homeless children. Also, learning <u>disabilities</u> among homeless children <u>have been linked</u> to these conditions (United States GAO, 1989, June). (7)

## The Women

Over half (58 percent) of all the individuals who are poor are female. Women comprise the majority (65 percent) of all adults among the poverty population. Nearly half (48.5 percent) of the families in poverty have a female head of the household. (8)

Diana Pearce's research on poor women provides an outline of the dis-

tinctive nature of women's poverty. Maintaining that the poverty of women is "fundamentally different from that of men," Pearce points out that there are two distinctly *female* causes of women's poverty: (9)

1. Women overwhelmingly bear the economic as well as the emotional burdens of raising children when the parents do not live together. (10)
2. Women enter the labor market handicapped by their gender, and thus earn considerably less than men (Pearce, 1984). (11)

## The Elderly

In the past, people 65 years old and older—the elderly—constituted the largest specific age category among the poor. Over three decades ago, in 1959 the poverty rate among the elderly was 35.2 percent; today that rate has dropped to a historic low of 12 percent. (12)

Certainly, cost of living adjustments for Social Security,[4] the establishment of Supplemental Security Income (SSI) in 1974, and the expansion of private pension programs have all contributed to the reduction of poverty among the elderly. Nevertheless, some subgroups of the elderly population remain at high risk for entering the ranks of the poor. Again, gender and race play a role in producing disproportionate rates of poverty in some groups. Among the poor, the percentage of elderly women (15 percent) is almost double that of elderly men (8 percent). Compared to elderly whites, elderly Hispanics are two and one-half times (and elderly blacks over three times) more likely to be poor (Gabe, 1989:29). (13)

Although the number of elderly who live below the official poverty line has dropped, the economic position of millions of America's elderly citizens is, at best, very <u>precarious</u>. In addition to the elderly who fall below the poverty line, another one-fifth of the elderly

---

[1]shelter: a temporary place where the homeless can live or sometimes only sleep at night; usually provided by charitable organizations

[2]poverty line: the level of yearly income below which the government determines that a family of four is living in poverty; amount is periodically adjusted; also called *poverty threshold*

---

[3]homeless: living without a home, sometimes in cars, in public places, or in shelters

---

[4]social security: a government pension provided to people who have been employed during their adult lives; amount is based on ten years of highest earnings; periodically adjusted

hover just above it, existing at 125 percent of the poverty threshold. (14)

**Minorities**

A popular stereotype depicts most of the poor as nonwhite. Technically, that stereotype is false. The basis for it, however, stems from the fact that a disproportionate percentage of the poverty population is nonwhite. In other words, the majority (69 percent) of poor people are white, yet only 12 percent of the entire white population is poor. On the other hand, 28 percent of the poverty population is black, but blacks make up only 11.9 percent of the entire general population. People of Spanish origin comprise only 6 percent of the general population, but 12.5 percent of the poverty population is Hispanic. These disproportionate differences have persisted since the government began collecting poverty data. (15)

**The Working Poor**

Some people distinguish between what they term the "deserving poor" and the "undeserving poor," a distinction based on whether or not the poor person is working or willing to work. The person who works full- or part-time is often regarded more sympathetically by society and considered to be more "deserving" of assistance than a poor person who is unemployed. In the United States, approximately 9 million people could be classified among the working poor. Of these working poor, 2 million work full-time, an increase of 50 percent since 1968. Although the majority of the poor are children, women, and the elderly, 60 percent of able-bodied, poor adults work full-time, part-time, or seasonally (Whitman et al., 1988:19). (16)

During the last decade, the number of people who work, yet remain poor, has burgeoned; this fully discredits the common, comfortable stereotypes often used to depict the poor. Furthermore, from 1979 to 1984, 60 percent of all new jobs that were created paid less than $7000 a year, suggesting the causes of poverty are not to be found in the personal characteristics of those who are poor, but reach far beyond their control. (17)

**The Rural Poor**

Poverty remains a predominantly urban problem, if for no other reason than the fact that 75 percent of the general population lives in urban areas. Rural poverty, however, is becoming a growing concern. Indeed, the poor, inner-city black represents another common stereotype of American poverty. Yet, the poverty rate in America's rural areas is as great as that in the central cities, and 50 percent higher than that of the entire urban population (O'Hare, 1988). In the late 1980s, 17 percent of rural Americans lived below the official poverty line. These statistics indicate a reversal of the 20-year trend toward declining rural poverty and increasing urban poverty. One out of every four children in rural America lives in poverty. Again overrepresented, blacks constitute 44 percent of the rural poverty population. This fact contradicts the stereotype that black poverty is a problem that is confined to the inner cities. (18)

Ropers, 1991, pp. 43–52.

## ELABORATING ON THE READING

1. With two or three of your classmates, create a small table, chart, or graph that compiles some of the statistics given for one of the demographic groups mentioned above.

2. Now, compare the stereotypes that you underlined or highlighted in the passage with tables which illustrate the facts.

*LEARNING STRATEGY*

**Managing Your Learning: Increasing your opportunities to talk with native speakers increases your ability to speak and listen effectively in a second language.**

## Gathering Data: Going to the Library

Send representatives from your group to the library to find the following information. The library's information or reference desk, usually near the entrance, has a librarian who will be glad to direct you to the proper resources and help you find out what those resources are.

Find out:

- the current U.S. poverty line for a family of four
- the U.S. minimum wage
  After finding this dollar amount, multiply it times 40 (for hours/week) and then times four (for weeks/month). Now, multiply this amount by .75 (for an approximate tax rate of 25 percent). This new amount is the full-time, minimum wage worker's net monthly income. What do rents cost in your area?
- the amount of financial assistance your state will provide to a mother with two young children (You may find a range rather than an exact dollar amount.)
- how much financial assistance increases if the mother has another baby

What conclusions can you and your teammates draw from the information you have found?

### SHORT WRITING (150–200 WORDS)

Choose one of the categories from the reading above, and imagine that you are a member of that group who is under or near the poverty line. Write a letter to your local newspaper (intended for a middle-class audience), and explain why the stereotypes about you and poverty are not true.

## Taking the Idea Farther: Developing Ideas

**EXERCISE:** Form teams with three members, and brainstorm information to fill in the following chart. Team members should identify the poverty victims about whom they plan to write in their major essays.

| VICTIMS TO BE DESCRIBED | CAUSES OF THEIR POVERTY | SOLUTIONS TO THEIR POVERTY |
|---|---|---|
| 1. | | |
| 2. | | |

| VICTIMS TO BE DESCRIBED | CAUSES OF THEIR POVERTY | SOLUTIONS TO THEIR POVERTY |
|---|---|---|
| 3. | | |

## Making Your Draft Clearer: Writing Skills

### ORGANIZING BY CLASSIFYING

When a large amount of information is to be presented about a complicated topic, it is usually useful to *classify* that information. This is done by following one guiding principle by which items can be grouped.

For example, when analyzing poverty, we might choose to present information in several ways (the classifying principles are underlined):

   **a.** by discussing each <u>type of victim</u> (children, elderly, minorities)
   **b.** by grouping the <u>reasons for poverty</u> (economic, social, personal)
   **c.** by grouping the <u>effects of poverty on a society</u> (economic, social)

Notice that it would be inappropriate to write a portion of paper (c) on the *psychological* effects of poverty since that aspect violates our stated principle: the effects of poverty on a society. Psychological effects are personal.

Once a guiding principle for classifying is determined, the paper typically discusses one member of the group at a time, in a single paragraph or several paragraphs. The In-Depth Reading "Who Are the Poor" on page 127of this chapter, provides an example of classifying information.

**EXERCISE—Part A:**   Find principles by which you could classify the following information on poverty in an essay and present it in an organized manner.

   **1. a.** child care for working parents
      **b.** job training programs
      **c.** raising the minimum wage
      **d.** adult educational benefits

   _____

   **2. a.** African Americans
      **b.** Native Americans[1]
      **c.** Latin Americans
      **d.** Asian Americans

   _____

---

[1]Native Americans are also sometimes referred to as American Indians.

**3. a.** persons with disabilities
   **b.** senior citizens[2]
   **c.** women
   **d.** children

___

**4. a.** Americans with Disabilities Act[3] (1990)
   **b.** Family Support Act (1988)
   **c.** Stewart B. McKinney Homeless Assistance Act (1987)
   **d.** Job Training Partnership Act (1982)

___

**Part B:**   Determine which of the following pieces of information do not fit the guiding principles named, and cross them out. You may find some disagreements in your team.

**1.** U.S. presidents' policies toward the poor:
   **a.** John F. Kennedy
   **b.** Lyndon Johnson
   **c.** Martin Luther King
   **d.** Mother Theresa
   **e.** Ronald Reagan
   **f.** Bill Clinton

___

**2.** professionals who try to alleviate poverty:
   **a.** social workers
   **b.** teachers
   **c.** journalists
   **d.** lawmakers

___

**3.** ways of making formal national policies about poverty:
   **a.** laws
   **b.** court decisions
   **c.** traditions
   **d.** elections

___

**4.** ways poverty affects society:
   **a.** loss of human resources
   **b.** increased crime
   **c.** increased medical costs
   **d.** lost self-esteem

___

   Now go back to your draft and find places where you can classify information more clearly. Make changes where necessary.

___

[2]Senior citizen generally refers to someone over the age of 60.

[3]An "act" is a national government law:

## Making Your Draft Clearer: Writing Skills

### PHRASAL TRANSITIONS[1]

Just as simple transitions like *however, therefore,* and *in addition* can be useful in guiding your reader toward a clearer understanding of your ideas if used in moderation, so too can <u>phrasal transitions</u> increase the coherence of your writing. Phrasal transitions not only point out the direction of information that is coming next but also remind the reader of the paper's thesis or the previous paragraph's main idea. They serve to remind the reader of the main points of the paper by reaching back to show connections between paragraphs.

Examine the following topic sentences. From their phrasal transitions, you should be able to tell what the whole paper or the previous paragraph was about.

    **a.** <u>Another group often victimized by poverty</u> is Native Americans.
    **b.** <u>Not only are women more often victims of poverty</u>, but so are children.
    **c.** <u>In addition to court decisions,</u> laws are formulated to enact poverty policies.

Sometimes, you may wish to write a whole sentence as transition:

    **d.** <u>There are even more complicated reasons for poverty than these</u>.
    **e.** <u>The business of creating poverty policies is also done in another important way.</u>

Now look at the following paragraphs, and identify the phrasal transition. How does it summarize? How does it lead the reader forward?

> Higher wages for men after World War II were truly a great achievement, but another effect of men's growing ability to support a family was the tendency not to regard female workers as serious workers. Younger women were believed to be working only until they found a husband or had a child.
>
> All of this allowed employers to treat women as second class workers and pay them less than men were paid. (Mattera, 1990, p. 141)

**EXERCISE:** Add phrasal transitions at the beginnings of the marked paragraphs in the passage below.

    **1.** One of the main causes of hunger worldwide is resource abuse. Human beings have a centuries-long history of resource destruction, most especially in the past century. There have been great resource losses in the U.S., Africa, central India, Latin America and in the Pacific Rim because of ignorance and neglect. The search for profit has led to numerous losses in land, forests,

---

[1]Please look at "Simple Transitions" in Chapter 4 for a review of when and how to use transitions.

water, and soil resources. As industries continue to try to satisfy consumption, the resulting damage reduces the earth's capacity to provide food for its inhabitants.

_____

_____

. . . there is very little usable soil on the earth's surface. Only twenty-five percent of the earth's surface is dry land. Of this amount, one fifth is too cold to cultivate, one fifth is too high, and one fifth is too dry. Thus, only 10 percent of the earth's surface remains, but some of this land is of very poor quality or too wet to cultivate crops. (Freudenberger, 1982, p. 90–91)

2. Some people would like to think that the relationship between poverty and employment is very simple: eliminate poverty by providing everyone with a job. However, it isn't this simple. Actually, a large number of people with a job find themselves in poverty anyway.

_____

_____

Economic security depends on how much one works and how much one earns for the work he does. In general, only those who work full-time throughout the year find themselves above the poverty line, though they may find themselves perilously close to it. (Schiller, 1989, p. 64)

3. Prejudice against low-income persons exists in any society. Many theorists contended in nineteenth-century England, for example, that persons in the lower class possessed character faults which caused them to have innumerable children, engage in crime, and be alcoholic.

_____

_____

One of the well-respected founding fathers of the United States, Benjamin Franklin, argued that "it seems to be a law of nature, that the poor should be to a certain degree improvident . . ." Americans have often believed that poor persons possess cultural predispositions that contribute to their economic status. As a matter of fact, they were thought to possess inferior genes. (Jansson, 1993, p. 332)

## Making Your Draft Clearer: Language Skills

### PASSIVE AND ACTIVE VERBS

We can think of the basic English sentence as having three parts:

- the do-er, the person or thing that does the action in the sentence
- the action, the verb

• the receiver, the person or thing that receives the action of the verb

**EXAMPLE:** The poor experience poverty.
*do-er/subj.* *action/verb* *receiver/object*

It's very common for the do-er to be the subject and the receiver to be the object, as in the above sentence.

Sometimes, however, we don't want to mention the do-er *or* we want to emphasize the receiver by moving it to the front of the sentence. In this case, we have to signal to our readers that we are putting the receiver in the subject position by changing the verb form. This change involves two steps: adding a form of the verb *be* and changing the main verb to the past participle form. We call this new verb form a *passive verb*.

**EXAMPLE:** Poverty is experienced by the poor.
*receiver/subject* *action/passive verb* *do-er*

If the do-er remains in the sentence, it is placed at the end and introduced with "by." In this sentence, we can ask "Who experiences?" If the answer is "the poor," then "poverty" is not the do-er, and the verb must be passive.

Practice this test with the following sentences. What should the correct verb form be?

1. Every social agency (develops) policies of its own to combat poverty. (Who/what develops?)
2. High rates of economic inequality (have tolerated) over the decades. (Who/what has tolerated?)
3. Some poverty policies (imply) in the preambles of many pieces of social legislation. (Who/what implies?)
4. Social workers (must decide) how to implement specific policies. (Who/what must decide?)

We can summarize this as follows. When the <u>do-er is the subject</u> of the sentence, use a regular verb form. When the <u>receiver is the subject</u> of the sentence, change the verb form to passive by adding the appropriate tense of the verb *be* and the past participle of the main verb.

When *forming* the passive we use a form of the verb *be* and the *past participle* of the main verb, no matter what the tense is. If the verb tense requires a helping verb (such as *have/has/had, can/will/should*), the form of *be* agrees with the helping verb before it. Otherwise, the form of *be* is either past or present. For example:

*is* taken
    (present, singular)
*are* taken
    (present, plural and "you")
*was* taken
    (present, singular)
were taken
    (present, plural)

*are being* taken
*were being* taken

has *been* taken
    (present perfect, singular)
have *been* taken
    (present perfect, plural)

will *be* taken
    (future, plural and singular)
can *be* taken
    (present, plural and singular)

to *be* taken

Notice that using the passive involves adding at least two words to the sentence (a form of *be* and *by*) if the do-er is included, and that it also reverses the normal order of the English sentence by putting the do-er last. Since two qualities of good writing are economy of words and directness, we use passive voice only when we are unable or unwilling to name the do-er or when we have a good reason to emphasize the receiver.

**EXERCISE 1—Checking the Form:** In the following passage, a number of verb phrases are underlined. Examine these with a partner and determine whether the phrases should be passive or active. Make changes where necessary. Use the test described above as an aid.

In its broadest social sense, social welfare policy represents a collective strategy to address social problems. Collective strategy <u>is created</u> by laws, rules, regulations, and budgets of government. . . . To understand how Americans <u>have been addressed</u> social problems in the past, various social welfare policy responses need to be identified.

Some social welfare strategies involve public policies, laws which <u>enact</u> in local, state, or federal legislatures. [*handwritten: are / have been enacted by*] The Chinese Exclusion Act of 1882, the Social Security Act of 1935, the Adoption Assistance and Child Welfare Act of 1980, and the Americans with Disabilities Act of 1991 are examples of public laws, as are state and local laws that established poorhouses and mental institutions in the nineteenth century.

Court decisions play important roles in American social policy. By overruling, upholding, and interpreting statutes of legislatures, policies <u>are established</u> in courts that significantly influence the American response to social needs. For example, in the 1980s, the courts <u>required</u> the Reagan administration to award disability benefits to many disabled persons even though many administration officials <u>were opposed</u> this policy.

Budget and spending programs are a kind of policy as well since it is difficult for society to respond to specific social problems if resources <u>are not allocated</u> to social programs and institutions. In understanding the response of Americans to social needs, for example, it is important to know that

Americans ~~are chosen~~ *Chose* not to expend a major share of their gross national

product on social spending prior to the 1930s but greatly increased levels of

spending in the Great Depression and succeeding decades. (Jansson, 1993,

p. 3-4)

Now go back to your draft, and check your verbs. Have you used the passive
form where necessary? Have you used it unnecessarily? Make changes where appropriate.

## Reflecting on Draft One

1. Highlight or underline the most useful facts you were able to include in your
   essay.

   _____

   _____

2. List a few places where your paper would be more effective if you could add
   more specific facts or statistics. How can you find this information?

   _____

   _____

3. Imagine that you are a reader of this paper rather than its author. How would
   this paper influence your opinions on its topic?

   _____

   _____

4. Imagine that your reader is from outside your culture. Are there any places in
   your paper that may require a bit more background information about your
   culture in order for your reader to understand?

   _____

   _____

**5.** Imagine that your reader's opinions about poverty are exactly opposite yours. Are there any places in your paper where you based your explanation on assumptions that your reader would have the same basic opinions as you?

_____

_____

# PART III: WRITING THE SECOND DRAFT

Revise the first draft of your major essay. In particular, concentrate on improving the quality of the information you provide, taking into account the various perspectives your reader may have about poverty and the ways your reader may react to your information based on his or her perspective. In addition, guide your reader's understanding by providing both simple and phrasal transitions. Check also to be sure that you have used passive verbs where necessary.

## FURTHER READING

**Vocabulary Enrichment**

### LEARNING STRATEGY

**Managing Your Learning: When trying to learn new vocabulary, you will often find it a useful memory aid to classify the words according to some similarity that they share. For example, in Chapter 5 you grouped words according to _roughness_ and _gentleness_.**

**EXERCISE 1:** Glance through the following passage noticing in particular the underlined words. List below those words underlined in the passage that are used to refer to each of the following.

**Housing**

1. _____

2. _____

3. _____

4. _____

**Losing or maintaining good health**

1. _____

2. _____

3. _____

**Government actions**

1. _____

2. _____

**Formal statistical data**

1. _____

2. _____

3. _____

4. _____

**Remember Your
Vocabulary Checklist!**

When you thought of the United States in the past, how did you imagine its standard of living to be? The following passage describes what a group of physicians found when they visited a poor area of Greenwood, Mississippi, in southern United States. While it is not representative of the average U.S. standard of living, such poverty does exist in the U.S. Their guide is a woman named Joie, who is a social worker and lives in the area. Are there areas such as this in your country? As you read this, try to imagine why the people of Greenwood find themselves in this situation.

## *LEARNING STRATEGY*

**Remembering New Information: As you read, do your best to create visual images in your mind of the action in the reading, as if you were watching a movie. This will help you understand the reading better and remember it longer.**

# A killer in the deep South

The image of the baby remained vivid in my mind as I tried to sleep. She was the first thing I saw as I entered the <u>dilapidated</u> house in Greenwood, Mississippi, that morning, a tiny creature whose brown skin was dusty and uncovered. She lay whimpering on a torn mattress as her little brother tried to put an empty bottle in her mouth while swatting at the flies around her face. (1)

An older girl stood in the doorway, silent and uncomfortable as the intruding doctors entered. Her father rose from his chair, gesturing to one of the visitors to take his seat, but no one moved. Behind him stood the mother, next to a pile of clothing that rose from the floor to the height of my eyes. (2)

My mind raced to keep up with the visual images my eyes recorded: a small mass of humanity existing in a <u>condemned</u> house, with no front door, no windows, no plumbing, a worn sofa, two beds without covers, a dirty blanket piled on a chair, and a bright yellow balloon. (3)

"These people are <u>starving</u>," said Joie Kammer, the seventy-seven-year-old worker from the St. Francis Center, our guide for the three-day field trip to the Mississippi Delta. The doctors had no reason to disagree. Joie had virtually adopted the family and had been supplying them with dried beans and other food items for several weeks. "It seems like I just can't do enough," Joie observed. "They got no job, no money, no food stamps."[1] (4)

In May 1984, government statistics placed unemployment in the area at 16 percent. A quarter of the state population lived in poverty, and very few of them received any aid. Some 300,000 poor residents were left out of the food stamp program. This family was among them. (5)

They had <u>subsisted</u> on handouts for almost two months. Their food stamp application had been held up because the father could not verify his recent income. Employers did not pay him by check for his odd jobs,[2] and federal rules designed to prevent cheating did not permit his personal declaration of income. "They're slowly starving," Joie repeated. "Sometimes I wish there could be a little bit of cheating so people like this could get food." (6)

As we left I was the first to exit the house, more to relieve my senses than to keep the team of doctors on schedule. Stepping to avoid the hole in the porch, I turned to the parents as we left, but I found that I had no idea what to

say. I muttered something and walked to the car. (7)

### Just Like South Africa

Everything is vivid in Mississippi. We drove down long roads of rich farmland, where cotton and soybean crops have been grown for two hundred years. Suddenly the panorama is broken by a stand of trees with a big house and several little <u>shacks</u> trailing off to the side, the homes for black families who have lived in the unheated <u>dwellings</u> for decades. (8)

Signs proudly display the names of the plantations. Little attempt is made to hide, excuse, or change the enormous <u>disparity</u> between rich and poor in this state. Most of the residents have lived in this environment for so long that they defend it without shame. "There's no hunger here," one local physician told us, generalizing from his wealthy patients to the poor he never treats. "Every specimen I see is fat and shiny." (9)

Hunger is easy to find for those willing to go into the homes of the poor. So are the other problems that accompany it, because people don't just get to be hungry in Mississippi without having other things wrong in their lives—dilapidated housing, no health care, no jobs. We saw <u>substantial</u> numbers of people whose lives are crippled by poverty and racism, lives that cannot be easily repaired. But the people we saw are also hungry, and that is a problem easier to remedy. (10)

### The Faces of Death

We were taken by the volunteer drivers to McClure's Alley, which is not really an alley, but a short dead-end dirt road within the town of Greenwood. Rows of six or seven houses face one another on each side. With white shacks with peeling paint and children sitting on the porches next to old-fashioned wringer washing machines, the place looked like something out of a Faulkner novel. (11)

Standing in the center of the dusty road, Joie called out to the residents who knew her as the social worker at the St. Francis Center: "We got here a group of doctors who have come from up North

to talk to you about your problems," she drawled. "They're good people, so let them in to talk with you and tell them what they want to know." (12)

We split into small groups, some going inside the houses and others talking with people on their porches. Gordon and I briefly spoke to a youngster playing in front of his home before a camera crew filming our conversation scared him into silence. (13)

We approached a woman on her porch; she was perhaps seven months pregnant. Her other child listened as we explained who we were. The mother had lost a baby the year before but didn't know exactly what caused the death. Her total monthly income consisted of $60 in food stamps, on which she tried to feed herself, her unborn child and a five-year-old son. We asked to go in the house, thinking she might be embarrassed to talk in front of the ever-present cameras. However, the camera crew followed us in as we went to the kitchen. (14)

After asking permission, Gordon opened the refrigerator to find three sticks of butter. In a cupboard were some dried beans. Nothing more to eat was in the house. The woman had had no milk for several days and her son had a cup the day before. She answered questions but ventured no information otherwise. (15)

"When did you last have milk?" I asked. (16)

"Day or two ago," she answered.

"How about your son?"

"Yesterday morning. He had a little yesterday morning."

"Are you hungry?" I asked.

"Yes, sir."

"Do you have any food besides the dried beans?"

"No, sir."

Formal politeness, no anger, no effort to tell it all. Nothing about her fears, about the infant she carried. Nothing about the baby who had died a year before. (17)

"What you're looking at are the faces of infant <u>mortality</u> statistics," I remarked to Steve Curwood, who asked me what I thought about what we had

[1] food stamps: coupons provided by the government to the poor for buying food

[2] odd jobs: short-term (perhaps a few days) jobs that generally pay little

seen. The faces behind the numbers that appear in government mortality data were staring at us from the porches of the little street. Steve nodded; one did not have to be a medical expert to see the connection. (18)

An hour later the change of location brought different skin color but not radically different circumstances. We met seventy-year-old Emma Ferris, who lived in an apartment and, by her own description, used to be middle class. Photographs around her apartment seemed to confirm her life had once been more comfortable. (19)

Bill Beardslee spoke with her at length, learning that Emma had been cut off the supplemental security income program for reasons she did not quite understand. When her daughter died of leukemia she sold her car, and this "income" apparently made her ineligible. She was to repay the money but had no income to do so. As she described her situation her grandmotherly disposition masked the problems she faced. While Bill spoke to her I opened the refrigerator to find four eggs, bread, mayonnaise, and a jar of honey. (20)

Emma Ferris cannot walk, but she is a resourceful woman. She somehow managed to plant a small garden that she was hoping would provide more food than she had on the day we visited her in May. How, we asked, does she get outside to the garden? We were startled to hear her answer: "I crawl." (21)

I remember feeling as if I could crawl from the house of this woman. So stressed did I feel at what we were finding in the Delta that I felt overwhelmed, but Ms. Ferris somehow made me ashamed to succumb to it all. She faced difficulty every day; she had little food, she couldn't even walk, yet she maintained a pleasant disposition even if her tone masked what the psychiatrist with me found to be deep depression. (22)

Maxine and Naomi made a house call to the Yates family, a white couple with three children living on a plantation near Phillips. Jerry, the father, brings home just over two dollars an hour working as a farmhand. The family gets some food stamps but has no medical coverage. Two of the children have seizure disorders that require regular medications which the family cannot afford. They owe $5,000 at the county hospital for one stay the prior autumn. (23)

"After we pay for rent, utilities, and medical bills there ain't[3] much left," the mother noted. "The kids get hungry, but what can I do?" (24)

Maxine inquired about the metal barrel which served as a wood stove. It looked like an accident waiting to happen, being neither safe nor efficient. "We all sleep in one room during the winter," the mother offered. "Last year we lost our house to a fire." (25)

Nearby lived seventy-six-year-old Laura Jane Allen, who had a social security income of $189 and got a bonus of $10 in food stamps. For days before our arrival she had eaten only peas, beans, and bread. Her weight was down considerably. (26)

"How are you feeling?" Naomi inquired. (27)

"Well, I got high blood pressure, I guess. The doctor, he say I'm suppose' to have fresh vegetables and fish, and to stay away from salt." The old woman paused before completing her response. "But I jus' can't buy them things on my money."[3] (28)

Laura Jane continued to eat what she could afford, a diet rich in the things which bring an earlier death. She was already older than most, but her health was going downhill for no good reason. We had seen many others that day who were far younger, who were experiencing the same fateful process. Hunger had become a real killer in the Delta. (29)

Brown and Pizer, 1987, p. 39-50.

[3]ain't, he say, them things: ungrammatical language often used by poorly educated people and some other speakers

---

**Remembering New Material: Check your understanding of the reading by speaking aloud its main points. Verbally repeating the most important information about a reading when you finish is a form of rehearsal that can help you check your understanding and remember the new information better.**

## Threads

**Only about 12% of American families have an employed father and a stay-at-home mother.**

*Prosperity Lost*

## ELABORATING ON THE READING

Discuss the following questions with at least two of your classmates.

1. What reasons were you able to discern directly from the reading to explain these people's poverty? Point to particular paragraphs to support your answers.
2. What reasons are you able to infer indirectly from the reading to explain these people's poverty? Point to particular paragraphs which provide the bases for your inferences.
3. Refer again to the categories of the poor mentioned in "Who Are the Poor?" in Part II of this chapter. Which categories are represented in "Killer in the Deep South"?
4. The author of this article has a great deal of sympathy for the impoverished people he describes. Point out some of the places where the sympathy is evident.
5. Why do you think the authors of the book from which "Killer in the Deep South" was taken wrote this passage? List as many reasons as you can.
6. How successful do you think the authors are, assuming you are correct in your evaluation of their purposes? What makes this passage successful or not, in your opinion?

## SHORT WRITING (150–200 WORDS)

The author of "Killer in the Deep South" shows a lot of sympathy for the people he describes in his writing. Imagine that you are a more conservative person who has little sympathy for most poor people. This article appears biased to you. Write to the author, and express the anger you feel at his uneven treatment of his subject. Suggest ways in which the author could provide a more balanced description of the situation. You might consider additions of information, deletions, and changes in language.

Go back to your major essay draft. Are there any examples from "Killer in the Deep South" that you could summarize in your draft to make it stronger or more interesting?

## Making Your Draft Clearer: Language Skills

## SENTENCE FRAGMENTS AND RUN-ON SENTENCES

If you were to program a computer to recognize English sentences, you would want the computer to recognize three separate components:

- the subject: the word or phrase which does the action of the verb and that controls the form of the verb
- the verb: the word or phrase that names the action or condition controlled by the subject
- the verb tense: the time reflected by the form of the verb, past, present, or future

We could then construct a formula for the computer to follow:

$$Sentence = Subject + Verb\ [+ tense]$$

Therefore, any collection of words that is missing a subject, verb, or verb tense could not be defined as a sentence.

The definition of a clause could be given in the same way:

$$Clause = Subject + Verb\ [+ tense]$$

The difference between clauses and sentences is only that clauses are linked together to form sentences. We do this by adding a fourth component, a <u>connector</u>. The purpose of a connector is exactly what its name implies; it connects at least two clauses together (some connectors can connect simpler phrases too). Consider the following examples. In each, identify the *connector, clauses, subjects,* and *verbs.*

1. When women suffer financial hardship, their children are affected. (Mattera, 1990, p. 143)
2. Fewer than 15 percent of divorced women are awarded alimony, and only 3 percent of the total actually receive their payments. (Mattera, 1990, p. 138)
3. The poverty rate for black women who head households while they work is about 32 percent. (Mattera, 1990, p. 139)

Notice each clause is complete in that it has a subject, verb, and verb tense. In addition, there is a connector each time an *additional* clause is written. So, for example, sentences 1 and 2 have two clauses and one connector apiece. Sentence 3 has three clauses and two connectors. Can you guess how many connectors would be necessary in a sentence with four clauses? five? 100? The answer is that you will virtually always need one fewer connector than the number of clauses in your sentence. This is because every English sentence must have one clause that is not introduced by a connector. (This is the independent clause.) Every other clause must be linked to the independent clause with a connector. (These are the dependent or subordinate clauses.)

## FRAGMENTS AND RUN-ONS

There are several ways that English sentences can be considered incomplete (fragments) or excessive (run-ons). Among them:

a. The sentence lacks one of the three essential components of a sentence (subject, verb, or verb tense).
b. The sentence has too many connectors (no independent clause).
c. The sentence has more than one clause but lacks a connector.
d. Two sentences are connected with a comma (,) which is incorrect in English.

Following is a list of connectors and transition words to help you determine whether your sentences are structurally correct. The connectors in the first two columns, coordinators and subordinators, are used to connect clauses. The last column summarizes transition words for you.

A Partial List of Connecting Words

| | COORDINATORS (with clauses) | SUBORDINATORS (with clauses) | CONNECTIVES (with phrases) | TRANSITION WORDS |
|---|---|---|---|---|
| **Time** | and | after<br>as<br>by the time<br>as soon as<br>before<br>since<br>until<br>when<br>whenever<br>while<br>if | after<br><br>as soon as<br>before<br>since<br>until | then,<br>afterward,<br>later on, |
| **Reason** | and<br>for | because<br>since<br>so that<br>in order that | because of<br>due to<br><br>(in order) to | |
| **Manner** | | as if<br>as<br>as though<br>how<br>however (in any way) | | |
| **Condition** | | as long as<br>if<br>in case<br>provided that<br>supposing<br>unless<br>whether (or not) | in case of | |
| **Result** | so<br>and | so (adj.) that<br>such (a) (N) that | | consequently,<br>as a result, hence,<br>therefore,<br>for this reason,<br>accordingly, |
| **Contrast** | but<br><br>yet<br>or<br>nor | although<br>while<br>though<br>even though<br>in spite of the fact that<br>despite the fact that | instead of<br><br><br><br>in spite of<br>despite | however,<br>on the other hand,<br>nevertheless,<br>on the contrary, |
| **Addition** | and<br>both . . . and<br>either . . . or<br>not only . . . but also<br>neither . . . nor | that, who, which,<br>whose,<br>why, what,<br>whatever,<br>whoever,<br>how much/many | | moreover,<br>furthermore,<br>also, besides,<br>in fact,<br>in addition,<br>for this reason,<br>as a matter of fact, |

144

**EXERCISE 1:** Practice identifying the components of the following complex sentences. Identify connectors, clauses, subjects, and verbs with tenses.

   **A.** A popular stereotype depicts most of the poor as nonwhite. Technically, that stereotype is false. The basis for it, however, stems from the fact that a disproportionate percentage of the poverty population is non-white. In other words, the majority (69 percent) of poor people are white, yet only 12 percent of the entire white population is poor. On the other hand, 28 percent of the poverty population is black, but blacks make up only 11.9 percent of the entire general population. People of Spanish origin comprise only 6 percent of the general population, but 12.5 percent of the poverty population is Hispanic. These disproportionate differences have persisted since the government began collecting poverty data. (Ropers, 1991, pp. 48-49)

   **B.** Although the number of elderly who live below the official poverty line has dropped, the economic position of millions of America's elderly citizens is, at best, very precarious. In addition to the elderly who fall below the poverty line, another one-fifth of the elderly hover just above it, existing at 125 percent of the poverty threshold. (Ropers, 1991, pp. 47-48)

   **C.** Many women lack medical care because they lack money. About one in six women of childbearing age has no health insurance, public or private. When those with health insurance that does not cover maternity benefits are taken into account, approximately 25 percent are completely unprotected against the cost of prenatal care. (Mattera, 1990, p. 145)

**EXERCISE 2:** Go back to the working draft of your paper. Choose one paragraph, and analyze each of the sentences in that paragraph, identifying the subjects, verbs, and connectors in those sentences. Have you used enough connectors? too many? Are there any missing subjects or verbs? Make any changes necessary. Discuss any questions you have with your instructor. Then go on to check the rest of your draft for fragments and run-ons.

# ALTERNATIVES FOR CORRECTING FRAGMENTS

As has been implied above, one simple way to correct a fragment is to insert the missing component (subject, verb, or connector). Another alternative, however, when the subject or connector is missing, is to change the form of the verb <u>from a main verb to a describing verb</u> using -ed for passive verbs or -ing for active verbs. Look at the following examples. (The asterisk [*] indicates poorly structured sentences.)

1. *Two of the children have seizure disorders require medications.

    *to:*

    Two of the children have seizure disorders *that* require medications.

    *or:*

    Two of the children have seizure disorders *requiring* medications.

2. *There is a need for basic changes in the social and economic conditions of many citizens, provide a reason for drastically increasing the size of the American welfare state.

    *to:*

    There is a need for basic changes in the social and economic conditions of many citizens, *which* provides a reason for drastically increasing the size of the welfare state.

    *or:*

    There is a need for basic changes in the social and economic conditions of many citizens, *providing* a reason for drastically increasing the size of the American welfare state.

3. *We do not know how many of the social problems inflict would be alleviated if the country spent all the money necessary to cure them.

    *to:*

    We do not know how many of the social problems that are *inflicted* would be alleviated if the country spent all the money necessary to cure them.

    *or:*

    We do not know how many of the social problems *inflicted* would be alleviated if the country spent all the money necessary to cure them.

    Turn to Chapter 4, Reduction of Adverb Clauses, for additional information.

## Making Your Draft Clearer: Language Skills

### A SPECIAL USE OF *THE*

There is one very specific use of the definite article *the* which allows writers to use adjectives as if they were plural nouns referring to groups of people. Look at the following examples.

EXAMPLES:    Some people believe that *the poor* are responsible for their own poverty. (*The poor* refers to the members of the group "poor people.")

*The elderly* are especially susceptible to poverty since they typically live on fixed incomes. (*The elderly* refers to the members of the group "elderly people.")

Notice in each case that the article *the* is used along with an adjective that functions as a noun. When this new nounlike form is used as the subject of the sentence, it is plural. Below are other sample words which, when used with *the,* function as nouns. Can you think of more?

| | |
|---|---|
| the rich | the powerful |
| the homeless | the unemployed / the employed |
| the disabled | the helpless |
| the poverty-stricken | the impoverished |
| the sick | the abandoned |

*NOTE:*    With nationality adjectives, this method only works if the adjective ends in one of the *-s* sounding suffixes. These include *-ese, -ch,* and *-ish.* For example, we can write "the Japanese, the French, and the British" to mean the members of these groups of people. We cannot write "the American, the New Zealander," or the Philippino," for example, unless we mean them as generic singulars. (See p. 103 for an explanation of the generic use of *the.*)

EXERCISE:    Check over your draft now. Have you used adjectives in this way? Be sure you've written *the* before them. Have you used the word *people* too often? Can you use an adjective with *the* instead? Make changes where appropriate.

## Editing Strategy: Nemesis Errors

Aside from editing by blocking off all but one line of your text and reading your text aloud, another way to edit efficiently is to look for particular types of errors that you know you are prone to making. Do you often make verb tense mistakes? fragments? spelling errors? Read your essay one time for each of the types of errors you make most often. Don't try to look for all your errors at once because you'll be sure to miss many. If you concentrate on examining only the verbs in your sentences, for example, you'll have a better chance of finding your verb errors and correcting them. Then you can edit again for another of your most common error types.

EXERCISE:    Edit your second draft by looking for your nemesis errors. Read your paper once for each type of error you make often. You will increase the efficiency of your editing if you combine this strategy with one or both of the strategies described in Chapters 4 and 5 (blocking off lines and reading aloud). A partial list of error types follows to help you focus on your most common problems.

**PARTIAL CHECKLIST OF ERROR TYPES**

- verb endings
- singular/plural nouns
- word order
- articles (a/an, the)
- fragments/run-ons
- spelling
- endings for part of speech (noun, verb, adj., or adv.)

## Student Writing: Practice Peer Response

The following essay was written by a student from Vietnam. In it she makes use of research to describe the plight of a particular homeless person whom she refers to as H.M. Homeless people live on the streets of cities rather than in apartments or houses for a variety of reasons, both social and personal. Sometimes even whole families with children are homeless.

After you finish reading the essay, fill out the peer response that follows to analyze it. Your instructor may ask you to do this with or without your classmates and may provide additional questions.

### H.M., A HOMELESS MAN

*Oanh Nguyen*

1 "They lack the political and cultural power to correct the stereotypes that other people hold of them and thus continue to be thought of as lazy people, spendthrifts, etc. . . ." (Gans, 1991, p. 330) Society sees only the most visible members of this class: the addicts, alcoholics, and the homeless, and forgets why people live this way. Only a small number choose to do so; the majority live this way because they do not have jobs. Poverty dominates the lower class and they are the most despised. Stereotyping can, in fact, harm the reputations of many innocent people. Such stereotypes do not benefit anyone. They can destroy the beliefs and trust that people have in each other. Stereotyping is a factor that contributes to separation among groups and individuals.

2 Poverty is not a disgrace; it is an unfortunate situation that can afflict anyone. For example, take a case such as an accident crippling a man, who, as a result, loses his job. Obviously this man is being discredited for his ability to perform his job; for this reason, he falls into despair and loses everything that he has ever owned.

3    In order to understand what this man has gone through, I will attempt to describe his lifestyle and the conditions that he has lived through since the accident. I will refer to this man as H.M.

4    In poor health, with little chance of improving his life, he is socially isolated and suffers from low self-esteem. Unless H.M. finds some way to regain all the possessions that he has lost, he will continue to live in an impoverished state. But for now, H.M. is living as a homeless man (where the street is his home), and his only possessions are the clothes that he has on. Every day he moves from one area to another in hope of finding a place to sleep (shelter from the freezing winter and shade from the hot, blazing sun). The basic necessities such as food, shelter, clothing, and health care do not come so easily to H.M. Finding enough to eat is a daily struggle. His only means of survival is the amount of change that others can spare (the amount he receives varies daily). How much he eats (and sometimes he doesn't eat at all) depends on how much change he gets a day. All day long, H.M. loiters in front of a market. He patiently awaits a shopper to enter or exit the market. Attentively watching, H.M. then approaches a shopper and politely asks for some spare change. With no stable source of income, H.M. panhandles all day long with uncertainty, never knowing whether he will have a bite to eat just for this day. Not only is H.M. suffering from malnutrition, but also from the lack of medical care. Having no home and, therefore, no address, H.M. cannot apply for medical care even though there are some medical facilities that are open to the public at low or no cost. These facilities are understaffed and low on supplies and equipment. Under these circumstances, I can imagine how difficult it is for H.M. to receive any care any time soon. My guess is that he will be assigned a number on a long waiting list. This situation is more or less like the temporary shelters for the homeless. Shelters are operating on tight budgets similar to the medical facilities. Because they are usually supported by charitable organizations, these shelters face the same problems of being understaffed and lacking supplies. If there were any programs that could help him, I think he would get help. For now, H.M. is condemned to a life of uncertainty.

5    Are people interested in helping someone like H.M. and others in similar situations? Personally, I think that there are some people who are really dedicated to helping others, but a majority are more concerned with their own lives. It is a struggle for everyone to work and support themselves and, in addition to that, they have to contribute part of their earnings to help others (in the form of taxes). I can understand the frustrations, but if the world is to live in harmony, then everyone must work together to lend a helping hand. In addition to this, people who hold authority positions in government should make it their responsibilities to be considerate of people living in poverty. "Solving the problems of poverty in the world, or even within the United States, is not a simple task. For the world, it would involve a change of the U.S. government's policy of providing more weapons than welfare. Here, it would involve changing the way we view the poor and supporting programs for better housing and education, as well as full employment at decent wages—the only real cure for poverty." (McNall and McNall, 256.)

*Sources*

Gans, J. Herbert. "The Uses of Poverty: The Poor Pay All." *Down to Earth Sociology,* 6th ed. Ed. James M. Henslin. New York: Macmillan, Inc., 1991, pp. 327-333.

McNall, G. Scott, and Sally Allen McNall, *Sociology.* Ed. Nancy Robert. Englewood Cliffs, N.J.: Prentice-Hall, Inc., 1992, p. 256.

## Threads

Based on gross domestic product (GDP) per person in 1988, the richest nation in the world was Switzerland ($27,748 per person), and the poorest was Mozambique, $78 per person) followed by Cambodia ($83 per person). The United States' GDP was $19,815 per person.

Rand McNally, *Almanac of World Facts*

**EXERCISE:**   Now, trade your paper with one of your classmate's papers and complete the same peer response after reading it.

## Peer Response to Draft Two

1. Tell the author what you think his or her purpose was in writing about this topic.

   _____

   _____

2. Tell the author your own opinion about this topic.

   _____

   _____

3. Tell the author about any places in his or her paper where you disagreed or were confused.

   _____

   _____

4. Tell the author about any places in his or her paper that you think were especially well done. Explain why.

   _____

   _____

5. Ask the author one question about his or her topic.

   _____

   _____

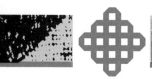

# PART IV: WRITING DRAFT THREE AND ASSESSING YOUR LEARNING

In Part IV, you will once again revise your essay. As you are doing so, be sure to consider your peer reviewer's comments, your teacher's comments, and any changes you have been planning. In addition, check the following things:

- Have you managed to use some phrases in your writing of which you can be proud? If not, revise to add some.
- Are you confident of your sentence structure? Are your sentences varied in both length and structure? If not, make changes to show a variety of sentence complexities.
- Have you adequately considered potentially opposing points of view when expressing your information? If not, make changes.

## Punctuation Note: Punctuating Clauses

You have already learned that a clause in English is composed of at least a subject and a verb with tense (with commands, the subject is assumed to be "you"). The way that you choose to combine clauses determines not only whether you will need to use a connector but also whether you will need punctuation between the clauses and, if so, what kind. There are four ways to combine clauses, each with its own style of punctuation.

1. *With simple transitions, use a period or semicolon before, a comma after:*

   The well-being of children depends on the economic condition of their parents; unfortunately, the parents are not doing very well nowadays. (Jansson, 1993, p. 304)

   There were many budget cuts in poverty programs in the 1980s. However, for the most part the elderly managed to evade these cuts. (Jansson, 1993, p. 306)

2. *Between two independent clauses (without connectors) use a semicolon:*

   Aging Americans appear to have improved their condition in the 1970s and 1980s; rates of poverty decreased sharply in this population, from 35 to 12.8 percent between 1959 and 1989. (Jansson, 1993, p. 306)

3. *Between a dependent clause (with a connector) followed by an independent clause, use a comma:*

   **Though** the welfare state remained intact and specific programs within it grew considerably from 1980 through 1992, the actual economic position of poor persons worsened because of lowered wages, reductions in social benefits, and increased taxes. (Jansson, 1993, p. 298)

4. *Between an independent clause (without a connector) followed by a dependent clause, use no comma:*

   In the 1980s, elderly persons paid roughly 50% of their medical costs **because** consumer fees associated with Medicare were so high and so many services were not covered. (Jansson, 1993, p. 306)

## Student Writing for Further Discussion

The following essay was written by a young man from Taiwan. In it, he makes use of research to show why women are so often the victims of poverty and to discuss ways of alleviating the "feminization of poverty."

### THE FEMINIZATION OF POVERTY

*Ronald Chen*

Why do women have a higher chance of being in poverty than any other group that is classified as poor? For one, in present day America, women are being treated unfairly at work. Because of this unfair treatment, they have a higher risk of becoming poor than men do. In order to provide better service to help the American women in poverty, equal participation in the government is needed to change the laws. Although there's no one answer to how to stop poverty, there are ways to alleviate it.

**Threads**

Sixty-one percent of divorced women with children under 21 years old are awarded child support by the courts from the father, but only one third of these women actually receive any of this money.

*Prosperity Lost*

2 The foremost thing women need to escape poverty is to have equality in the society. The stereotype about women not being able to perform as well as, or better than, men in certain jobs is the central cause for the lower wages women receive. As women constitute a major percentage of the people who live in poverty, once equality has been achieved, a much lower percentage of women will be in poverty. In the past, women have increased their participation in the labor force from 29.6 percent to 44.8 percent between 1950 and 1987. (U.S. Department of Labor, 1989) In 1980, 59 percent of all workers in service occupations were women, and they also constituted 95 percent of all household workers, which is an unpaid job. (Reskin and Hartmann, 1986) In 1985, the average income for full-time working females was about 25 percent less than males received. (U.S. Bureau of the Census, 1985) With the same amount of education, men received more money, on the average, than women. In 1985, women earned on the average between 70 and 73.3 percent of what men earned with the same amount of education. (U.S. Bureau of the Census, 1989) If women are doing as much as men do, they deserve the same pay as well.

3 The low income for some women is not the only cause for their poverty; much of their income is being used to support their dependents. Almost two-thirds of working women is widowed, divorced, separated, never married, or has husbands with annual incomes under $15,000. (Christensen, 1988) Death in the family, divorce, separation, or desertion, and other problems cause most of the women to be working parents with dependents. The effects of such changes are the interruption of their careers, lost opportunities for promotion, and increases in responsibilities at home. Since women are generally thought to have responsibility for children, they often receive custody of the children when their marriages end, and the fathers often provide no monetary support for these children. Fewer men would be impoverished with a dependent because they have a better chance at finding a well-paying job than women. In 1960, 30.4 percent of women with dependents under age 18 were employed. This number increased to 65.6 percent in 1987. (U.S. Department of Labor, Bureau of Labor Statistics, 1989) In 1987, the total number of single-mother families exceeded the number of female headed families with children by 1.5 million (about 23 percent). (Goldberg, 1990) In 1976, families with a female head of household and no husband present constituted one-half of the poor families. (U.S. Bureau of the Census, 1989) Women have a harder time to survive with less pay for the same job, and even harder if they have a dependent. Because of the high percentage of women, who have almost no other sources of income, working to support themselves combined with the fact that they receive less pay, it's no wonder that women have a higher risk of becoming poor.

4 Because household responsibility is easily taken up by the women, women allow more compromise in finding a job; they want to have work where they can spend the time they want with their children. Because of this compromise, in the United States, about two thirds of the part-time work force is made up of women. (Goldberg, 1990) Part-time workers get lower wages than full-time workers. Also, part-time workers are much less likely than full-time workers to be covered by health insurance and pension plans. (Miller, 1990)

5 Women need to have more representation in the government to achieve equality. Discrimination against women is being formed by the concept of men being better. In 1987, the earnings of 45 percent of women workers were below the poverty level for a three-person family. As women press for better treatment, they might succeed if they have the power to change it. This power can be obtained by participating in the government. Once women participate in government more, new legislation can be written to ensure their equal treatment in social and economic situations. (Miller, 1990)

6 Women and their families who are living in poverty may consider welfare programs as a temporary solution. There are many unclaimed welfare funds.

Only about two percent of the people who receive welfare are receiving it constantly for over eight years. (Miller, 1990) The majority of the financial aid that poor single-parent families rely on is Aid to Families with Dependent Children (AFDC). AFDC has offered poor women the choice of staying home with their children. In 1988, Congress decided to reduce that option by imposing a work requirement in AFDC for mothers of very young children. Although it is a type of financial support, "the benefits of AFDC are below the poverty level in all states, even when the value of food stamps is counted." (Goldberg, 1990) In forty-one states, these combined benefits were less than 75 percent of the poverty level in 1987. (Center of Social Welfare Policy and Law, 1987)

7    With all of these barriers women have to cross to be out of poverty, the society has to stop gender-typing in jobs, undervaluing women's work, monopolizing most power systems, and maintaining economic inequality. (Zopf, 1989) In order to increase women's economic opportunities, equal pay legislation or affirmative action is a step the government can take. A gradual increase of equality for all people can then be seen. The stereotype that a woman's place is at home and a woman is less capable of doing the same work as a man should be perceived as a myth to everyone.

*ending thought*

*(citation)*

*Sources*

Center on Social Welfare Policy and Law. *Analysis of 1987 Benefit Levels in the Program of Aid to Families with Dependent Children.* Washington, DC: Center on Social Welfare Policy and Law, 1987.

Christensen, K. "Women's labor force attachment." In U.S. Department of Labor, Women's Bureau. *Flexible Workstyles: A Look at Contingent Labor: Conference Summary.* Washington, DC: U.S. Department of Labor, Women's Bureau, 1988.

Goldberg, Gertrude Schaffner, and Eleanor Kremen. *The Feminization of Poverty: Only in America?* New York: Greenwood Press, 1990.

Miller, Dorothy C. *Women and Social Welfare.* New York: Praeger Publishers, 1990.

Reskin, B. F., and H. Hartmann. *Women's Work, Men's Work: Sex Segregation on the Job.* Washington, DC: National Academy Press, 1986.

U.S. Bureau of the Census. *Poverty in the United States: 1987.* Current Population Reports, Washington, DC: U.S. Government Printing Office, 1987.

U.S. Bureau of the Census. *Women in the American Economy.* Current Population Reports, Series P-23, No. 146 by C. M. Taeuber and V. Valdisera. Washington, DC: U.S. Government Printing Office, 1986.

U.S. Department of Labor, Bureau of Labor Statistics. *Labor Force Statistics Derived from the Current Population Survey, 1948–87.* Bulletin 2307. Washington, DC: U.S. Government Printing Office, 1989.

Zopf, Paul E. *American Women in Poverty.* Greenwood Press, 1989.

## DISCUSSION

1. What causes of women's poverty does Chen give in his essay? Do you agree with his analysis?
2. What suggestions does he offer for alleviating the poverty of women? How valuable do you find each of his suggestions?
3. How effective do you think Chen's essay is? What makes it effective? What could make it more effective?
4. What assumptions does Chen appear to believe his audience will share with him about women and poverty? Do some people in your class disagree with some of Chen's basic assumptions? Does Chen address the concerns of these people in his essay?

## Reflecting on Draft Three

1. Once again, highlight or underline phrases of which you are particularly proud.

   _____

   _____

2. Explain one thing your peer reviewer said that influenced your revision of this paper.

   _____

   _____

3. Identify one part of your paper that you developed further. Explain why you did so.

   _____

   _____

4. Explain the effect you'd like your paper to have on your reader.

   _____

   _____

5. Explain the effect writing this paper had on you.

   _____

   _____

## Writer's Notebook

Consider the following questions in your writer's notebook after you write the drafts of this chapter's major essay.

### LEARNING STRATEGY

**Managing Your Learning: Evaluate your progress as a writer by comparing your own development as a writer with what you know of professional writing. Gauge where you are in your development, formulate specific goals that you would like to achieve in the next chapter, and follow up on those goals.**

1. Which qualities would you say characterize the sentences of professional writers? Do you think long sentences are more sophisticated-sounding than short ones? Do you think professional writers write short sentences too? Can you imagine why?

2. What kind of vocabulary do you think professional writers prefer? Do you think more formal or sophisticated words are automatically better than short simple words? When might more sophisticated words be useful? simpler ones?

3. How do your own sentences and vocabulary choices compare to what you know about professional writing? What might you do differently?

4. Have you achieved as much control over error as you would like? How important are (a) the time you spend, (b) your grammatical knowledge, and (c) editing strategies in your ability to control error? What else can you do to improve your ability to control errors?

5. What can you do to move your writing in the direction of those characteristics of professional writing that you admire most?

## Vocabulary Checklist

Add vocabulary words from the chapter that you believe will be useful to you. Several additional useful words have been added for you.

| WORD | PART OF SPEECH | MEANING | PREPO-SITIONS | SAMPLE SENTENCE |
|---|---|---|---|---|
| 1. impoverished | adj. | poor | ø | The impoverished people in the Mississippi Delta had given up. |
| 2. poverty line | n. | level of income considered poverty | under/at above | A large number of children live at or under the poverty line. |
| 3. | | | | |
| 4. | | | | |
| 5. | | | | |

| WORD | PART OF SPEECH | MEANING | PREPO-SITIONS | SAMPLE SENTENCE |
|------|----------------|---------|---------------|-----------------|
| **6.** | | | | |
| **7.** | | | | |
| **8.** | | | | |
| **9.** | | | | |
| **10.** | | | | |

## Sample Footnotes[1]

**Important characteristics of footnotes**
- contents
- order of contents
- punctuation
- capitalization

**Single author/book**
David Stockman, *The Triumph of Politics: Why the Reagan Revolution Failed* (New York: Harper & Row, 1986), pp. 376–411.

*NOTE:* When italic lettering is unavailable, <u>underline</u> book, journal, and magazine titles.

---

[1]Based on the *Modern Language Association Handbook.*

### Multiple author/book

Stanley Wenocur and Michael Reish, *From Charity to Enterprise: The Development of American Social Work in a Market Economy* (Urbana, Ill.: University of Illinois Press, 1980), pp. 211-213.

### Organization as author/book

Children's Defense Fund, *State of America's Children* (Washington, D.C., 1991), pp. 24-25.

### Article in edited book

Martha Ozawa, "Introduction: An Overview." In Martha Ozawa, ed., *Women's Life Cycle and Economic Security* (New York: Greenwood Press, 1989), pp. 2-8.

### Article/newspaper (with author)

Linda Greenhouse, "Justices Bar Using Civil Rights Suits to Enforce U.S. Child Welfare Law," *New York Times,* March 26, 1992, A15. [section A, page 15]

### Article/scholarly journal; no volume

Amy Butler, "The Attractiveness of Private Practice," *Journal of Social Work Education* (Winter 1992), 47-60. [notice no "pp." for page numbers]

### Article/journal with volume

Linda Demkovitch, "Hospitals That Provide for the Poor Are Reeling from Uncompensated Costs," *National Journal,* 16 (November 24, 1984), 2245-2249.

### Article/journal with volume and number

Donald Chambers, "Policy Weaknesses and Political Opportunities," *Social Service Review,* 59:1 (March 1985), 1-17.

### Article/weekly magazine (no author)

"Selling Fear to L.A.'s Poor," *Newsweek,* October 22, 1990, p. 33.

## Bibliography

Brown, J. Larry, and H. F. Pizer. *Living Hungry in America.* New York: Macmillan Publishing Company, 1987.

Freudenberger, C. Dean. "Resource Abuse: 'The Land Does Not Lie,'" *The Causes of World Hunger.* Ed. William Byron. New York: Paulist Press, 1982.

Gabe, Thomas. *Progress Against Poverty in the United States (1956-1987).* Washington, D.C.: Congressional Research Service, The Library of Congress, 1989.

Green, Bob. "Homeless Boy Sought Escape in Death," *Las Vegas Review Journal,* April 17, 1989.

Jansson, Bruce S. *The Reluctant Welfare State: A History of American Social Welfare Policies.* 2nd ed. Pacific Grove, Cal.: Brooks/Cole, 1993.

Mattera, Philip. "Women and Children Last," *Prosperity Lost.* Reading, Mass.: Addison-Wesley, 1990.

O'Hare, William. *The Rise of Poverty in Rural America.* Washington, D.C.: Population Reference Bureau, Inc., 1988.

Pearce, Diana. "Farewell to Alms: Women's Fare under Welfare." In Terry Reuther, *Sociology: Empowerment in a Troubled Age.* Boston: Copley Publishing Group, 1990, pp. 121–130.

Ropers, Richard. *Persistent Poverty: The American Dream Turned Nightmare.* New York: Plenum Press, 1991.

Schiller, Bradley R. *The Economics of Poverty and Discrimination.* Englewood Cliffs, N.J.: Prentice-Hall, 1989.

UPI. "Number of Homeless Rises 18% in 15 Months to about 2 Million." Iron County, Utah, *Daily Spectrum,* October 13, 1989.

U.S. Bureau of the Census, "Poverty in the United States: 1985," *Current Population Reports.* Series P-60, No. 158. Washington, D.C.: Government Printing Office, 1987.

U.S. General Accounting Office. *Children and Youths: About 68,000 Homeless and 186,000 in Shared Housing at Any Given Time.* GAO/PEMD-89-14, Washington, D.C., June 1989.

Whitman, D., et al. "America's Hidden Poor." *U.S. News & World Report,* January 11, 1988, pp. 18–24.

# Challenges and Choices

Think about the following questions as you work on this chapter.

1. What does the word challenge mean to you?
2. What are some of the toughest challenges people regularly face in their lives?
3. What are some of the choices available to them for solving these challenges?

## Topic Orientation

This chapter is a little different from the previous ones in that two very different aspects of the main topic will be presented, and you will have many more choices of subtopics to write about. In order to begin understanding the topics for this chapter, discuss the following questions with two or three of your classmates.

1. Make a list of some of the challenges you've heard about in world news that people are facing nowadays. How are they handling these challenges?
2. What are some of the challenges you have faced (or are facing) in your life? How have you dealt with these challenges?
3. What is the best general advice you could give people who are facing a tough challenge?
4. Do you believe it is appropriate to ignore or avoid certain challenges? Is it appropriate to seek certain challenges?

# PART II: WRITING THE FIRST DRAFT

## Major Essay Assignments

Write the first draft of a major essay of approximately 750 words on one of the following topics (or a topic of your choice that you have discussed with your instructor). Choose the type of essay that you feel competent to write but that will also provide a challenge for you. Notice that there are two persuasive essay topics to encourage you to stretch your abilities. Use the questions in the assignments to help you begin the assignment, not to limit your ideas.

**1. Analytic Essay.** Find a newspaper or magazine article which describes a challenge that someone is facing. Analyze what causes the situation to be challenging and what choices are available for coping with the situation. Do these choices represent successful or unsuccessful coping strategies? Finally, analyze the coping strategy the person in your article adopted. Does it result in success or not, in your opinion? Why?

**2. Persuasive Essay.** Argue whether or not suicide is a successful coping response to imminent death or grave illness. As your starting point, you might consider the situations presented in one of this chapter's readings, "Choosing Not to

Die Alone," but there are many other articles available in newspapers and magazines which you can find by using your library's *Reader's Guide to Periodical Literature,* to which your information desk librarian can refer you. While this is certainly an emotional issue, and it may be appropriate to base part of your argument in emotion, avoid the "knee-jerk response" (explained in detail on page 173). Readers on both sides of the issue are likely to have strong feelings. Your paper will be most effective if you can provide solid, expert evidence to support your views.

**3. Persuasive Essay.** Virak Khiev, whose article is reprinted in this chapter, faced several challenges that ultimately led him into crime. Kevin, whose story is also told in this chapter, faced similar challenges but was able to cope differently. Argue that there is one particular way to help kids like Virak and Kevin successfully deal with the challenges that might lead them into taking part in criminal activities such as drugs, theft, or murder. You might begin by considering Virak and Kevin as representatives of many young people and asking yourself what made the difference for them and what other strategies might have been used. Then narrow down these answers to the one you would like to persuade your audience to adopt. Why is it necessary to deal with this problem? Why is the method you have chosen to discuss important? Why will it make a difference? How can it be implemented? If it costs money, how can the money be raised?

## INTRODUCTORY READING

### Vocabulary Enrichment

Using your dictionary, fill in the following chart with the missing word forms indicated. Then write a brief definition in the last column.

| | NOUN | VERB | ADJECTIVE | ADVERB | DEFINITION |
|---|---|---|---|---|---|
| 1. | _____ | _____ | strategic | _____ | _____ |
| 2. | appraisal | _____ | XXX | XXX | _____ |
| 3. | competence | XXX | _____ | _____ | _____ |
| 4. | mastery | _____ | _____ | _____ | _____ |
| 5. | _____ | assess | XXX | XXX | _____ |
| 6. | denial | _____ | XXX | XXX | _____ |
| 7. | _____ | avoid | XXX | XXX | _____ |
| 8. | _____ | withdraw | XXX | XXX | _____ |
| 9. | _____ | XXX | _____ | impulsively | _____ |
| 10. | _____ | XXX | aggressive | _____ | _____ |
| 11. | _____ | XXX | passive | _____ | _____ |

***VOCABULARY LEARNING STRATEGY:*** Choose one or more of the words from this vocabulary exercise that you feel will be useful in your writing. Enter them into the Vocabulary Checklist at the end of this chapter.

In the following passage, author Chris L. Kleinke explains some of the basics of coping (or dealing) with life's challenges.

## LEARNING STRATEGY

**Personalizing: Applying a reading to your personal experiences can help you understand it more completely.**

Before you read this short passage, think of a challenge you are facing in your own life right now. Then apply what you read in the passage to your own challenge. Does this help you understand the passage? Does the passage help you understand your challenge?

# Some conclusions about successful coping responses

What conclusions can we reach from research studies on coping responses? People who cope most successfully are those who are equipped with a battery[1] of coping strategies and who are flexible in gearing[2] their responses to the situation. Good copers have developed the following three skills (Atonovsky, 1979): (1) *flexibility:* being able to create and consider alternative plans; (2) *farsightedness:* anticipating long-range effects of coping responses; and (3) *rationality:* making accurate appraisals. (1)

. . . A number of research studies analyze the effectiveness of people's coping responses. Although these studies used somewhat different terms for their coping measures, they all agreed on the following conclusions: (2)

• Successful copers respond to life challenges by taking responsibility for finding a solution to their problems. They approach problems with a sense of <u>competence</u> and <u>mastery</u>. Their goal is to <u>assess</u> the situation, get advice and support from others,

and work out a plan that will be in their best interest. Successful copers use life challenges as an opportunity for personal growth, and they attempt to face these challenges with hope, patience, and a sense of humor. (3)

• Unsuccessful copers respond to life challenges with <u>denial</u> and <u>avoidance</u>. They either <u>withdraw</u> from problems or they react <u>impulsively</u> without taking the time and effort to seek the best solution. Unsuccessful copers are angry and <u>aggressive</u> or depressed and <u>passive</u>. They blame themselves or others for their problems and don't appreciate the value of approaching life challenges with a sense of hope, mastery, and personal control. (4)

We live in a society where people want easy answers to their problems—a pill, a quick fix, or a guaranteed solution that doesn't require much cost or effort. Successful coping does not result from discovering a single fail-

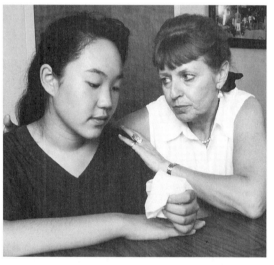

proof[3] response. It is an attitude and a life philosophy. Successful copers teach them-selves to use primary and secondary appraisal[4] for deriving coping responses best suited for a particular life event they are facing.(5)

Kleinke, 1991, p. 11.

[3]fail-proof: sure not to fail (-*proof* is a suffix meaning "able to resist")

[4]primary and secondary appraisal: primary appraisal is the immediate judgment we make about a challenge; secondary appraisal is the later judgment after more careful thought (Kleinke, 1991, p. 16–24)

[1]battery: a social science word for collection

[2]gearing: matching or adapting

## ELABORATING ON THE READING

With two or three of your classmates, consider the following situations in which people face challenges. Using the information in the reading above, imagine how a successful coper would handle each situation. Then imagine how an unsuccessful coper might handle each. Share and compare your answers with your classmates.

### *LEARNING STRATEGY*

**Forming Concepts: Applying theories to real-life situations helps you understand the theories better.**

1. A forty-six-year-old man is laid off from his job because his company is curtailing production.
2. A university student realizes three weeks before the end of the semester that she will probably fail her history course.
3. A fifteen-year-old boy's parents work such long hours that he can never spend enough time with them. He misses them terribly.
4. A middle-aged woman finds she has incurable cancer.
5. (Supply your own challenge!)

### SHORT WRITING (150–200 WORDS)

Describe a challenge that you are facing now (or have faced recently). What choices do you have for coping with the situation, either successfully or unsuccessfully? What coping strategy do you expect to choose? Why do you expect it to be successful?

### FIRST IN-DEPTH READING

**Vocabulary Enrichment**

**EXERCISE:**  Find each of the following words in the reading that follows this exercise and determine which of the three given meanings best defines each word. You may have to read both the sentence before and the sentence after each word in order to determine its meaning.

1. longed for
   a. wanted strongly
   b. increased
   c. stretched

2. deceptive
   a. rich
   b. smart
   c. untruthful

3. unscrupulous
   a. without morality
   b. dependable
   c. experienced

4. peers
   a. skills
   b. friends
   c. family members

5. mentality
   a. mental illness
   b. way of thinking
   c. level of intelligence

6. adversaries
   a. enemies
   b. the authorities
   c. criminals

7. immortalized
   a. killed
   b. illegal
   c. living forever

8. broke
   a. without any money
   b. tired
   c. miserable

9. halt
   a. start
   b. continuation
   c. stop

10. ignorance
    a. understanding
    b. caring
    c. lack of knowledge

**Threads**

**War is for everyone, for children too.**

Robert Frost, "The Bonfire"

**Remember Your
Vocabulary Checklist!**

The article below was written by a nineteen-year-old man, now living in the United States but originally from Cambodia. In it, he describes some of the difficulties he had adjusting to the U.S. culture and changing his expectations. What challenges did he face both in his country and in the United States? How did he choose to deal with these challenges?

# Breaking the bonds of hate

Ever since I can remember, I wanted the ideal life: a big house, lots of money, cars. I wanted to find the perfect happiness that so many people have <u>longed for</u>. I wanted more than life in the jungle of Cambodia. America was the place, the land of tall skyscrapers, televisions, cars and airplanes. (1)

In the jungles of Cambodia I lived in a refugee camp. We didn't have good sanitation or modern conveniences. For example, there were no inside bathrooms—only outside ones made from palm-tree leaves, surrounded by millions of flies. When walking down the street, I could smell the aroma of the outhouse; in the afternoon, the 5- and 6-year-olds played with the dirt in front of it. It was the only thing they had to play with, and the "fragrance" never seemed to bother them. And it never bothered me. Because I smelled it every day, I was used to it. (2)

The only thing that bothered me was the war. I have spent half of my life in war. The killing is still implanted in my mind. I hate Cambodia. When I came to America nine years ago at the age of 10, I thought I was being born into a new life. No more being hungry, no more fighting, no more killing. I thought I had escaped the war. (3)

In America, there are more kinds of material things than Cambodians could ever want. And here we don't have to live in the jungle like monkeys, we don't have to hide from mortar bombing[1] and we don't have to smell the rotten human carrion.[2] But for the immigrant, America presents a different type of jungle, a different type of war and a smell as bad as the waste of Cambodia. (4)

Most Americans believe the stereotype that immigrants work hard, get a good education and have a very good life. Maybe it used to be like that, but

not anymore. You have to be <u>deceptive</u> and <u>unscrupulous</u> in order to make it. If you are not, then you will end up like most immigrants I've known. Living in the ghetto[3] in a cockroach-infested house. Working on the assembly line or in the chicken factory to support your family. Getting up at 3 o'clock in the morning to take the bus to work and not getting home until 5 p.m. (5)

If you're a kid my age, you drop out of school to work because your parents don't have enough money to buy you clothes for school. You may end up selling drugs because you want cars, money and parties, as all teenagers do. You have to depend on your peers for emotional support because your parents are too busy working in the factory trying to make money to pay the bills. You don't get along with your parents because they have a different <u>mentality</u>: you are an American and they are Cambodian. You hate them because they are never there for you,[4] so you join a gang as I did. (6)

You spend your time drinking, doing drugs and fighting. You beat up people for pleasure. You don't care

about anything except your drugs, your beers and your revenge against <u>adversaries</u>. You shoot at people because they've insulted your pride. You shoot at the police because they are always bothering you. They shoot back and then you're dead like my best friend Sinerth. (7)

Sinerth robbed a gas station. He was shot in the head by the police. I'd known him since the sixth grade from my first school in Minneapolis. I can still remember his voice calling me from California. "Virak, come down here, man," he said. "We need you. There are lots of pretty girls down here." I promised him that I would be there to see him. The following year he was dead. I felt sorry for him. But as I thought it over, maybe it was better for him to be dead than to continue with the cycle of violence, to live with hate. I thought, "It is better to die than to live like an angry young fool, thinking that everybody is out to get you."[5] (8)

*Mad-dog mind-set:* When I was like Sinerth, I didn't care about dying. I thought that I was on top of the world, being <u>immortalized</u> by drugs. I could see that my future would be spent working on the assembly line[6] like

---

[1]mortar bombing: large bombs sent through the air to explode in a large area

[2]carrion: dead flesh

[3]ghetto: area of a city which is isolated from the majority of the city because its residents are impoverished or members of a minority group, often a racial minority

[4]there for someone: available to give support and encouragement

[5]out to get someone: looking for revenge

[6]assembly line: industrial era method of production involving rote, specialized tasks

most of my friends, spending all my paycheck on the weekend and being broke again on Monday morning. I hated going to school because I couldn't see a way to get out of the endless cycle. My philosophy was "Live hard and die young." (9)

I hated America because to me, it was not the place of opportunities or the land of "the melting pot"[7] as I had been told. All I had seen were broken beer bottles on the street and homeless people and drunks using the sky as their roof. I couldn't walk down the street without someone yelling out, "You —— gook" from his car. Once again I was caught in the web of hatred. I'd become a mad dog with the

_____

[7]the melting pot: a metaphor for the mixing of ancestries in the United States; this term is often used sarcastically nowadays to express the isolation of minority groups in the United States

mind-set[8] of the past: "When trapped in the corner, just bite." The war mentality of Cambodia came back: get what you can and leave. I thought I had come to America to escape war, poverty, fighting, to escape the violence, but I wasn't escaping; I was being introduced to a newer version of war—the war of hatred. (10)

I was lucky. In Minneapolis, I dropped out of school in the ninth grade to join a gang. Then I moved to Louisiana, where I continued my life of "immortality" as a member of another gang. It came to an abrupt halt when I crashed a car. I wasn't badly injured, but I was underage and the fine took all my money. I called a good friend of the Cambodian community in Minneapolis for advice (she'd tried to help me earlier). I didn't know where to go or

_____

[8]mind-set: a preconceived way of understanding new information

whom to turn to. I saw friends landing in jail, and I didn't want that. She promised to help me get back in school. And she did. (11)

Since then I've been given a lot of encouragement and caring by American friends and teachers who've helped me turn my life around. They opened my eyes to a kind of education that frees us all from ignorance and slavery. I could have failed so many times except for those people who believed in me and gave me another chance. Individuals who were willing to help me have taught me that I can help myself. I'm now a 12th grader and have been at my school for three years; I plan to attend college in the fall. I am struggling to believe I can reach the other side of the mountain. (12)

Khiev, 1992, p. 8.

## ELABORATING ON THE READING

**EXERCISE 1:** Conduct an analysis of the reading by scanning it for information to fill in the following chart. You may also infer some of your entries.

| | VIRAK'S CHALLENGES IN CAMBODIA | VIRAK'S CHALLENGES IN THE UNITED STATES | VIRAK'S COPING STRATEGIES IN RESPONSE TO THE CHALLENGES |
|---|---|---|---|
| 1. | | | |
| 2. | | | |
| 3. | | | |
| 4. | | | |
| 5. | | | |

**EXERCISE 2:**   Discuss the following questions with two or three of your class-mates.

1. How do you feel about the choices Virak made in response to his challenges?
2. What reason(s) can you give for Virak's changing to the pronoun *you* in para-graphs 5 and 6? Would you say it is generally a good idea to write with the pronoun *you*?
3. What was it that finally caused Virak to turn his life around?
4. What aspects of Virak's story are designed by him to make you feel sorry for him? Do you feel sorry for him? Why or why not?
5. How can Virak's situation be understood in light of what you learned in Chapter 4 (Education and Empowerment), Chapter 5 (Fatherhood), and Chapter 6 (Poverty)?
6. Would you say Virak was a successful coper as a teenager or an unsuccessful one? Why? Are his coping responses better now?

### *LEARNING STRATEGY*

**Personalizing: Putting yourself in another person's situation can help you better understand that situation.**

**EXERCISE 3—Role-play:**   Working in small groups of two or three members, play the roles of the following people in conversations about one of the following situations. Afterward, perform the conversation for your classmates. Ask them whether they agree with your interpretation of Virak's life.

a. *Virak and his parents*
   Virak's parents work long hours, and Virak is angry because they don't spend enough time with him.
b. *Virak and his friend Sinerth*
   Sinerth is inviting Virak to come to California to live.
c. *Virak and a couple of police officers*
   Virak thinks the police are bothering him once again.
d. *Virak and his helpful friend from Minneapolis*
   What did they say the first time she tried to help him?
e. *Virak and his helpful friend from Minneapolis*
   What did they say when Virak asked her for help again?

## Preparing for Short Writing: Writing Skills

### REPETITION OF KEY WORDS

Inexperienced writers often make one mistake when they choose words to express their ideas: They avoid repeating the same words again and again. They often go to great trouble to find synonyms in a *thesaurus,* a book which provides a wide range of synonyms for more common words. As a result, they often choose inappropriate words, sometimes even ridiculous words.

As a matter of fact, experienced writers make great use of repetition, that is, repetition of key words. Key words refer to writers' main points. When key words are repeated, they serve to reinforce in the readers' minds the main points being expressed. Good writers understand that it is easy for many readers to lose track of the main point. By repeating the words related to the essay or paragraph's main points, readers are reminded of those points and find it easier to understand and remember them.

Consider the following paragraphs from the Introductory Reading. Key words that match are highlighted in similar typefaces.

**Successful copers** respond to *life challenges* by taking responsibility for finding a solution to their *problems.* They approach *problems* with a sense of competence and mastery. Their goal is to assess the situation, get advice and support from others, and work out a plan that will be in their best interest. **Successful copers** use *life challenges* as an opportunity for personal growth, and they attempt to face these *challenges* with hope, patience, and a sense of humor.

**Unsuccessful copers** respond to *life challenges* with denial and avoidance. They either withdraw from *problems* or they react impulsively without taking the time and effort to seek the best solution. **Unsuccessful copers** are angry and aggressive or depressed and passive. They blame themselves or others for their *problems* and don't appreciate the value of approaching *life challenges* with a sense of hope, mastery, and personal control." (Kleinke, 1991, p. 11)

Notice that it is only the key words that are repeated often. Repetition of words other than key words can be confusing or tedious to readers.

**EXERCISE:** Analyze the following piece of text from "Breaking the Bonds of Hate" for repetition of key words. Mark matching repetitions in matching colors or styles. Why do you think Virak chose to repeat these particular words?

Ever since I can remember, I wanted the ideal life: a big house, lots of money, cars. I wanted to find the perfect happiness that so many people have longed for. I wanted more than life in the jungle of Cambodia. America was the place, the land of tall skyscrapers, televisions, cars and airplanes. . . .

The only thing that bothered me was the war. I have spent half of my life in war. The killing is still implanted in my mind. I hate Cambodia. When I came to America nine years ago at the age of 10, I thought I was being born into a new life. No more being hungry, no more fighting, no more killing. I thought I had escaped the war.

In America, there are more kinds of material things than Cambodians could ever want. And here we don't have to live in the jungle like monkeys, we don't have to hide from mortar bombing and we don't have to smell the rotten human carrion. But for the immigrant, America presents a different type of jungle, a different type of war and a smell as bad as the waste of Cambodia. . . .

I hated America because to me, it was not the place of opportunities or the land of "the melting pot" as I had been told. All I had seen were broken beer bottles on the street and homeless people and drunks using the sky as their roof. I couldn't walk down the street without someone yelling out, "You —— gook" from his car. Once again I was caught in the web of hatred.

### Threads

The country with the lowest murder rate in 1988 was Mali at 0.0 per 100,000 people; the country with the highest murder rate was the Philippines at 38.70 per 100,000 people.

Rand McNally, *Almanac of World Facts*

I'd become a mad dog with the mind-set of the past: "When trapped in the corner, just bite." The war mentality of Cambodia came back: get what you can and leave. I thought I had come to America to escape war, poverty, fighting, to escape the violence, but I wasn't escaping; I was being introduced to a newer version of war—the war of hatred." (Khiev, 1992, p. 8)

## SHORT WRITING (150–200 WORDS)

Write a letter to Virak explaining why his coping responses have been successful or unsuccessful in your opinion. You may choose either his early coping responses or his most recent ones. Be sure to *repeat key words* to make your writing clear.

Now go back to your major essay draft and find places where you can reinforce your readers' understanding of your ideas by repeating key words. Make changes where appropriate.

## SECOND IN-DEPTH READING

**Vocabulary Enrichment**
Examine the underlined words from the passage, and determine which of the given meanings on the right is correct. Write the letter of the correct definition next to its word.

| | | |
|---|---|---|
| 1. _____ modest | **a.** according to everyone |
| 2. _____ valid | **b.** mixed feelings |
| 3. _____ weariness | **c.** expectation |
| 4. _____ propelled | **d.** acceptable |
| 5. _____ profound | **e.** intense |
| 6. _____ barred | **f.** incentives |
| 7. _____ revocation | **g.** fatal |
| 8. _____ motives | **h.** tiredness |
| 9. _____ by all accounts | **i.** fallen apart |
| 10. _____ prospect | **j.** caused |
| 11. _____ deteriorated | **k.** cancellation |
| 12. _____ ambivalence | **l.** middle-sized |
| 13. _____ terminal | **m.** feeling great sorrow |
| 14. _____ mourning | **n.** made it known |
| 15. _____ revealed | **o.** prohibited |

**Remember Your
Vocabulary Checklist!**

The article that follows describes the choice of some patients who faced either death or a great deal of pain. Each chose to go to Dr. Jack Kevorkian in Michigan so that he could help them end their lives with a "suicide machine" he invented that delivers deadly carbon monoxide to patients. Dr. Kevorkian has said that he enables people to kill themselves in a painless way out of pity for the patients. The patients themselves operate the machine, and Dr. Kevorkian is said to take certain measures to assure himself that the patients truly want to commit suicide.

## LEARNING STRATEGY

**Understanding and Using Emotions: Avoiding forming an opinion too soon keeps you open to learning more.**

# Choosing not to die alone

On a glass-top table in the center of the family room, Catherine Andreyev's medicines were sorted out in coffee cups. There were sleeping pills, Tylenol with codeine, barbiturates, tranquilizers, narcotics and a mug full of morphine patches. (1)

"I fully expected to walk in there one morning and find the cups empty and Catherine dead," recalls her neighbor, Diane Collins. Each sleeping pill was tiny, a grain of sand. You could pop 20 of them down in a gulp of Jell-O[1]. . . . But, of course, that's not what she did." Instead, Andreyev, who had cancer, persuaded two friends to drive her six hours from her suburban Pittsburgh home to a <u>modest</u> house outside Detroit for an appointment with Dr. Jack Kevorkian. (2)

No one knows for certain why Andreyev made that choice. But Collins has an idea: "I think Catherine was saying 'I didn't have enough time to make anything out of my life, so I'll make something out of my death.'" (3)

Since June of 1990, Jack Kevorkian has helped 15 people "make something" of their deaths. Although the

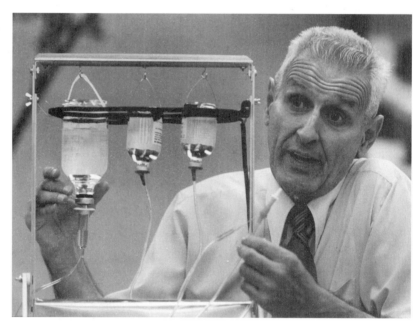

*Dr. Jack Kervorkian*

numbers of patients who have done this are too small to be statistically <u>valid</u>, some patterns are beginning to emerge. Eleven of the patients were women; all were ill, all were white, most middle-aged. In addition, most: (4)

- Had months, even years of life ahead of them. They said it was not pain but their <u>weariness</u> with life that made them want to die. (5)
- Were divorced, widowed or lifelong

singles. Many had recently suffered the loss of a loved one. (6)
- Seemed depressed or withdrawn to their families and friends. (7)

Suicide experts recognize such themes. But what <u>propelled</u> *these* four men and 11 women to kill themselves? Why did they seek out a high-profile stranger at life's most private and <u>profound</u> moment? "It's a paradox, but sometimes people who kill themselves

---

[1]Jell-O: A particular brand of gelatin, a sweet, clear dessert which usually comes in fruit flavors

are trying to connect with life by taking leave of life," says sociologist Ronald Maris, who heads the Center for the Study of Suicide at the University of South Carolina. (8)

Through the highly public exit offered by Kevorkian, some connections are assured: with the media, with a famous doctor, with a cause, even with history. Kevorkian, who has been <u>barred</u> from practicing medicine in Michigan and faces license <u>revocation</u> in California as well, refused to discuss his patients' <u>motives</u> in seeking him out. "For some, choosing Dr. Kevorkian may be a way of finally—for the first time perhaps—creating a social contact . . .," says Janet Billson of the American Sociological Association. (9)

For the never-married Catherine Andreyev, who was a schoolteacher, friends say the need to be a part of something grander than her own modest life may well have been a factor in her decision to go to Michigan to die. "In life, she was practically invisible," says one longtime acquaintance. "There is no doubt that, because of Kevorkian, Catherine was larger in death than she ever was in life." (10)

Andreyev, like most of Kevorkian's patients, lived alone. "We know that people who are alone tend to commit suicide more often. Life seems to have less meaning," says Faye Girsh, a San Diego psychologist and right-to-die advocate. "Living alone is harder. . . ." And so is dying. Like most of Kevorkian's patients, Andreyev had access to enough prescription medicines to kill herself without help. But, <u>by all accounts</u>, she

never tried. "People don't like the <u>prospect</u> of sitting in their apartments alone, brewing a lethal cup of tea, possibly vomiting everything up and never being found until they are totally <u>deteriorated</u>," says Girsh. "If people had a choice of having a nice, kind doctor give them an injection and sit by their bedside until they die, wouldn't that be better?" (11)

The Kevorkian guarantee of success also may help relieve the <u>ambivalence</u> that tortures most people who contemplate suicide, says Dr. Joseph Richman, a New York psychologist and author of several books on suicide. "For some, Dr. Kevorkian seems quite magical, a true angel of death. . . . By going to this man, they may be saying 'I've put myself in this wonderful person's hands and now I don't have to go through any more of this pain of deciding whether to live or die.'" (12)

For 47-year-old Elaine Goldbaum, who was suffering form multiple sclerosis,[2] Kevorkian was an angelic guide to the afterlife. In a letter Goldbaum wrote to Kevorkian before her death last February 8, she said, "I am Jewish and have been raised to believe that suicide is a mortal sin. . . . Your assistance in medicide [Kevorkian's term for physician-assisted suicide] will get me into heaven." Goldbaum's condition was not <u>terminal</u> but her family said she was depressed by her progressive loss of muscle control. Still, Goldbaum

---

[2]multiple sclerosis: a disease of the nervous system resulting in loss of muscular control

was mobile enough to go out to have her hair done for her appointment with Kevorkian. At the end, her neighbors say, she seemed in high spirits. "You'd never imagine she was getting all fixed up to *die,*" says one. (13)

The typical suicide victim is a white, middle-aged male. Among those who sought Kevorkian's help in dying, only two fit that description—Jack Miller, 53, and Jonathon Grenz, 44. Both men had spreading cancers. Grenz, an Orange County (California) real estate broker whose sister—a physician—accompanied him to Michigan, was <u>mourning</u> the loss of his mother as well as his own recent loss of speech to throat cancer, say friends. (14)

Although Kevorkian and his lawyers insist physical pain drove most of his patients to their deaths, autopsies[3] on the men and women <u>revealed</u> fewer than half were taking any medications for pain when they died. Stanley Ball, 82 and suffering from terminal pancreatic cancer, had been to his own doctor 10 days before his Feb. 4 Kevorkian appointment. Although his doctor gave him a prescription for a powerful painkiller, Ball never filled it. Instead, he dictated a letter to his daughter to be shared later with the press. "I've lived a great life," he wrote, adding, "I want to end my life at the earliest opportunity." (15)

Warrick, 1993, Sec. E, pp. 1, 4.

[3]autopsies: physical examinations to determine cause of death

## ELABORATING ON THE READING

**EXERCISE 1:**   Identify the challenges the people in "Choosing Not to Die Alone" faced by filling in the following chart with two or three of your classmates. Notice that some of their challenges are directly stated but others may be inferred by the reader. Brainstorm choices they could have made instead of suicide. The chart is begun for you.

| CHALLENGES | | | |
|---|---|---|---|
| CATHERINE ANDREYEV | ELAINE GOLDBAUM | JONATHAN GRENZ | STANLEY BALL |
| 1. | | | |
| 2. | | | |
| 3. | | | |

| CHOICES | | | |
|---|---|---|---|
| CATHERINE ANDREYEV | ELAINE GOLDBAUM | JONATHAN GRENZ | STANLEY BALL |
| 1. | | | |
| 2. | | | |
| 3. | | | |

**EXERCISE 2:**   Discuss for each person above whether you think his or her choice was a successful or unsuccessful way of coping with these challenges.

## LEARNING STRATEGY

**Managing Your Learning: Increasing your contact with native speakers increases your ability to speak and listen effectively in a second language.**

## Gathering Data: A Poll

In small groups of three or four students, prepare a very short poll on either "Physician-Assisted Suicide" or "Juvenile Crime." Then go out into the community around your school or neighborhood, and ask people to answer your questions, being careful to keep a record of their answers. Prepare your results and explain them to your class.

*HINT:*  Be sure to limit the number of questions—no more than five. Also be sure that your questions can be answered in a short answer.

## Preparing for Short Writing: Writing Skills

### RECOGNIZING THE KNEE-JERK RESPONSE

When we visit a doctor's office for a physical examination, the doctor might tap a spot on our knees to check our reflexes. All is fine when our lower leg jerks forward uncontrollably. We use this situation as a metaphor for voicing our opinions. Someone mentions a complicated or controversial topic, and we voice opinions as if by reflex, without careful thought or logic. We make knee-jerk responses.

Because writers are people, they are also vulnerable to knee-jerk responses in their writing. However, just like in conversation, when we have to justify our opinions in writing, we may find that it becomes very difficult or even impossible. There are warning signs that the knee jerk is at work:

- Your arguments are based on emotion rather than fact.
- You can't find any statistics to support your assertions, or you realize that the statistics you have found are questionable.
- You can't think of an illustration or example to support your opinion.
- You can't use an example of people you know in the situation you are describing because they don't support *your* opinion but rather its *opposite*.
- You start to hear a little voice in your head arguing against the points you are trying to make, and that voice seems more authoritative than your own.

Inexperienced writers ignore these warning signs of the knee-jerk response and persevere. They are unwilling to start over and throw out what they've written because they're reluctant to lose all the hard work they've done already. As a result, they produce poor essays that are incapable of convincing their readers because they did not even convince their writers.

Experienced writers, however, recognize that the process of writing is also a process of discovery. Writers may *begin* writing with a particular opinion in mind, but they are willing to alter that opinion as they think more carefully about the topic. They recognize that it is sometimes necessary to discard large amounts of their written material and start over. More importantly, these writers recognize that the rewriting will go faster and more smoothly the second and third times because they can benefit from the large amount of thought they've already invested in their topic.

You may already have experienced the knee-jerk response. In the chapter on fathers, you may have tried to write an essay saying that mothers should receive custody of their children because it is natural. But as you were writing, did you start to wonder whether there might be a good argument for fathers' receiving custody? What did you do with this "little voice"? When you were writing about poverty, you may have expressed the opinion that some people are poor because they want to be or because they are lazy. As you were saying this, did you notice that the statistics in the readings did not support your opinion? Did you realize that you had no evidence to prove this? Did these realizations affect your writing?

## SHORT WRITING (150–200 WORDS)

In order to feel what the knee-jerk reaction is like, choose one topic below with which you do NOT agree, and write about it as if you did.

1. People should be required to end their lives at age 65 because they are relatively useless after that anyway.
2. Everybody who has an illness that is expensive to cure should be refused treatment because he or she will only become a drain on society's resources.

Now check your major essay draft. Are you a victim of the knee-jerk response? Are you having trouble supporting your opinion? Consider starting over.

## Making Your Draft Clearer: Writing Skills

### CAUSE/EFFECT DEVELOPMENT

When you are analyzing choices and challenges or persuading your audience to adopt certain strategies to cope with challenges, you are essentially dealing with causes and effects. The challenges we face are the catalysts (or causes) of the emotions we feel and the actions we take (effects). In turn, the choices we make in response to these challenges (causes) also lead to certain results (effects). We engage in analyzing causes and effects for two basic reasons:

#### 1. To Learn About Situations in Order to Make Good Decisions

How you analyze the causes of a situation determines the decisions you make about the situation. If you believe Virak is simply a bad person and became involved in crime as a result of this, you will probably decide simply to send him to jail and forget about him. However, if you analyze the cause of his problem as that his parents were too busy, and further, that they were too busy because it is difficult for immigrants to stay out of poverty, you might decide to develop a program that helps immigrant families financially, or you might develop a program that provides adult role models for young people like Virak. (One program in the United States which does this is Big Brothers/Big Sisters of America. See "A Little Push from Big Brother Goes a Long Way" on p. 182) How you analyze the causes of his situation determines your response to the problem.

Keep in mind, however, that it is very important for you to analyze all the possible causes of the situation, called *causal factors*. It is simply not good enough to say that Virak is a bad person. We cannot take responsible action if we are uninformed about the factors involved. Additionally, even if you do not discuss all the factors involved, your readers are likely to think of these factors and respect your discussion less because you did not.

There are two different kinds of causal factors to consider: *direct* and *indirect*. A direct cause of Catherine Andreyev's physician-assisted suicide is her disease. An indirect cause is her loneliness. It is important to consider both types of causes because it is likely that one of these causes alone would not have led to the suicide. Many people have terminal diseases, but not all commit suicide. Many people are lonely but do not kill themselves. These causes together plus others led Catherine to commit suicide. We cannot understand and learn from her situation without analyzing all the causes. When writing about causes, it is common to discuss direct causes first, then indirect causes.

**EXERCISE:**    List the direct and indirect causal factors in the following situations.

| | DIRECT CAUSES | INDIRECT CAUSES |
|---|---|---|
| **1.** Stanley Ball dies with Kevorkian's help. | | |
| **2.** Virak leaves his gang. | | |
| **3.** You are learning English. | | |

### 2.  To Predict the Results of Actions We May Take

When you recommend a course of action to your readers, it is very important for you to analyze completely the results this action will have. You must consider not only the *direct* effects of the action but also the *indirect* effects. For example, a direct effect of suicide is the lost opportunity for the patient to live a full life. An indirect effect is the grief the patient's family feels after its loved one's suicide. An indirect effect of physician-assisted suicide is the physician's possible lost feeling of professionalism. You must analyze all *important* effects of an action for your reader so that your reader will respect your analysis. (You will also identify unimportant effects and decide not to write about them. For example, the landlord of the apartment the suicidal patient was renting will lose rent, but you need not mention this in your paper!)

## Coincidence

Be careful! When two actions occur in sequence, they are not necessarily cause and effect. For example, Virak mentions in his article that his friend Sinerth died. It is tempting to think that this caused Virak to change his ways. But Virak doesn't say this. What he does say is that his "life of immortality . . . came to an abrupt halt" when he crashed his car and lost all his money. When analyzing causes and effects, make sure they really are related as causal factors and don't just happen coincidentally.

**EXERCISE:** Identify the following events as *cause/effect* (CE) or *coincidental* (CO). Be prepared to defend your answers.

1. _____ Kevorkian assists suicides. / His medical license has been revoked.

2. _____ Catherine Andreyev was lonely. / She requested "medicide."

3. _____ An economic recession began in 1990. / Dr. Kevorkian began assisting suicides in 1990.

4. _____ Virak lived in Minnesota. / Virak joined a gang and committed crimes.

5. _____ Elaine Goldbaum was Jewish. / She didn't want to keep living.

6. _____ Sinerth was involved in crime. / Sinerth was shot by the police.

## Causal Chains

When causes lead to effects and these effects become the causes of still more effects, we call this a *causal chain*. You are quite likely to deal with causal chains in your writing for this chapter. Consider the following example of a causal chain:

> A teenager is often left alone at home; he becomes lonely and angry; he joins a gang; he begins to drink, take drugs, fight a lot; his neighbor becomes afraid; his neighbor buys a gun to protect himself from the boy's friends; one night the teenager and his friends have too much to drink and get into a fight in front of the neighbor's house; the neighbor becomes afraid and shoots one of the teenagers.

The ultimate cause of the shooting in this scenario might be that the teenager was left alone at home too much. Yet clearly there is much more to the story that must be explained. When analyzing complicated situations, keep in mind that most of them are caused by many factors, sometimes by factors which occur in chains like the one above.

**EXERCISE:** Construct causal chains for the following results, following the example of the one given above.

1. Virak's family leaves Cambodia.
2. Elaine Goldbaum seeks physician-assisted suicide.
3. Virak joins a gang.

## Organizing Causal Factors

It is likely that the essay you write for this chapter will include multiple causes and effects or a causal chain. If you describe multiple causes and/or effects, it is important to describe each separately, probably each in its own paragraph if there is enough information to do so. Certain language is especially useful in describing causes and effects, whether or not they are in chains.

| | CAUSES | EFFECTS |
|---|---|---|
| **Verbs** | causes, leads to, stimulates, produces, brings about, provokes, makes, promotes, compels, propels | results in, ends in, affects, reacts to |
| **Nouns** | a cause of, an impetus for, a catalyst for, a stimulus for, a reason for, a source of | an effect of, a result of, a reaction to, a consequence of, an outcome of |
| **Transitions** | | As a result (of . . .), Thus, Therefore, In consequence, Consequently, As a consequence, In turn,[1] In return, |

[1] Used in detailing causal chains: Loneliness leads to depression; depression, in turn, can bring about physical problems.

**EXERCISE:**   Circle the language that makes the causes and effects clear in the following paragraphs.

 A.   What causes anger? When asked, most people answer that someone else provoked their anger. Family members and close friends are often identified as common sources of anger whereas strangers and even enemies make up a small portion of those who make people angry. One of the most common catalysts of anger is unexpected interruption of one's plans. Other reasons include failure to satisfy one's personal expectations which, in turn, results in harm to one's self-esteem. (Kleinke, 1991, p. 100)

 B.   How do people react to anger? Most people say they experience negative consequences when they are confronted with other people's anger. The most common reactions are indifference, sorrow, anger in return, or hurt feelings. Unfortunately, these reactions rarely lead to positive outcomes in relationships. Although we may feel satisfaction as a result of expressing our anger, our relationships are likely to suffer from this expression. This may then lead to a lost opportunity to achieve our goals and, ultimately, increase our anger. (Kleinke, 1991, p. 100.)

Now check your first draft of the essay for this chapter. Have you expressed the causes and effects effectively, using clear cause-effect language? Have you avoided assuming that any coincidences had a cause/effect relationship? Have you managed to avoid knee-jerk reactions? Make changes where necessary.

## Making Your Draft Clearer—Language Skills

### EXPRESSING INTENSE CAUSES AND THEIR EFFECTS

Sometimes we want to indicate that we are facing an intense situation that causes us to take action or have certain feelings. Examine the following sample sentences and answer the questions beneath them.

1. Virak's family had <u>such a difficult life</u> in Cambodia <u>that</u> they left.
   Some patients have <u>such painful diseases</u> <u>that</u> they seek physician-assisted suicide.
   There was <u>such terrible poverty</u> in Cambodia <u>that</u> Virak's family left.

What parts of speech are *life, diseases,* and *poverty*? Why is the word *a* used in the first sentence but not the second and third? What kind of grammatical structure follows *that*?

2. Some people feel <u>so much pain</u> <u>that</u> they prefer to take advantage of physician-assisted suicide.
   Anger occurs for <u>so many different reasons</u> <u>that</u> it is hard to give advice on how to deal with it.

What part of speech are *pain* and *reasons*? Why do you think the first sentence uses *much* but the second *many*? Which part of each sentence is the cause? which part the effect? (Note: We can also use the words *little* and *few* in place of *much* and *many,* and it is possible to use these without a noun: I like my car so much that I'll never sell it.)

3. Perhaps Catherine Andreyev's life was <u>so lonely</u> <u>that</u> she had no reason to keep on living.
   Virak was <u>so angry</u> about his unfulfilled hopes in the United States <u>that</u> he turned to a life of crime.

What part of speech are *lonely* and *angry*? Why are *much* and *many* not used in these examples? Which part of each sentence is the cause? which part the effect?

---

### *LEARNING STRATEGY*

**Remembering New Material: By using summary charts, you can easily remember new material.**

---

#### Summary

| |
|---|
| so + **adj.** . . . that |
| so much/many/a little/a few + **noun** . . . that |
| such (a/an) + **noun** . . . that |

**EXERCISE 1:** Write intense cause-effect sentences with *so/such (a) + that* for the following situations. The first is done for you.

1. (your money situation)

   *I have so little (or so much!) money that I can't even buy a newspaper.*

2. (your good friends)

   _____

3. (your feelings about being in the United States)

   _____

4. (your homework situation)

   _____

5. (your feelings about your family)

   _____

6. (your favorite activity)

   _____

7. (your feelings about the English language)

   _____

8. (your major personality strength)

   _____

9. (your major personality weakness)

   _____

10. (your biggest need)

    _____

**EXERCISE 2:** Now write five intense cause-effect sentences analyzing the situations *either* of Virak Khiev *or* of the patients who seek Dr. Kevorkian's help.

1. _____
2. _____
3. _____
4. _____
5. _____

Now, go back to your draft of this chapter's major essay. See if you can better express your ideas in some places by using intense cause-effect expressions. Make changes where necessary.

## Reflecting on Draft 1

After you complete your first draft to your satisfaction, consider the following questions.

1. What was your main purpose in writing on the topic you chose for this essay?

   _____

   _____

2. Would you say that your essay focuses more on causes, effects, or a balance of both? Why?

   _____

   _____

3. What specifically did you do in your writing to make the cause and effect factors clear to your reader? Do you think they are clear enough?

   _____

   _____

4. Which part of your paper do you expect to be most interesting to your reader? Why?

   _____

   _____

5. Describe one thing you discovered about your topic while you were writing. Did you discover any knee-jerk responses in the early stages of your writing?

   _____

   _____

# PART III: WRITING THE SECOND DRAFT

Write a second draft of your major essay. Take into consideration your teacher's comments on your first draft and your own reflection on that draft as you revise your ideas. Also be careful to analyze causes and effects clearly, especially watching out for causal chains and coincidences. You have already learned how to use *so/such (a) + that,* and you will soon learn how to use correlative conjunctions to provide emphasis where needed. You will also learn how to make your sentences adhere to the requirements of parallelism so that they will be clearer.

## FURTHER READING

### Vocabulary Enrichment

**EXERCISE:**   Words from the following story are in Column A and are underlined. Find the *one word* in Columns B, C, or D that is *not* related in meaning to the word in Column A. You will probably need a dictionary.

### LEARNING STRATEGY

**Managing Your Learning: Purposely learning several ways to say the same thing can give you more flexibility in your language use.**

| | A | B | C | D |
|---|---|---|---|---|
| 1. | scrape by | subsist | survive | prosper |
| 2. | whiz | dolt | genius | prodigy |
| 3. | befriend | nurture | foster | neglect |
| 4. | link | connect | sever | unite |
| 5. | role model | underachiever | ideal | hero |
| 6. | sharp | clever | quick-witted | stupid |
| 7. | perceptive | alert | observant | dull-witted |
| 8. | manners | rudeness | civility | courtesy |
| 9. | pay off | reward | penalty | profit |
| 10. | crucial | important | essential | trivial |
| 11. | mentor | derelict | role model | guide |
| 12. | credit | blame | praise | commend |
| 13. | mind | approve | complain | oppose |
| 14. | prejudice | admiration | bias | preconception |
| 15. | steer | point | hinder | direct |

The following story provides a counterpoint to Virak Khiev's challenges and the coping strategies available to him. In this story, Kevin Moore is a fatherless black boy living in a poor, tough neighborhood. How was he able to cope?

### LEARNING STRATEGY

**Forming Concepts: You can understand better if you compare new experiences with previous ones. While reading this story, consciously make comparisons between Virak's and Kevin's challenges and choices.**

# A little push from big brother goes a long way

**K**evin Moore did not have much to look forward to—until he found a stranger to look up to. (1)

The fatherless 8-year-old watched as his mother scraped by in one of Los Angeles' toughest neighborhoods. He saw his two older brothers on a downward spiral: one would soon be murdered, the other would be lost to drugs. (2)

Then computer tax whiz David Anderson stepped in. The man from El Segundo befriended the boy from South-Central Los Angeles, introducing him to museums and camping trips, professional football and pizza parlors. The friendship thrived for more than four years. When it ended about five years later, Kevin was enrolled in a junior high school program for gifted students and the newly married Anderson was settling down to raise his own family. (3)

. . . Seventeen years later, the pair has been reunited on a happy note. Anderson was a guest of honor this week at a party celebrating Moore's graduation from the Stanford University School of Medicine. (4)

"He had a positive influence on me," said Moore, now 30. "Who knows? The time Dave was with me might have been the time I went into a gang." (5)

Said the 49-year-old Anderson: "I was very surprised when he tracked me down. But he said he was graduating and felt I contributed to him going on the right path." (6)

Stanford officials said Moore will be near the top of his class of 84 students on commencement day, June 13, 1993. Starting July 1, Dr. Kevin Moore will specialize in emergency room medicine at Atlanta's Grady Memorial Hospital as he begins a three-year residency, which will be administered by Emory University. (7)

Moore and Anderson praise the Big Brothers program that united them in 1972. The organization has linked 8,500 pairs of boys and men in Los Angeles over the past 38 years, including 520 current pairs. (8)

Anderson said he signed up with the Big Brothers program after having spent four years as a big brother to a boy in San Francisco. That experience had been a positive one, and Anderson discovered that Los Angeles officials had a waiting list of boys looking for older role models. (9)

There was no awkwardness when he met Kevin, then a skinny boy with a large Afro and a quick wit. "He was a kick. No matter what we discussed, he was with me. He was very sharp and perceptive," recalled Anderson, now retired and living in Napa (California). "He was good to be around. He and I hit it off." (10)

Moore said he never noticed if the sight of a white man and a black boy raised eyebrows 21 years ago. "It was the first time I'd ever been around white folks," Moore said. "I'd seen them on the streets, but never had any interaction. I'd watched 'The Brady Bunch' on TV and thought that all white people were rich, had great manners and were smarter than the rest of us." (11)

He said his friendship with Anderson showed him that people are alike. "That was a huge thing for me to learn—definitely a lesson that paid off," Moore said. "It's hard to succeed in life if you think other people are better than you." (12)

Self-esteem was crucial for Moore after he became bored with studies at Dorsey and Inglewood high schools and dropped out before his senior year. He landed a job as a bank teller. "At the bank, I was working under people who weren't using their brains," he said. "I realized that because they had college degrees, they had power over me. I realized that without a degree, nobody would ever take me seriously." (13)

Moore enrolled at West Los Angeles college and graduated from Occidental College. At Stanford's medical school, he became a student leader and worked as

a mentor for disadvantaged high school students in the Palo Alto area. . . . He decided to go into medicine for the good of the community and for personal satisfaction, he said. (14)

Moore credits his mother, Brenda, for his academic skill. "She bought a set of World Book encyclopedias for me when I was 5," he said. "I remember the day the lady came by selling them—we were on welfare and we spent money that we really didn't have. But my mother wanted me to have them. I read the World Books until I was 16. I'd sit in front of the TV set and read them for fun." (15)

It was Brenda Moore who sought help from Big Brothers for her son. "I could see the mistakes I was making with my two other sons. I saw that Kevin needed a strong father figure, a role model, around," said Ms. Moore, who is now a nurse. "They asked me if I minded if his big brother was white. I told them I wasn't teaching Kevin prejudice, that we're all brothers." (16)

Kevin Moore doubts that he would have dropped out of high school if he had continued with Anderson. He said his friend would have probably <u>steered</u> him directly to college admissions offices. (17)

In Atlanta, Moore plans to become involved with the Centers for Disease Control and Prevention to do research into violence prevention. Eventually, he hopes to teach emergency medicine. (18)

Pool, 1993, Sec. A, p. 14.

## ELABORATING ON THE READING

### Discussion

1. What challenges did Kevin Moore face as a child?
2. How do the challenges Kevin Moore faced as a child compare to the challenges Virak Khiev faced?
3. How did Kevin's brothers cope with those challenges?
4. How was Kevin able to cope more successfully with those challenges?
5. What connections can you make between the challenges Kevin Moore faced and what you learned in Chapter 4 (Education and Empowerment), Chapter 5 (Fathers), and Chapter 6 (Poverty)?

**EXERCISE:** Consider some of the challenges that young people like Virak Khiev or Kevin Moore face when their families live in poverty and/or their fathers are absent. Then brainstorm some coping strategies for these challenges that might be used by the young people themselves, their families, or society in general. An example is given for you.

| WHAT THE YOUNG PEOPLE CAN DO | WHAT THEIR FAMILIES CAN DO | WHAT SOCIETY CAN DO |
|---|---|---|
| 1. | | Big Brothers/ Big Sisters program |
| 2. | | |
| 3. | | |
| 4. | | |

**Threads**

**A brother is a friend given by nature.**

Gabriel Marie Jean Baptiste Legouve

## SHORT WRITING (150–200 WORDS)

Describe a time, when you were young, when you faced a challenge that you thought was difficult. How did you cope with it? Were there any adults to whom you could turn for help? If not, how did you feel having to cope alone?

### *LEARNING STRATEGY*

**Forming Concepts: Learning alternative sentence structures provides you with more choices in your writing style.**

## Making Your Draft Clearer: Language Skills

### CORRELATIVE CONJUNCTIONS

We can connect clauses quite simply with the conjunctions *and, or,* and *but.* However, sometimes we want to add extra emphasis to each clause. We do this by using *correlative* or two-part conjunctions. There are four correlative conjunctions, each with a meaning similar to the simple conjunctions named above but with added emphasis. The most important point grammatically is *whatever grammatical form follows the first conjunction must also follow the second conjunction.* Compare the following pairs of sentences. Notice the differences in emphases between sentences (a) and (b) and the similarity of grammatical forms which follow each conjunction.

1. *both . . . and . . .*
   a. Keeping realistic expectations *and* maintaining a sense of humor are important aspects of pain control.
      *Both* keeping realistic expectations *and* maintaining a sense of humor are important aspects of pain control. (gerunds)
   b. Men *and* women suffer from chronic pain.
      *Both* men *and* women suffer from chronic pain. (nouns)

2. *not only . . . but (also) . . .*
   a. Pain leads to inactivity *and* depression.
      Pain leads *not only* to inactivity *but also* to depression. (preposition phrases)
   b. Chronic pain can lead to helplessness, *and* it can cause drug addiction.
      *Not only* can chronic pain lead to helplessness, *but* it can cause drug addiction.* (clauses)

3. *either . . . or . . .*
   a. When patients suffer from chronic pain, physicians recommend self-relaxation techniques *or* one of several other coping strategies.
      When patients suffer from chronic pain, physicians recommend *either* physical pain management techniques such as medication, massage, *or* cold/warmth; *or* psychological coping strategies such as relaxation techniques, creative imagery, or altering expectations. (noun phrases)
   b. The chronic pain patient learns to manage his pain, *or* he succumbs to the pain and sacrifices his normal lifestyle.
      *Either* the chronic pain patient learns to manage his pain, *or* he succumbs to the pain and sacrifices his normal lifestyle. (clauses)

4. *neither . . . nor . . .*
   a. Physicians and pain treatment clinics have not had success in curing chronic pain.
      *Neither* physicians *nor* pain treatment clinics have had success in curing chronic pain.
   b. Because pain treatment clinics are designed to help patients cope with their pain, they do not try to cure it, *nor* do they offer medical treatments.*

Because pain treatment clinics are designed to help patients cope with their pain, *neither* do they try to cure it, *nor* do they offer medical treatments.* (Kleinke, 1991, p. 161–167)

*NOTE:* Sentences 2b and 4b are a special type. When you use *not only* or *neither ... nor ...* before complete clauses, the clauses take the question form (auxiliary + subject + main verb) even though they do not express questions. Notice the auxiliary verbs and the word order in these sentences.

## LEARNING STRATEGY

**Forming Concepts: Trying out what you've learned by using it with real information helps you develop stronger skills.**

**EXERCISE:**  Using the information in the following chart, write sentences in the four patterns above.

### Dealing with Chronic Pain Sufferers

| PERSON | HELPFUL ACTIONS | UNHELPFUL ACTIONS |
|---|---|---|
| Spouse and family | just being there to listen | criticizing the patient's response to his or her problem |
| | showing concern | being too worried |
| | showing affection | being pessimistic |
| | being calm about the patient's problem | expressing too little concern |
| Friends | helping with day to day needs | avoiding social contact with the patient |
| | showing affection | showing fear of the patient's condition |
| | showing concern | worrying too much |
| Nurses and physicians | providing useful information | providing insufficient information |
| | being optimistic | criticizing the patient's reactions |
| | providing competent care | providing incompetent care |

Adapted from: Dakof and Taylor, 1990, pp. 80–89.

Write two sentences for each conjunction. Be sure to practice using both phrases and clauses with these correlative conjunctions.

**A.** both . . . and . . .

    **1.** _____

    **2.** _____

**B.** not only . . . but (also) . . .

    **1.** _____

    **2.** _____

**C.** either . . . or . . .

    **1.** _____

    **2.** _____

**D.** neither . . . nor . . .

    **1.** _____

    **2.** _____

## Making Your Draft Clearer—Language Skills

### PARALLELISM

In English, particularly in writing, there are certain situations where items must be named in a similar grammatical form, a practice which is called *parallelism*. Parallelism is employed when listing, coordinating, and comparing. Similar grammatical form is defined as "all noun phrases" (whether or not they all include articles or adjectives), "all verb phrases," "all adjectives," "all infinitives," and so on. Examine the following samples of parallelism.

**Listing:** Use similar grammatical forms when making lists. For example:

*My hobbies:* bicycling, swimming, cooking, and eating (all *-ing* gerunds)

*A good physician:* competent, intelligent, compassionate (all adjectives)

*My goals:* to learn English, to get a good education, to enjoy myself (all infinitive phrases)

**Coordinating:** Use similar grammatical forms before and after *and, or, but, so, yet, not only . . . but also, both . . . and, either . . . or, neither . . . nor.*

Many suicide victims not only *suffer* from an incurable disease but also *have* few friends or family. (all verb phrases)

Suicide victims often suffer from incurable *diseases* or *pain.* (nouns)

Neither *killing* oneself nor *joining* a gang seems to be a successful coping strategy. (gerunds)

Someone *who kills herself* or *who asks another to kill her* must be experiencing a lot of emotional pain. (clauses)

**Comparing:** We also make items that we are comparing parallel in grammatical structure:

> *Lonely people* are more likely to commit suicide than *people with close relationships.* (noun phrases)
>
> Catherine Andreyev may have been more *lonely* than *ill.* (adjectives)
>
> It is preferable *to live poor* than *to die rich.* (infinitives)
>
> *A patient's* situation is more difficult than *a doctor's.* (possessives)

*NOTE:* It is important to identify the items that must be parallel carefully, particularly when verbs like *could, can, should, will,* or *must* or prepositions like *in, on, for,* or *with* are involved. When prepositions and these particular verbs, called modal verbs, introduce items in a series, they apply to each item in the series even when they are not repeated. Examine the following sentences. Note that they mean the same thing but it is unnecessary to repeat "can" because it applies to all three verbs, even without repetition, because of parallelism.

1. Even several years ago, teenagers facing difficult challenges *could ask* their teachers for help, *discuss* their situations with friends, or *call* one of the hotlines that exist for teenagers to talk over their problems with trained counselors over the telephone. (The modal verb "could" applies to "ask," "discuss," and "call" even though it is not repeated.)

However, when the same verb or preposition does not apply to all items in a series, you must repeat all verbs or prepositions, regardless of whether or not some of them are the same.

2. Working *on the assembly line, in the chicken factory,* or *in the corner grocery* to support your family is really hard. (Two different prepositions are necessary, so "in" is repeated.)
   Teens face challenges in school, (in) their neighborhoods, even (in) churches. (The same preposition for each item need not be repeated.)

**EXERCISE 1:** Study the first sentence of each group below to understand how the underlined items are parallel. Then underline the parallel items in the rest of the sentences in each group.

### Noun Phrases
1. America was the place, the land of tall *skyscrapers, televisions, cars* and *airplanes.* (Khiev, 1992, p. 8)
2. But for the immigrant, America presents a different type of jungle, a different type of war and a smell as bad as the waste of Cambodia. (Khiev, 1992, p. 8)
3. We didn't have good sanitation or modern conveniences. (Khiev, 1992, p. 8)

### Adjectives
1. You have to be *deceptive* and *unscrupulous* in order to make it. (Khiev, 1992, p. 8)
2. They seemed depressed or withdrawn to their families and friends. (Warrick, 1993, Sec. E, p. 1)
3. The typical suicide victim is a white, middle-aged male. (Warrick, 1993, Sec. E, p. 4)

**Threads**

. . . give us grace to accept with serenity the things that cannot be changed, courage to change the things which should be changed, and wisdom to distinguish one from the other.

Reinhold Niebuhr,
*The Serenity Prayer*

### Verb Phrases

1. I could have failed so many times except for those people who *believed in me* and *gave me another chance.* (Khiev, 1992, p. 8)
2. Most Americans believe the stereotype that immigrants work hard, get a good education and have a very good life. (Khiev, 1992, p. 8)
3. Eleven of the patients were women; all were ill, all were white, most middle-aged. In addition, most:
   • Had months, even years of life ahead of them. They said it was not pain but their weariness with life that made them want to die.
   • Were divorced, widowed or lifelong singles. Many had recently suffered the loss of a loved one.
   • Seemed depressed or withdrawn to their families and friends. (Warrick, 1993, Sec. E, p. 1)

### -*ing* Forms (Participles or Gerunds)

1. You spend your time *drinking, doing* drugs and *fighting.* (Khiev, 1992, p. 8)
2. It meant no more being hungry, no more fighting, no more killing. (Khiev, 1992, p. 8)
3. I could see that my future would be spent working on the assembly line like most of my friends, spending all my paycheck on the weekend and being broke again on Monday morning. (Khiev, 1992, p. 8)
4. People don't like the prospect of sitting in their apartments alone, brewing a [lethal] cup of tea, possibly vomiting everything up and never being found until they are totally deteriorated . . ." (Warrick, 1993, Sec. E, p. 4)

### Infinitive Phrases

1. . . . maybe it was better for him *to be* dead than *to continue* with the cycle of violence, *to live* with hate. (Khiev, 1992, p. 8)
2. It is better to die than to live like an angry young fool, thinking that everybody is out to get you. (Khiev, 1992, p. 8)

### Commands

1. My philosophy was "*Live* hard and *die* young." (Khiev, 1992, p. 8)
2. The war mentality of Cambodia came back: get what you can and leave. (Khiev, 1992, p. 8)

### Prepositional Phrases

1. Imagine working *on the assembly line* or *in the chicken factory* to support your family. (Khiev, 1992, p. 8)
2. Through the highly public exit offered by Kevorkian, some connections are assured: with the media, with a famous doctor, with a cause, even with history. (Warrick, 1993, Sec. E, p. 1)

### Clauses

1. And here *we don't have to live in the jungle like monkeys, we don't have to hide from mortar bombing* and *we don't have to smell the rotten human carrion.* [This could also have been done without repeating "We don't have to . . ."] (Khiev, 1992, p. 8)
2. You don't get along with your parents because they have a different mentality: you are an American, and they are Cambodian. (Khiev, 1992, p. 8)
3. Cancer victims who have lost all hope and who are unable to continue coping with pain or the certainty of death may choose to die.

**EXERCISE 2:**    There are parallelism errors in the following paragraphs. Find and correct them. The number of errors in each paragraph is given above it.

**A.** (*four errors*)    "Stress is an event or series of events that leads to strain, both physical and psychologically. Everyday living involves dealing with frustrations, conflicts, experiencing pressures, and change. At certain times in our lives, moreover, most of us are confronted with severely stressful situations that are difficult to cope with, such the death of a family member or a close friend, lose a job, a personal failure, or an injury. Even changes that we perceive to be positive, such as a promotion or moving to a new location, can be stressful and often require a period of adjustment. If stress is severe enough, it takes its toll on us physically and psychologically." (adapted from: Corey and Corey, 1990, p.152)

**B.** (*five errors*)    In order to cope with stress effectively you first need to face up to the causes of your problems, including your own part in creating them. Instead of adopting destructive reactions to stress, you can use task-oriented, or constructive, approaches aimed at realistically coping with stressful events. Weiten (1986) describes constructive coping as behavioral reactions to stress that tend to be relatively healthy or adaptive. He lists the following characteristics of constructive coping:

- it involves a direct confrontation with a problem;

- staying in tune with reality;

- based on an accurate and realistic appraisal of a stressful situation, rather than on a distortion of reality;

- it involves learning to recognize and inhibit harmful emotional reactions to stress;

- a conscious and rational effort to evaluate alternative courses of action; and

- it is not dominated by wishful or irrational thinking.

This section focuses on several positive ways to deal with stress: leading a low-stress lifestyle, meditation, relaxing, and therapeutic massage. (adapted from: Corey and Corey, 1990, pp. 162–163)

Now go back to your draft. Are there places where you listed, coordinated or compared but neglected to make the items parallel? Make changes where necessary.

## Editing Strategy

### A. THE DOMINO EFFECT

If you are a good self-editor, whether you block all lines but one, read aloud, look for nemesis errors, or do all three, you will find many errors to correct and other changes to make that will strengthen your sentences. However, as you make changes in your text, you must realize that some of the changes you make will necessitate still more changes. We call this the domino effect, a type of causal chain for editors.

Dominos are black tiles with white dots which we read as numbers when playing with them. If you stand them on their ends and arrange them next to each other, you can knock the first one over, making it fall, and watch all the others fall in turn. Similarly, touching or changing one thing in writing can necessitate other changes as well.

For example, consider the following sentence:

Chronic pain patients hope for a cure, but most don't find one.

Now, imagine that you want to add *every* before the subject. By doing so, you will also have to change *patients* to *patient* and *hope* to *hopes* since *every* is grammatically singular. The new sentence will now read:

Every chronic pain patient hopes for a cure, but most don't find one.

When you make changes in your text as you edit, it is always very important to check the whole sentence to see if any other changes will be needed as a result of the first change. In some cases, particularly when you change verb tenses, you may have to make changes in the rest of the paragraph or even the essay.

**EXERCISE:** Now go back to your second draft, and edit carefully using one or more of the strategies described in the previous units. Be aware of the domino effect!

**Managing Your Learning: When you look at others' work, try to find techniques that you can use successfully in your own writing.**

## Student Writing: Practice Peer Response

The following is the second draft of an essay by a young man from Hong Kong. Because of the length of the paper and its lack of detail, the author clearly needs suggestions for developing his thesis further. As you read the paper, make a mental note of ways that the author could expand his topic and make it more persuasive to a large audience. Then complete the Peer Response questionnaire below. Your teacher may ask you to work together with some of your classmates.

### HELL

*Sam Luk*

For some unknown reason, we are all afraid of the word "death." Whenever the word "death" comes up in a conversation, people all become quiet and serious. The word "death" seems to have some sort of magical power over us.

"Suicide" is another one of those magical words. Do we like to talk about "suicide" in any social gathering? No. We don't like words such as "suicide" or "death."

Since the beginning of human history, "death" has been viewed as something that is negative and evil; therefore, it should be avoided. "Suicide," a word closely related to death, has been viewed as an act of foolishness and emotion. The politically correct[1] statement is no one should ever commit suicide.

However, mankind has overlooked the fact that death is part of life. Everything in this universe has a beginning and an end. Nothing lasts forever. If we enjoy the birth of a child, we should enjoy death as much as the birth of anything.

Besides, this place called "earth" is not for everyone. We don't have the right to choose to be born or not. That choice is made by our parents. We have no choice except to accept the fact that we are here.

If you were healthy or rich, the chances are you would want to live. Would you still have the will to live if you had an incurable disease and suffered from pain every day until the day you died? Some people might pray for a miracle to happen until the day they died. Nevertheless, some people don't want to struggle with suffering. That's why some of the people have chosen the right to die: to commit suicide. It's their lives and they have the right to do it. As outsiders, we can't possibly feel how those sick people feel. Only the insiders, the sick ones, know what to do with their lives. The greatest thing about life is we can do whatever we want with it. We have the power to choose, whether it's justified by other people's beliefs or not. They are the ones who know it's a successful coping response for them.

Now trade papers with a classmate, read each other's paper and discuss the questions in the peer response below.

> **Threads**
>
> **Nearly 30,000 Americans commit suicide each year.**
>
> L. DeSpelder and A. Strickland, *The Last Dance: Encountering Death and Dying.* Mayfield Publishers, 1983

---

[1]"Political correctness" involves recognizing, especially speaking about, various groups of society without prejudice or bias.

## Peer Response to Draft Two

1. Explain to your author what you think some of his or her main points are in the essay.

   _____

   _____

2. Tell your author which part of his or her paper is likely to be most memorable or interesting to you. Explain why.

   _____

   _____

3. Tell your author about a part of his or her paper that you think was especially well explained. Explain why.

   _____

   _____

4. Tell your author about any places in his or her paper where you were confused, disagreed, or didn't quite believe what he or she was saying.

   _____

   _____

5. Give your author suggestions for developing the paper further in the next draft.

   _____

   _____

# PART IV: WRITING THE THIRD DRAFT AND ASSESSING YOUR LEARNING

In Part IV, you will once again revise your essay. While you are working, consider the following points:

- Have you emphasized your points as strongly as you would like by repeating key words, using correlative conjunctions, and subordinating with *so/such (a) + that*?
- Have you used expert evidence to strengthen your views, including, perhaps, the readings in this chapter as well as information you have found in the library or community?
- When coordinating, comparing, or listing have you maintained parallelism?
- Have you made your causes and effects, both indirect and direct, clear by the ways you have chosen to organize information?

- Have you considered all the feedback you have been given while writing previous drafts?

## Punctuation Note: Commas with Coordinators

Whether you need to use commas with coordinators (such as *and, or, but, both . . . and, not only . . . but also*) depends on what type of structure you are connecting.

When you are coordinating independent <u>clauses</u>, use a comma between each clause and before *and:*

**EXAMPLES:** Not only do low achievers forget how to savor their successes, but they also tend to blame many of their failures on lack of ability. (one comma for two independent clauses) (Kleinke, 1991, p. 47)

A natural reaction when other people don't meet our needs is to get angry or pout, but we often have to be the first to give when we want something from others. (one comma, two independent clauses) (Kleinke, 1991, p. 57)

When you are coordinating <u>*phrases or single words*</u> (such as verb phrases, noun phrases, adjectives, or adverbs), use commas between each only when you are coordinating <u>more than two</u> items:

**EXAMPLES:** A sense of control reinforces our commitment to take responsibility and to use our problem-solving skills to find solutions. (no comma, only two items) (Kleinke, 1991, p. 59)

Nondepressed people know how to get their minds off sadness, give themselves a break when judging themselves, and balance happy life events against sad ones. (two commas; three verb phrases) (Kleinke, 1991, p. 60)

## Student Writing for Further Discussion

The following essay was written by a student from Korea. In it, he expresses some of the challenges he and the Korean-American community have experienced as they try to fit into U.S. culture.

### BEING A "KOMERICAN"

*Sung Hong*

Seven years ago I immigrated to the United States, so I had to learn its language and culture to live here. During the past seven years I've tried hard to assimilate into western culture. Now I believe I am half American and half Korean, but I have no idea to which group I really belong. My largest problem is Koreans treating me as an American and Americans treating me as a Korean.

Whenever I talk to Americans, they always ask me about Korea and about Korea's culture. I don't have many ideas about Korea and its culture since I immigrated

## Threads

Between 1980 and 1990, nearly 6 million people immigrated from other countries to just ten cities in the United States: Los Angeles, New York, San Francisco, Miami, Chicago, Washington, D.C., Houston, Boston, Dallas, and Philadelphia.

Rand McNally, *Almanac of World Facts*

when I was only eleven. I wish they would treat me as an American, but they never do, so it is hard for me to be a true friend to Americans. They always treat me as a guest and they never talk to me as they would talk to their American friends. There is always a glass wall between them and me. Some Americans even look down on me, as if Orientals[1] are peasants and Americans are kings and queens. So I've tried to be Americanized but there are always differences between Americans and Americanized Koreans. The biggest difference is my "veneer." Even though I speak their language and dress like them, I still have the hair color and eye color of an Oriental.

Yet when I visited Korea last summer, I had a feeling that I didn't belong there either. Everything was strange to me. There were so many changes in six years. Towns and cities had changed and people also had changed. My friends were not the people I used to know and my childhood memories were gone forever. Whenever I talked to my friends I couldn't understand what they were saying because I still had the language skill of an eleven-year-old kid and my friends had the language skill of adults in Korea, probably better than most of the adults.

Korean-American immigrants call themselves Komericans. As you can perceive from the word "Komerican," we don't belong to any group. Why do Koreans call us Americans and Americans call us Koreans? It is because they don't welcome us. We Komericans know that we are not Americans but we are not foreigners either. And since Koreans and Americans don't welcome us, we Komericans had to form our own government. The government is called Han-In-Hwe. Han-In-Hwe tries to help Korean immigrants. Whenever Komericans need counseling, Han-In-Hwe will provide it for free and when Komericans need translators, they will provide one; most of them are volunteers. During the Los Angeles Riot, Han-In-Hwe gathered young men to help

---

[1]Many people from Asia who are now living in the U.S. consider it more acceptable usage to say *Asian* rather than *Oriental* in the United States.

Korean businesses.[2] Even though this brought bad results and reputations to immigrants, they tried their best to help Korean immigrants.

Being a Komerican doesn't always give me problems. Actually it gives me more benefits than problems. Speaking two languages almost fluently is one of many benefits of being a Komerican. Even though it is not really useful right this moment, I believe and know that some day I will use this skill very well. Another benefit is experiencing many different cultures. This benefit is not only because I am a Komerican but also because I live in California. In California there are so many immigrants from all over the world that I can learn and experience many different cultures and meet diverse people. One other benefit is that I have experiences that non-immigrants never have. Non-immigrants don't know what it means to encounter two cultures at the same time. Encountering two cultures at the same time when you are young gives you a chance to be one hundred percent Korean and one hundred percent American.

When I was younger I had to encounter two cultures at the same time. When I was with my friends, I had to act like an American. Then when I was with my parents, I had to act like a Korean. I had to act totally opposite with each group. When I was with my friends, I said I liked rock and rap music, and when I was with my parents I said I liked quiet and soft music. I also told my American friends that I liked playing basketball and hated studying, but to my parents I said I liked studying and playing golf. From my friends I learned how to speak English and how Americans think. From my parents I learned respect for elders and the traditions of Korea. It was very hard for me to encounter these two different cultures at the same time but it was also beneficial. Now I know how to act in front of an American and how to act in front of a Korean. These experiences have given me a chance to be one hundred percent Korean and one hundred percent American.

There are some Komericans who try to assimilate themselves totally into the second culture and some people who resist assimilating into the second culture at all. It depends on what kinds of friends they have. But I try to make myself one hundred percent Korean and one hundred percent American, which means speaking both languages fluently and understanding both cultures completely.

There are benefits and problems with being an immigrant, but I believe there are always problems and benefits when a person changes, when someone tries to assimilate into a new culture. There also is a problem because Komericans don't belong to Korean or American society, but some day Komericans will be welcomed by both Korean and American society. Bilingual skills will be very useful that day and our experiences will be very highly valued.

## DISCUSSION

1. What specific challenges has Sung Hong faced in his seven years in the United States?
2. What challenges has the Korean community in general faced, according to Hong?
3. How has Hong chosen to cope with his challenges? Do you think he is coping successfully?
4. How is the Korean community coping with its challenges? Do you think their strategy is successful?
5. What is the significance of the term "Komerican"?
6. Where in this paper would you recommend more information or different information?

---

[2]The Los Angeles Riot occurred in 1992 as a result of a court decision finding police officers innocent who had been videotaped beating a suspect during his arrest. During the riot, Korean stores were often targets of violence.

## Reflecting on Draft Three

1. With a highlighter or colored pen, mark some places in your text that you think were especially clearly or strongly phrased. What makes them so good?

   _____

   _____

2. Which part of your paper would you expect your reader to enjoy the most? Why?

   _____

   _____

3. Which part of your paper are you most satisfied with? What were you hoping to accomplish with that part, and how were you able to make it work so well?

   _____

   _____

4. Describe one important change you made in your essay between your second draft and your third draft. Why did you make this change? Does the change satisfy you?

   _____

   _____

5. Which part of your paper would you continue to work on if you had more time? What would you do to it?

   _____

   _____

### *LEARNING STRATEGY*

**Managing Your Learning: By evaluating your progress, you can determine what your strengths and weaknesses are and what you should work on next. Improvement in your writing shouldn't end simply because your course ends.**

## Writer's Notebook

Since this is the last chapter of this text, you have an opportunity to look back and describe what you have come to learn about writing in general and yourself as a writer in particular.

1. Try to remember back to the beginning of the course. How did you feel about your own writing then? Were you confident? knowledgeable? capable?

2. How confident are you about writing now? If there is a change, what do you think has caused it? What can you do to continue developing your confidence?

3. How knowledgeable are you about writing now? If you were giving a friend advice about writing, what would you say is the most important thing to know? Are there any opinions you used to have about writing that you no longer have?

4. List some skills you have developed in your writing that you can use in future writing, outside this course. Do you have enough skills to handle any writing assignment you might have in the future (whether given by a teacher, supervisor, or yourself)? What can you do to continue developing your skills?

5. In this course, you have had feedback on your writing from your teacher, your classmates, and from yourself via reflections. How did these types of feedback influence your writing? Do you believe you have developed enough skill in reflecting on your own writing to depend on yourself in the future when necessary?

## Vocabulary Checklist

Add vocabulary words from the chapter that you believe will be useful for your essay or your life in general. Several additional useful words have been added for you.

| WORD | PART OF SPEECH | MEANING | PREPO-SITIONS | SAMPLE SENTENCE |
|---|---|---|---|---|
| 1. challenge | n./v. | risk | ø | All of us face a challenge at one time or another. |
| 2. cope | v. | handle | with | It's hard to cope with some of the difficulties of life. |
| 3. commit suicide | v. | kill oneself | ø | To commit suicide is a choice of last resort. |
| 4. | | | | |

| WORD | PART OF SPEECH | MEANING | PREPO-SITIONS | SAMPLE SENTENCE |
|------|----------------|---------|---------------|-----------------|
| 5. | | | | |
| 6. | | | | |
| 7. | | | | |
| 8. | | | | |
| 9. | | | | |
| 10. | | | | |

## Bibliography

Atonovsky, A. *Health, Stress and Coping.* San Francisco: Jossey-Bass, 1979.

Corey, Gerald and Marianne Schneider Corey. *I Never Knew I Had a Choice.* 4th ed. Pacific Grove, Cal.: Brooks/Cole, 1990.

Dakof, G. A. and S. E. Taylor. "Victim's Perceptions of Social Support: What Is Helpful from Whom?" *Journal of Personality and Social Psychology,* 58 (1990), 80–89.

Khiev, Virak. "Breaking the Bonds of Hate." *Newsweek, April 27, 1992, p. 8.*

Kleinke, Chris L. *Coping with Life Challenges.* Pacific Grove, Cal.: Brooks/Cole, 1991.

Pool, Bob. "A Little Push from Big Brother Goes a Long Way." *Los Angeles Times,* June 5, 1993, Sec. A, p. 14.

Warrick, Pamela. "Choosing Not to Die Alone." *Los Angeles Times,* March 30, 1993, Sec. E, pp. 1, 4.

Weiten, W. *Psychology Applied to Modern Life: Adjustment in the 80s.* 2nd ed. Pacific Grove, Cal.: Brooks/Cole, 1986.